SEASONS OF
THE MIND

SEASONS OF THE MIND

Norman E. Rosenthal, M.D.

BANTAM BOOKS
NEW YORK · TORONTO · LONDON · SYDNEY · AUCKLAND

The suggestions, ideas, and procedures contained in this book are in no way
intended as a substitute for consulting with your physician. All matters regarding
your health require medical supervision.

SEASONS OF THE MIND

A Bantam Book
Bantam hardcover edition / December 1989
Bantam trade paperback edition / December 1990

Photos on page 229 courtesy of Scott Johnston.

ISBN 0-553-34993-7

Published simultaneously in the United States and Canada

*Bantam Books are published by Bantam Books, a division of Bantam Doubleday
Dell Publishing Group, Inc. Its trademark, consisting of the words "Bantam
Books" and the portrayal of a rooster, is Registered in U.S. Patent and Trademark
Office and in other countries. Marca Registrada. Bantam Books, 666 Fifth Avenue,
New York, New York 10103.*

PRINTED IN THE UNITED STATES OF AMERICA

0 9 8 7 6 5 4 3 2

For my father and mother, who sent me north.

CONTENTS

Epilogue

Resources

Acknowledgments

I owe thanks to many who helped plant the seeds of this book, nurture them, and see them through to fruition. For the past ten years, Dr. Tom Wehr has been mentor, colleague, friend, and closest associate in the work that is the subject of this book. Other mentors, Drs. Dave Dunner, Fred Goodwin, and Chris Gillin, helped me become a research psychiatrist. My colleagues, Drs. Al Lewy, Dave Sack, Barbara Parry, Steve James, Fred Jacobsen, Bob Skwerer, Connie Duncan, Jean Joseph-Vanderpool, and Michael Genhart, contributed to different aspects of the seasonal story in important ways. Connie Carpenter, Todd Hardin, and Paul Gaist were the glue that held the seasonal program at the National Institute of Mental Health together. Although I have written this book in my private capacity, the NIMH, with its creative administration and its stimulating and exciting atmosphere, has provided the matrix in which many of the ideas contained in this book were able to flourish.

I wish to acknowledge my appreciation to the other researchers who picked up the seasonal story and ran with it. Their work has been critical to the rapid and widespread acceptance of Seasonal Affective Disorder and light therapy. Drs. Bud Brainard and Bill Sonis in Philadelphia, Richard Depue in Minnesota, Carla Hellekson in Alaska, Siegfried Kasper in

West Germany, Michael Terman in New York, Christopher Thompson in England, and Anna Wirz-Justice in Switzerland have all made—and continue to make—important contributions to this field.

In the production of this book, many have exerted an important influence. I owe thanks to my agent, Faith Hampton Childs, for her personal and professional interest; to my official editor, Michelle Rapkin, for her creative editing; and to my unofficial editors—Ardyce Asire, Gertrude Eaton, Elise Hancock, Barbara Ingersoll, Herb Kern, Desmond and Wendy Lachman, David Leibow, Susan and Wilfred Lieberthal, Dan Oren, Lydia Polonsky, Leora Rosen, and Richard Ross—all of whom offered invaluable suggestions, and stopped me from becoming too "academic." I believe that, because of their advice, this book is more interesting and useful to all readers than it would otherwise have been. Jenny Burris, Michael Bryant, and Scott Johnston helped with various aspects of the research. Barbara Hass constructed the diets and directed me to the recipes in the Resources section.

Much credit is due to all my patients with Seasonal Affective Disorder for teaching me about the condition, granting lengthy interviews, writing wonderful letters, and directing me to interesting literature on the subject. Finally, thank you, Josh, for allowing me to disappear into the "other world" of the writer, and thank you, Lee, for your advice and support, and for putting up with me through all seasons.

Part 1:

Seasonal Syndromes

1

SAD and Light Therapy: Discovery or Rediscovery?

Four seasons fill the measure of the year;
There are four seasons in the mind of man.
—John Keats

Like the bears, squirrels, and birds, humans have evolved under the sun. We incorporated into the machinery of our bodies the rhythms of night and day, of darkness and light, of cold and warmth, of scarcity and plenty. Over hundreds of thousands of years, the architecture of our bodies has been shaped by the seasons and we have developed mechanisms to deal with the regular changes that they bring. We continue to respond to these rhythms in the way we feel and behave. For some of us, however, these changes can disrupt our lives.

The effects of the seasons on humans were all well known by the ancients, but have largely been forgotten by modern medical practitioners. Their importance has been kept alive only by artists, poets, and songwriters. Shakespeare, for example, observed that "a sad tale's best for winter," while Keats wrote of a nightingale "singing of summer with full-throated ease," and the singer of a modern ballad calls his beloved the sunshine of his life.

In the past ten years, science has caught up with the arts, and the medical importance of the seasons has been recognized anew. Surveys have shown that most people experience some alteration in mood or behavior with the changing seasons and, for as many as one in four,

3

these changes present a problem. Natural and effective treatments have been developed to help people with seasonal problems, known as Seasonal Affective Disorder, or SAD. We are also aware of a milder version of this condition—the winter blues—and summer depression or heat intolerance. At the same time, our understanding of the emotional impact of the seasons—of light and temperature—has advanced. We are now better able to understand our relationship to the physical world around us. How these developments came about and what we have learned about the effects of the seasons on emotions and behavior are the subjects of this book. In addition, I will discuss how we can modify these emotions, as well as the impact of seasons and light on our minds and brains.

There are indeed seasons of the mind, though they are not the same for everyone. Autumn may enchant some with its grand colors, but for others it carries the threat of winter. Winter, cheerless and forbidding for many, has associations with stagnation, decay, and loss. But some people experience a different type of winter—one that finds them snug and cozy by the fireside, with chestnuts popping. Spring brings buds and blossoms, rebirth, with sap stirring, feverish urges, and a longing to go on pilgrimages. But we are also told that "April is the cruelest month . . . mixing memory and desire." Summer yields a harvest of fruit and flowers, but in the words of the Bard, "sometimes too hot the eye of heaven shines." Had they heeded the words of the poets, modern physicians would have realized much sooner that the seasons can have a profound effect on the way we feel, and that people experience them in different ways.

States of mind evoked by the seasons and the weather form part of our language. A person is said to have a sunny disposition, a radiant smile, to be warm or cold. Every news program carries a section on the weather. This curiosity goes way beyond wanting to know whether to take along an umbrella or not. The weather and the changing seasons affect the way many of us feel, how we sleep, what we eat, whether we can concentrate on our work, and even whether we are able to love.

This idea seems so obvious now that it is hard to believe that there was a time when we paid no heed to the effects of the changing seasons on humans. Only fifteen years ago, when I was in medical school, we were not taught about the effects of the seasons. According to the view handed down to us, man was a seasonless creature. Electricity provided us with light and heat. Food was available all year round. We were not like other animals, that have to cope with the challenge of the changing seasons.

Had we studied the ancients, we might have recognized that a seasonless view of human physiology and behavior is incorrect. Hippocrates, for example, observed in the fourth century B.C. that "whoever wishes to pursue the science of medicine in a direct manner must first investigate the seasons of the year and what occurs in them." Many physicians who followed him emphasized the effects of the different seasons on the mind and body. Apparently that wisdom was buried by the wonders of the industrial revolution. We forgot that we were once much closer to nature than we are today. Our responses to the changing seasons are programmed into us—presumably into our genetic code.

Man-made methods of escape from darkness, cold, moisture, and extreme heat have provided us with considerable protection from the effects of the seasons on our bodies, minds, and spirits. With this protection, the changing seasons are for many people merely the backdrops against which to go about their daily business. But others experience them with extreme intensity. Perhaps among these people are poets and artists who have seen the changing seasons as metaphors for our lives—whose emotional surges have produced some of the most beautiful products of the human mind.

However, there are also those for whom seasonal transitions trigger extreme changes in mood and energy, and produce sadness and despair. In this book I will describe not only the types of marked responses that some people have to the changing seasons, but also how to recognize these problems and treat them. Of course, our responses to the changing seasons should not be examined only through the microscope of pathology. They are part of our response to our world as a whole, enhancing the range of our emotions. I will also deal with this aspect of human emotional response, about which I have learned more from the intense experiences of my patients than from the most rigorous medical texts.

MY OWN SAD STORY

I trained as a doctor in South Africa, a country which, for all the turbulence of its politics, can truthfully boast about its climate. In

Johannesburg, where I grew up, there were really only two seasons: summer and winter. During summer one could swim outdoors and eat summer fruit: peaches, papaya, mangoes. During winter one could not do these things. It was warm outdoors during the day, though at night you needed a sweater. Spring and autumn were transition times. After several months of winter the blossoms would appear, and you knew it was spring. Similarly, when the long summer was over, the leaves would turn a simple brown and fall off the trees without much fuss or fanfare, and winter was there. But despite the mildness of the seasons, I was aware at some level of the effect they had on my mood. I had even considered writing a novel in which the mood of the central character changed regularly with the seasons. The novel was never written, but the seed of the idea stayed with me, germinating quietly.

It required the intense seasonal changes of the higher latitudes to which I moved to activate that kernel of thought, as well as my encounters with some inspiring people, who are central to this story. I arrived in the United States in the summer of 1976 and began both my psychiatric residency at the New York State Psychiatric Institute and research into disorders of mood regulation. The summer days felt endlessly long and my energy was boundless. I had never experienced such long summer days in Johannesburg, which is much nearer to the equator than New York City.

As the months passed, I was struck by the drama of the changing seasons. I had been unprepared for the brilliant colors of the autumn leaves in the north, the crisp days and cold nights, and most of all, for the disappearance of the light. I had not anticipated how short the days would be. When the sun shone, its rays struck the earth at a strange, oblique angle, and I understood what Shelley meant when he wrote:

> *Bright Reason will mock thee*
> *Like the sun from a wintry sky.*

Then daylight saving time was over and the clocks were put back an hour. I left work that first Monday after the time change, and found the world in darkness. A cold wind blowing off the Hudson River filled me with foreboding. Winter came. My energy level declined, and I wondered how I could have undertaken so many tasks the previous summer.

Had I been crazy? Now there seemed to be no alternative but to hang in and try to keep everything afloat. I understood for the first time the stoic temperaments of the northern nations. Finally, spring arrived. My energy level surged again, and I wondered why I had worried so over my work load.

I registered all these impressions, but I did not put them together into a cohesive story—and I probably would never have done so had it not been for the events that followed and the remarkable people I was to meet. At the end of my residency I went to the National Institute of Mental Health (NIMH) in Bethesda, Maryland, to undertake a research fellowship with Dr. Frederick Goodwin, whom I had heard speak on the topic of manic-depressive illness from both biological and psychological points of view. Dr. Goodwin made the subject come alive, describing how our shifting moods and fluctuating perceptions of the world correspond to certain changes in our brain chemistry. Since mind and brain seemed equally fascinating frames of reference, I wanted to use both models to try to understand mood disorders.

Shortly before my first visit to the NIMH, I met Dr. Alfred Lewy, one of several psychiatrists working with Fred Goodwin at the time. Dr. Lewy had just developed a technique to measure the hormone melatonin, in collaboration with Dr. Sanford Markey. Melatonin is produced by the pineal gland, a pea-sized structure tucked underneath the brain. Each night, like clockwork, the pineal releases melatonin into the bloodstream in minute quantities, and continues to do so until dawn. The secretion of melatonin signals the duration of darkness and thus serves as an important seasonal time cue in animals. Although it is unclear whether melatonin is instrumental in causing seasonal changes in humans, the research in this area proved to be a critical step in the rediscovery of SAD and light therapy.

Dr. Lewy and I spoke about our common interests and the various directions in which our research might take us. On occasion we chatted over a mass spectrometer, the instrument he had used to develop his technique for measuring melatonin. It looked like a very large washing machine. He injected samples of clear fluid into a small hole in the top, and reams of paper rolled off it, while inked pens traced out a graph upon the paper. He pointed to one blip on the graph and said, "That's melatonin." I was suitably impressed.

After I joined Dr. Goodwin's group, I was assigned to work most closely with Dr. Thomas Wehr, an outstanding clinical researcher, who had for some years been studying biological rhythms in an attempt to learn whether abnormalities in these rhythms might be at the basis of the mood disturbances in depression and mania. Shortly before my arrival at the NIMH, Lewy and Wehr had shown that bright light was capable of suppressing the secretion of human melatonin at night—a finding that was to have great influence over the events that followed. There was a buzz in Goodwin's group at that time—a sense of excitement—and I felt certain I had come to the right place.

A LIGHT-SENSITIVE SCIENTIST

Although many people were responsible for the rediscovery of SAD, our steps toward this end can all be traced back to the actions of one man: Herb Kern. In some ways, Herb might have appeared to be an unlikely person to initiate a new area of medical investigation, for he was not himself a medical professional, but a research engineer with a major corporation. I met Herb a year after arriving at the NIMH. At sixty-three, he was a youthful-looking man with a wiry build, a crew cut, and a twinkle in his eyes. He was intensely curious, and he had noted in himself a regular pattern of mood and behavior changes going back at least fifteen years. A scientist by nature and training, he had kept careful notes of these changes in numerous small notebooks. He observed that each year, from July onward, his energy level would decline and he would withdraw from the world. At these times he lacked energy, had difficulty making decisions, lost interest in sex, and felt slowed down and "ready for hibernation." He found it difficult to get to work in the morning, and once there he would sit at his desk, fearful that the telephone would ring, obliging him to have a conversation with someone. It is typical for a depressed person to withdraw—to have neither the desire nor the energy to interact with others. In fact, in many cases, he or she may feel it is an impossible task. People who are depressed simply want to be left alone.

More bothersome to Herb than his social isolation was the decrease in his creative powers during his depressed periods. He would procrastinate at work because "everything seemed like a mountain" to him, and his productivity decreased markedly. It was only by grim perseverance that he was able to write up his studies from the previous spring and summer. His sleep was disrupted, and his characteristic enthusiasm for life evaporated.

The months would drag on like this for Herb until mid-January when, over a two-week period, his energy would return. As he put it, "The wheels of my mind began to spin again." He had ample, even excessive energy at these times, and needed little sleep. Ideas came freely and he was eager to communicate them to others. For five or six months he was very confident of his abilities and felt that he could "tackle anything." He was very efficient and creative, needed only four hours of sleep per night, was more interested in food and sex, and admitted to a "tendency to go overboard" in buying luxuries.

Herb had observed that his mood improved as the days lengthened and declined as they shortened, and he had actually developed a theory that this might be due to changes in environmental light. He attempted to interest several people in his hunch that his mood and energy levels were related to the time of year. One of these, Dr. Peter Mueller, a New Jersey psychiatrist in private practice who had a research background, listened to Herb and subsequently looked for other patients with a similar history. Herb was treated with several different antidepressant medications, all of which resulted in unacceptable side effects without correcting his symptoms. Herb read about the work of Drs. Goodwin, Wehr, and Lewy and found his way to the NIMH, where he asked us to work with him on his seasonal difficulties.

Dr. Lewy suggested that we treat Herb by lengthening his winter day with six hours of bright light—three before dawn and three after dusk—in an attempt to simulate a summer day. He reasoned that since bright light is necessary for melatonin suppression in humans, it might similarly be necessary for altering mood and behavior. This reasoning was based on two pieces of information: first, the secretion of melatonin is an important chemical signal for regulating many different seasonal rhythms in animals; second, the nerve pathways involved in the suppression of melatonin secretion by light pass through parts of the brain that we believe are important in regulating many of the physical functions that are disturbed in depression, such as eating, sleeping, weight control, and sex drive. If the suppression of melatonin required much brighter light than ordinary indoor fixtures provided, then perhaps bright light might also be necessary in order for the brain to perform other mood-related functions.

We asked Herb to sit in front of a metal light box, about two feet by four feet. The box emitted as much light as one would receive while standing at a window on a spring day in the northeastern United States. We chose full-spectrum fluorescent lights—a type that mimics the color range of natural sunlight coming from a summer sky in order to replicate the conditions that appeared to bring Herb out of his winter depressions. We covered the lamps in the light box with a plastic diffusing screen in order to create a smooth surface. The type of light box used today for light therapy is very similar to the one we used for his original treatment.

Within three days, Herb began to feel better. The change was dramatic and unmistakable. He was moving into his spring mode several weeks ahead of schedule. We wondered what to make of this. Was it a new type of treatment for depression? Our scientific instincts immediately tempered our excitement. Herb had been heavily invested in the light therapy. Might his response not have been due to something other than the light—the wish to feel better, for example, or the emotional impact of entering an experiment in which three research psychiatrists were studying the outcome of a treatment based on his ideas? The so-called placebo effect had to be seriously considered. It has dogged behavioral researchers for years, and we could not rule it out in evaluating the effects of light therapy on Herb's depression.

A HUMAN BEAR

During the same winter that Herb was receiving light treatment at the NIMH, Dr. Peter Mueller, in consultation with Al Lewy, tried artificial light treatment with another patient, whom we will call "Bridget." She also appeared to benefit from light, and had an unusually good winter that year. The following summer, as luck would have it, Bridget moved to the Washington metropolitan area, and Dr. Mueller suggested that she contact us. Bridget's history and ingenuity in fitting the details of her seasonal problems into a coherent story were as remarkable as Herb's.

She was a professional in her mid-thirties, who had been aware of disliking winter since childhood. But it was not until her early twenties that a regular pattern of seasonal changes emerged. Bridget's problem would begin each year in August or September, as she anticipated the forthcoming winter with increasing anxiety. She was mystified about what subtle cues might have caused her premonitory dread, since this feeling began during the summer, when the days were still warm. She wondered whether it might be the fall catalogs, with their pictures of winter clothes, that triggered the memories of unpleasant winters of earlier years? Regardless, when the leaves began to turn color, she would have a strong urge to take out her winter clothes and stock her cupboards with food, "like a squirrel getting ready for winter."

As winter approached, Bridget experienced many symptoms similar to those described by Herb, such as feelings of extreme fatigue—a leaden sensation that made her want to lie down and sleep all day long. She would overeat at these times, and observed a marked craving for sweets and starches. As in Herb's case, Bridget continued to struggle in to work each day, though her productivity declined markedly. In addition to her seasonal mood problem, Bridget also felt depressed and irritable for a few days before each menstrual period, regardless of the season. When spring arrived, her depression lifted and was replaced by elation. In her earlier years she would forget her winter difficulties once they were over. "I was like the grasshopper," she remarked, "singing and playing all summer long," indifferent to the next winter that was to come.

Bridget had also observed that other changes in the environment besides the seasons seemed to affect her mood. She had visited the Virgin Islands during the two winters before her first light treatment. Both times she had been impressed by the marked improvement in her mood just days after her arrival, and the relapse a few days after her return to the north. She had lived for some years at different latitudes: Georgia, New York, and Quebec. The farther north she lived, the earlier her depression began, the more depressed she felt, and the later was her remission in the spring. She began to suspect that something in the environment was influencing her mood, and that perhaps it was the light. Why else did she seem to crave it so? Why else did she hate her poorly lit office? She made up any excuse to seek out the brightly lit photocopying room. Light treatment made good sense to Bridget. She was eager to try it and was delighted to find that it worked for her.

IN SEARCH OF SAD

Unusual individual cases have historically played an important role in medical research, in general, and psychiatry, in particular. We wondered whether Herb and Bridget might be examples of a special seasonal kind of depression, and whether they might help us understand how others respond to the changing seasons and environmental light.

Although single cases may be of great importance in generating new hypotheses, we generally need groups of patients to prove them experimentally. Dr. Mueller said he had encountered several other patients with seasonal depression. We wondered how common the problem was. Were there any other such patients in the Washington, D.C. area who might be interested in participating in a research program? I called a few local psychiatrists who specialized in treating depression, but they said they had not encountered the problem. I concluded that it must be quite rare and that the only chance we had of finding such a group was by publicizing our interest in the *Washington Post*.

Sandy Rovner, a journalist who specializes in health issues, sat across the room from me, tape recorder in hand, and listened to my story. She decided it would be of interest to her readers and wrote an article for the *Post,* which launched an entire field of research. Rovner's article began with Bridget's own words: "I should have been a bear. Bears are allowed to hibernate; humans are not."

The response to the article took us all by surprise. Instead of hearing from a handful of afflicted people, the phones rang for days and we received thousands of responses from all over the country. We sent out screening questionnaires, which were returned by the hundreds. I read them with a growing sense of excitement. In psychiatric research, heterogeneity is a major problem. In other words, the same condition may differ greatly in character from one patient to another, which has proven to be an enormous obstacle to psychiatric researchers, especially in the area of schizophrenia. As I read the questionnaires, it seemed as though Bridget had been cloned, as one person after another reported the symptoms of the condition that we went on to call Seasonal Affective Disorder, or SAD. I wondered whether this similarity in symptoms might correspond to a similar underlying disturbance in brain chemistry, which might imply a favorable response to light, as we had had with Herb Kern and Bridget.

We interviewed many people and admitted into our program all those with clear-cut histories of winter depression. During that summer, as expected, all the participants felt well and showed an unusually high level of energy. This generated considerable skepticism among some of my colleagues, who speculated that we might be dealing with a group of suggestible people who had read the article and persuaded themselves that they had the syndrome. That seemed unlikely to me, but I had no way of disproving it, and could not help feeling slightly uneasy when one of my colleagues pointed out that if none of the participants became depressed when winter arrived, we would all look a little foolish.

THE FIRST CONTROLLED STUDY OF LIGHT THERAPY FOR SAD

The days grew shorter and in October and November, right on schedule, the participants began to slow down and experience their winter syndromes, just as they had described. Although clearly not affected to the same degree as my seasonal patients, I noticed that I too had to push myself harder to get anything done. It was more difficult to get up in the morning, and even the project did not seem so exciting as it had the previous summer.

We planned to treat the patients with light as soon as they became moderately depressed—just enough so that we would be able to measure an effect of the treatment, but not to a degree where they felt incapacitated. We decided to use full-spectrum light, as we had with Herb Kern, for three hours before dawn and three hours after dusk. In any experiment designed to show the effectiveness of a treatment, it is important to have a control condition—one which incorporates all the ingredients of the "active treatment" condition, except the one believed to be crucial for achieving the desired effect. In this study we believed that the brightness of the light would be crucial, so we used dim light as a control. In order to make the control treatment more plausible, we chose a golden-yellow light—a color associated with the sun and one to which the eye is highly sensitive.

We treated each patient with two weeks of bright light and two weeks of dim light, then compared the effects. This type of treatment design—called a "crossover" because the individual is "crossed over" from one treatment condition to the other—has since become a standard format for light therapy studies. We presented the two conditions to the patients in random order. In other words, some began with the bright white and others with the dim yellow light, so as not to bias the outcome. It is also important for psychiatrists evaluating the effects of a treatment not to be aware of which treatment a patient has received, so that their prejudices cannot be reflected in their ratings. For this reason, treatment conditions were known only to me, not to my collaborators in this study, Drs. Thomas Wehr, David Sack, and J. Christian Gillin.

I will never forget the first patient who underwent the bright treatment—a middle-aged woman, markedly disabled by SAD. During the winter she was barely able to do her household chores, get to work, or attend her evening classes. After one week of treatment she came into our clinic beaming. She was feeling wonderful, keeping up with all her obligations, and mentioned that her classmates were regarding her with a new competitive respect as she answered questions in her evening classes, as if to say, "Where have you been hiding all this time?"

The second patient who received the bright-light condition was treated around Christmas. I called the ward from New York City, where I was spending the holiday with friends, and asked Dave Sack how things were going with the study. He replied, "I don't know what treatment 'Joan' is receiving but she's blooming like a rose."

And so it went. Nine patients responded to bright light and the dim light proved ineffective. I began to use the lights myself and was sure that they made me feel better. Some of my colleagues requested them, too. After a few weeks I had to put a big sign in front of the dwindling stack of light boxes, asking anyone who wanted to borrow a fixture to discuss it with me first so that we would have enough for the study. A local psychiatrist, whom I had initially polled about the existence of SAD patients, and who had told me that he did not know of any, called to say that he had realized that he himself had the syndrome and asked about how he might use the lights himself.

Many questions were raised by the results of our first study. Was it really possible that light was affecting mood? Could there be some explanation for the improvement, other than the light itself? Was it all a placebo effect? And if it was the light, how was it working? These were all important questions, and in due course, we and other researchers would address them, one by one. But as we reviewed the study in the spring of 1982, we realized that the patients had become depressed during fall and winter as they had predicted they would. The light treatment had worked more dramatically than we had ever hoped it might. The azaleas and the dogwoods were in bloom. Spring had arrived and, at that moment, nothing else seemed to matter very much either to our patients or ourselves.

In the years that followed we continued to treat new waves of SAD patients each winter, as did researchers at other centers. Light studies performed in Switzerland, Oregon, Alaska, and New York corroborated our experience. SAD is common and light treatment works. In view of this general consensus, the American Psychiatric Association recognized a version of SAD in its diagnostic manual, *DSM-III-R,* in the spring of 1987. In a brief six years since the first SAD patients were treated with light, a variant of depression that appeared at first to be a rare curiosity, was recognized by the psychiatric community as an important clinical condition.

2

SAD: The Clinical Profile

What is Seasonal Affective Disorder (SAD)? What are its symptoms? Who tends to get it and when does it usually begin? How long does it last? How does it affect people at home, at work, in their relationships? How does the SAD syndrome relate to the "winter blues" or "February blahs" that so many people complain about?

Since our first controlled-light treatment study we have learned that the great majority of the population experiences some seasonal changes in feelings of well-being and behaviors, such as energy, sleep, eating patterns, and mood. People vary in the degree to which they experience them. At one end of the spectrum are those who have few, if any, symptoms. Then there are those who experience mild ones that can easily be accommodated in the course of their everyday lives. A third group finds them a nuisance—not worth taking to the physician, but troublesome, nonetheless. This group may be suffering from what is commonly known as the "winter blues" or "February blahs." At the far end of the spectrum are patients with SAD, whose changes in mood and behavior are so powerful that they produce significant problems in their lives.

Such changes were well expressed by "Jenny," who suffers from a typical case of SAD. She has observed that she feels like "two different people—a summer person and a winter person." Between spring and fall she is energetic, cheerful, and productive. She initiates conversations and social arrangements, and is regarded as a valuable friend, co-worker, and employee. She is able to manage everything that is expected of her with time and energy to spare. During the winter, however, her energy level and ability to concentrate are reduced, and she finds it difficult to cope with her everyday tasks. She generally just wants to rest and be left alone, "like a hibernating bear." This state persists until the spring, when her energy, vitality, and zest for life return. It is easy to understand why she thinks of herself as two different people, and why her friends wonder who the "real Jenny" is.

This same theme is echoed by a variety of other seasonal people I have encountered. For example, a man from Missouri writes:

> I feel as though I "live" only during the sunny months. The rest of the time I seem to shut down to an idle, waiting for spring, enduring life in general. This is no joking matter to those of us who are like this. We, in effect, live only half our lives, accomplishing only half of what we should. It is really rather sad, when you think of it.

One woman wrote about her elderly mother, who has suffered from SAD for her entire adult life:

> In late spring or early summer she is full of energy, requiring only five or six hours of sleep. She talks incessantly and tries to do too many things. Then in late fall (occasionally she makes it to Christmas), her personality takes a complete turn. She sleeps twelve hours at night, cries all morning, and then takes a nap. She won't drive the car, seldom leaves the house, and won't answer the telephone.

Who are the victims of SAD? All sorts of people. The hundreds of SAD patients I have known have come from all different walks of life: different races, ethnic groups, and occupations. The disorder is four times more common among women than among men. Although people in their twenties through forties appear to be most susceptible, SAD occurs in all age groups. I have encountered children and adolescents with the problem, as well as the elderly.

We have estimated that approximately 6 percent of the population of the United States suffer from SAD and a further 14 percent suffer from a milder form of the condition—the winter blues. Those rates are equivalent to a total number of ten million and twenty-five million people respectively.

Just as the degree of seasonal difficulties may vary from one person to the next, so may the timing of the problem. For example, one person may begin to feel SAD symptoms in September, whereas another will feel well till after Christmas. The more severely affected person might only emerge from the winter slump in April, whereas a mildly affected one may feel better by mid-March. Many people can predict almost to the week when they will begin to experience their winter difficulties and when they will begin to feel better in spring, almost as one can predict when different flowers will begin to bloom.

The timing of the appearance of symptoms also depends on where a person lives. My colleague, Dr. Carla Hellekson in Alaska, has noticed that the patients in her SAD clinic become depressed about a month earlier, on average, than my patients in Maryland, and begin to feel better, on average, about a month later. "Terry," a thirty-eight-year-old realtor, is typical of many who have lived at different latitudes when she reports that during her years in Canada and New York, her problems began earlier than when she moved south to Washington, D.C.

"Merrill," an attractive vocational guidance counselor, sits in front of me, checking off on her fingers the symptoms she has during successive months. She has come to know her internal calendar well over the past eighteen years during which she has suffered from SAD. Since she is thirty-two years old now, these problems have been going on for more than half of her life.

> I only feel good for two or three months: May, June, and July. By August my energy level has already begun to slip. I begin to sleep later in the morning, but I can still get to work on time. In September, things are a little worse. My appetite increases and I begin to crave candy and junk food. By October I begin to withdraw from friends and I tend to cancel engagements. November marks the onset of real difficulties for me.
>
> I become sad and worry about small things that wouldn't bother me at all in the summer. My thinking is not as good as usual and I begin to make stupid mistakes. Other people notice that I am not looking well. Preparing

for Christmas is always an enormous chore. I am bad about getting my cards off and my gifts wrapped. I tend to avoid the usual round of parties: I don't want people to think I am being rude, but I find it very difficult to pretend to be cheerful and make conversation when all I feel like doing is going home and sleeping.

January and February are my worst months. On many days it's all I can do to get into work, and often I don't. I call in sick. Once I'm there it's very hard to get my work done. I procrastinate as much as possible and hope that I'll be able to handle things later.

In March and April my energy begins to come back, and that's a relief, but my thinking is still not back to normal and I continue to feel depressed at times. They are tricky months because you never know what the weather will be like. You can feel good for a few days and then wham, you're down again. And then it's late spring and summer and once again I feel myself again: friendly and happy. I can do my work and can be available to the people I care for. But it's so hard to have to cram everything you want to do into three months.

In Washington, D.C., November seems to be the month when people begin to feel really bad. Again, this differs from one person to the next. Merrill's sense of dread—having the joy of summer slip away, only to be replaced by the grim drudgery of winter—is very familiar to those who have experienced it or seen it in others. Henry Adams, the famous chronicler of American life, wrote from Washington, D.C., to Charles Milnes Gaskell, in November 1869, a description of his feelings about that month, which sound remarkably similar to those sentiments I have heard many times from patients with SAD:

Dear Boy:

I sit down to begin you a letter, not because I have received one since my last, but because it is one of the dankest, foggiest, and dismalest of November nights, and, as usual when the sun does not shine, I am as out of sorts as a man may haply be, and yet live through it. . . . This season of the year grinds the very soul out of me. My nerves lose their tone, my teeth ache, and my courage falls to the bottomless bottom of infinitude. Death stalks about me, and the whole of Gray's grisly train, and I am afraid of them, not because life is an object, but because my nerves are upset. I would give up all my pleasures willingly if I could only be a mouse, and sleep three months at a time. Well! one can't have life as one would, but if I ever take too much laudanum, the coroner's jury may bring in a verdict of willful murder against the month of November.

The three months during which most patients with SAD would like to be a mouse or bear and sleep are December, January, and February. These months could well be called the SAD months. Then comes the thaw of March, April, and May. People emerge from their low winter state in different ways. Some glide gracefully through April and May into feeling cheerful and well in June and July. Some have a bumpy course over the spring, especially in places where it is dark, stormy, and unpredictable. Others emerge into an exuberant state where they may be excessively energetic, needing little sleep, and feeling "wired" or "high." At times this state of excessive energy, known clinically as hypomania, can constitute a problem in its own right. A final group of people with SAD never quite emerge completely from their winter depressions and remain somewhat down all year round, though less so in the summer.

PROFILES OF SAD

Below are four profiles of SAD patients whose symptoms include the full range of seasonal changes. The first two, Neal and "Angela," suffer from milder and more common forms of SAD. The second two patients, "Peggy" and Alan, have suffered rather severely and have participated in the Seasonal Studies Program at the National Institute of Mental Health for several years. While such severe SAD symptoms are less common, they are capable of interfering markedly with the lives of those who suffer from them, and it is particularly important that they be recognized and treated.

Neal and Angela: Light for a Living and Light to Write By

Neal Owens is currently the president of the Sunbox Company, which sells lights for the treatment of SAD. He is thirty-one years old and has had difficulties during the winter for the past four years. His problems occurred mostly in the sphere of his work as a sales representative, as he found his productivity declining markedly in the winter months. He would sleep late, cancel appointments, and spend much of the day at home, depressed. It is not surprising that for a salesman, who needs to be upbeat, energetic, and eager to interact with others and promote his product, the symptoms of SAD would be rather disabling.

He consulted a psychiatrist at the urging of his girlfriend, and was given a series of antidepressants, none of which proved helpful. After seeing a television documentary about SAD, he mentioned light therapy to his doctor, who was not supportive of the idea. He then obtained information about it from the NIMH, constructed his own light box, and began therapy on his own. He switched therapists and improved noticeably, using a combination of light and psychotherapy. Neal's positive experience with light therapy inspired him to change careers and start a business to help others, by selling light boxes and providing information on SAD. He recently married and feels very hopeful about the future, now that his winter depressions are under control.

Angela is a writer in her mid-fifties, with a long history of winter difficulties too mild either to meet criteria for a diagnosis of SAD or to lead her to seek medical help. Since her childhood she has disliked winter and dark climates and places, which she has avoided whenever possible. She thought of herself as entering a "little hibernation" in the winter, when she would feel less creative than usual and "slightly melancholy," if not actually depressed. She had never consciously associated her low energy states with the quality of winter light, but when she first heard about SAD, she immediately identified herself as having a minor version of the condition.

Angela first found out about light therapy when she was writing a magazine article on the subject, for which she interviewed me. But she did nothing about her own winter problems until four years later, when she had strenuous writing deadlines to meet. She installed a set of lights on her desk, and they have been there ever since. She uses the lights both summer and winter, whenever she happens to be working. She observes:

> Since I started using the lights in winter, my brain seems to be clearer, I seem to be happier, and the writing goes better. Not only am I much more productive, but I also seem to be much more creative. The words come more easily and I seem to get more images. I also don't mind being at my desk and writing as much as I did before. When I used to think of having to write in the winter, it was a great effort. I felt almost as though I would have to pull the resistant words out of my head by force and sheer will. Now I have a much lighter feeling about it. It's more fun.

Peggy: Forty-one Grim Winters

Peggy is an attractive, youthful-looking woman in her late fifties, with blue eyes, fair skin, and silver-gray hair. Retired now, she worked as a medical statistician for many years. She was married twice and now lives alone. She grew up in the Midwest and has had difficulty with the winter since she was eleven years old. She was always an excellent student. She would start out particularly well in the fall semester, but when winter came, there were always problems. Her teachers, who regarded her as one of their best students, would register surprise and dismay at the sudden change in her work. Her parents would also become "disgusted" with her performance, which would decline for no apparent reason.

This seasonal problem in school performance increased over time. In her senior year of high school she was an honors student, and was given the responsibility for keeping a log of student aid contributions. The task simply involved putting a check mark next to the name of every student who had donated a nickel. Although she applied herself to the job enthusiastically in the fall, by the time November came, she found it overwhelming. Having such difficulties with so simple a task was confusing for Peggy, but typical of her state of mind every winter. She scored above the 99th percentile in intelligence tests, but when she found herself having difficulties with simple things, she believed she was a fraud and that the test results must have been wrong; that teachers must have given her good grades just because she was a nice person.

Peggy is sure that her mother had SAD as well. During the winter her mother would nap most of the day, whereas in summer she was energetic and vivacious. Both Peggy and her sister were conceived in August. Winter seemed like a low time for the whole family, and Peggy's own difficulties went unnoticed by the other family members. These troubles reached a crisis during her junior year of high school:

> It was mid-January. There had been a string of gray days but nothing bad had happened. I hadn't failed any exam or lost a boyfriend, but I felt so weighed down and in such a state of despair that I saw no future for myself. Everything I looked at was wrong. I went down into the basement, found a water pipe, got a piece of clothesline and tried to make a noose out of it, but I was unable to do so. I just didn't have the energy to figure out how to do it properly or the strength to do it.
>
> I went back upstairs to the bedroom I shared with my sister, and lay down on my bed crying, disgusted that I couldn't even commit suicide properly. I kept the whole thing to myself. The next day was sunny and I said to myself, "Had you committed suicide yesterday, you wouldn't be alive to see this beautiful day," and I felt better. I always thought that it was a miracle that the sun was shining the next day. I wonder what would have happened had it been cloudy. That experience taught me not to try and predict the future—that one day can be bad and the next day good.

Although Peggy had thoughts of killing herself on several subsequent occasions, that was the only time she ever came close to trying.

During adulthood Peggy's seasonal cycles continued. She would find herself beginning to prepare for winter in September, buying a six-month supply of toilet paper and all other nonperishable goods, "like a squirrel about to hibernate." In November, she notes:

> The physical difficulties start first: eating more, sleeping more, and the slowing down of brain functioning. Initially, I'm not sad. I can still sit down and laugh with friends and enjoy my favorite TV shows. As it becomes obvious that I'm less able to function at work or with friends, mental depression starts taking over. I have trouble writing Christmas

cards, which adds to my depression, since I am unable to communicate with people I really care about. Even though I really don't want to lose touch with them, I simply want to be left alone from December until April.

Needless to say, this wish to withdraw caused Peggy difficulties both at work and in her personal relationships:

I worked in an office where there was a lot of gift-giving. I would feel very upset with people who got their gifts out before December 20. I would wonder, "Why can't I get my gifts out on time?" By then I was closing the door to my office. I didn't want anyone to come in, and I would select only those phone calls I wanted to take. It was okay if people just wanted to chat, but I would hate it when they wanted me to dig up data, or worse still, to do a computer run. In the summer, doing that stuff was like a game. It was fun to sit in front of the computer. But in the winter any task was daunting.

The winter changes also caused problems in Peggy's relationships with men, in part due to her irritability and fault-finding—common early signs of her winter depressions. She would drive to work in the winter "cussing out the other drivers." It was hard for her to believe that this was the same morning commute that she found enjoyable during the spring. The same relationships to which she was open in the summertime seemed unappealing in the winter:

I had several relationships with men I met in the fall, during the beautiful, sunny October days, and managed, because of the early passion of the relationship, to make it through the first winter. Summer was great. Then the next winter came along and the relationship would collapse. During the winter, when someone canceled an evening social engagement, I generally felt relieved and spared the guilt of having canceled the engagement myself.

The memory and thought-processing problems that troubled Peggy during her school and college days continued to cause difficulties later on, as well. She would forget to set her burglar alarm, where she had put the keys, and other things that she would take for granted in the summer. Every chore seemed to take much longer in the winter, and complex tasks, which were easy for her in the spring and summer, were quite impossible during the winter months. She would become anxious at her failures, irritated by her ineptitude, and accuse herself once again of being a fraud.

She would eat more in the winter, particularly carbohydrates. When she lived in the Northeast, she would have to drive home from work for an hour each evening through the gray New England landscape, and when she finally reached home, as she confessed to the minister at her church one Lent, she would not be able to resist gorging on cookies. Was she not guilty of gluttony?

Her energy level stayed low all winter long. Over the years, she developed strategies for coping. For example, she would buy lots of winter clothes and let the laundry pile up for months until the spring, when she could finally face doing it all.

Peggy's sex drive was low during the winter. She recalls with amusement how there were two workmen in the house one winter. In the late afternoon, she was unable to stay awake, so she retired to bed and asked them to tell her husband that he could find her there when he got home from work. When he returned he was incensed, "as though I were this terrible seductress who had gone to bed, tempting the workmen in the house. He felt as though I had destroyed his honor. I laugh when I think of it now. All I wanted to do was sleep, and the last thing I was interested in was seducing those men."

Peggy was in classical psychoanalysis for three years, "five days a week, every month of the year except for August," but the seasonal pattern of her problems never emerged as an issue for discussion in the analysis. She had no other formal treatment for her seasonal difficulties.

During the summer she would often feel even more energetic and enthusiastic than the average person. Her high energy level would keep her working in the garden till nine at night and she would stay awake until two in the morning. She required only six hours of sleep. She recalls with amusement the summer day when she went rowing on a lake with a very large man. She felt so energetic that she did all the rowing, and the sight of a small woman rowing a two-hundred-pound man across a lake caused a group of passing fishermen to whistle catcalls at him.

It was her winter depressions, not her summer highs, that brought Peggy to the NIMH Seasonal Studies Program. She was beginning to enter her November decline when she received a tax audit notice. The thought of having to collect and submit all the necessary records threw her into an intense depression and induced her to seek psychiatric help. She was fifty-two at the time and had suffered regular winter depressions for forty-one years, though she had never recognized them as such. On being asked how that could have happened, she replied, "I thought it was normal to feel like that in the winter."

Peggy has been treated successfully with light therapy for the past four years and has participated in several studies of light treatment. Shortly after treatment was first started in January, she managed to refinance her house within a week—something she would never have been able to do before during the winter months. Since entering the Seasonal Studies Program, Peggy has learned to take winter vacations in the sun. She moved into a house with large windows and decorated it in light colors. She has been in weekly psychotherapy for the past few years to deal with a variety of psychological issues. Having retired from her former job, she busies herself with volunteer work and has been a founding member of a new support group for patients with SAD. As a result of her treatment, Peggy now feels fulfilled and much happier with her life than ever before.

When she thinks of what her understanding of SAD and her light treatment have given her, Peggy concludes:

> Now I don't have to blame myself for what happened in past winters. It's liberating to know that SAD is a physical disorder—not my fault. I can give myself some leeway for what happens now. I don't have to be so critical of myself. I have a tool to make myself feel better.

Alan: Too Low or Too High

Alan is a divorced electronics technician in his late thirties. Well-built, dark, and handsome, he has a wry smile, a twinkle in his eyes, and a cynical attitude toward life. This view of the world may have been partially shaped by his Seasonal Affective Disorder and its consequences. Since about age seven, he has had winter difficulties—times when he didn't want to be around people, accompanied by changes in sleep and appetite. Considered a "moody" child, his greatest early difficulties were in relation to school, where his dyslexia was aggravated during the winter. He remembers reversing numbers and letters, writing on the wrong side of the page, and having great difficulty spelling. Yet somehow he managed better in the summer and fall. In winter his increasing difficulties made him panicky about going to school, which he perceived as "an institution where I would have to go in order to be humiliated."

By age twelve he was refusing to go to school on a regular basis. He was taken to a psychiatrist and given electroshock therapy, apparently to cure him of his "fears, phobias, and dread of going to school." Not only was it unhelpful, but Alan has grim memories of the experience. By thirteen, the problem was so severe that reform school was considered and, later, when his parents agreed to go regularly to see a psychiatrist with him, the county provided him with a tutor a few days a week. With this help Alan was able to pass seventh and eighth grades. Eventually, the tutor was dropped and Alan played hooky regularly until he was fifteen. By then he was aware that his problems were not only related to school, but in some way also to the changing seasons, as he continued to feel bad in the winter.

At fifteen, Alan began to work and, after a series of jobs, became an electronics technician. He dated girls extensively in his late teens and, at age nineteen, entered into a stormy marriage that was to last eight years. The turbulence in his work and domestic life was dictated to a large extent by his dramatic responses to the seasons:

> By October I would definitely start to feel a little gray. My performance at work would start falling off, as would my strength, and my sleep would begin to increase. At work, my output would suffer and I'd begin to start charging less for the same job. I lost confidence in the quality of my work. I'd start worrying about everything and ask myself, "Why the hell am I doing this? What's the use?" It was somewhere between apathy and panic because I knew something was going wrong, but had no idea at the time what the heck it was.

His difficulties at work caused Alan to lose jobs on a regular basis, usually around Christmas. Four to five months of unemployment would follow, when he would live on the money he had earned and saved.

During that time I would feel very depressed. My wife would do all the grocery shopping. In the early years she was worried and panicky and would try to come home and be a cheerleader. I was usually so disagreeable to be around that she didn't say anything about my behavior. If anybody said, "What's the matter, why aren't you up getting a job?" I would get very upset, scream and yell. Usually, after one of those encounters, people would stay clear of me.

If money ran out, Alan would "get some kind of a job, moving pianos, driving semis, fixing cars, collecting loans, or bouncing at nightclubs"—anything except work at electronics repairs. He was unable to figure out the logic of the circuitry, diagnose a problem, and find a solution to it—all things that came easily to him during the summer months.

During the winter, Alan found little pleasure in anything. Occasionally he would forget himself and his misery for a few minutes, but would soon be engulfed again by helplessness and despair. He considered suicide many times. Standing by the roadside, he would think of walking in front of a truck; or he would stand on a balcony or bridge and consider "flopping over onto the asphalt below." While taking a bath or shaving himself, he would contemplate his razor and think of cutting his wrists. On one occasion, in the winter, Alan actually tried to kill himself. His winter problems had been getting worse during his late twenties and early thirties, and during that particular winter he felt the worst ever—"incapacitated, hospital material." One day he sat for a long time with the barrel of a gun in his mouth, the hammer cocked and his finger on the trigger. He still doesn't know exactly what stopped him from pulling the trigger.

By mid-March, Alan would be aware of a difference in the way he was feeling, and by mid-April he would begin to emerge from his depression. Between spring and summer he would move "along a pretty even curve" from depression to exuberance or even mania.

Usually by the time something was green, I was beginning to feel better. It's frightening at first. You begin to wonder, "Is it a teaser? Am I going to feel better for a few days and then bad again?" By May I was feeling pretty damn good. By June and July I was feeling like it was very urgent to do things. With a lot of enthusiasm and exhilaration, I'd think, "I beat the beast again.'' I felt fantastic compared with how hellacious I had felt in the winter.

By July 4 I would really begin to accelerate, to feel extremely strong and healthy, definitely virile, much more likely to be at all the parties. I'd work as much overtime as I could get. I was on top of the world. By August things were going even faster, and I was needing less sleep. A lot of people thought I was doing speed during the summer, especially at the time when a lot of people were doing speed. People were amused, shocked, or irritated. For example, at the beach or a party, if I wanted to go into the water nude, I would just do it. But I wasn't using drugs; my mood was simply high—it was summer, after all.

My sex drive would increase and become just about my reason for being. Trying to find one individual who had the same drive was kind of tough to do. I usually ended up seeing a lot of people during the summer months.

By August my temper was much worse. If nothing drastic happened, I would generally get through the summer with just a couple of fights. If I really got speeded up, which happened one particular year, I got into trouble with the police. By September I'd mellow out a little. I'd usually be licking my wounds from what happened in July and August.

Although Alan had made a connection between his changing behavior and the seasons, he had never specifically connected his behavioral changes to the light. But he had always been fascinated by light: "colored light, sunlight, white light, reflections, and, in the sixties, strobe lights.'' He even built some colored strobe lights for himself. However, he was skeptical when his psychiatrist recommended the NIMH Seasonal Studies Program to him. It sounded "absolutely bizarre— right up there with shock treatments and sleeping under the full moon. It was kind of a lunatic idea.'' But antidepressants, lithium, and psychotherapy had been of no help to him, so he thought he had little to lose.

His first light treatment was given as part of a study on an inpatient unit. He recalls that "about the third day I said to one of the nurses, 'I feel kind of funny, light-headed. Something's happening.' I got the dose of light that night and I knew what the feeling was—exhilaration. It was like compressing two or three months into four days. By the fourth day, I asked a nurse to marry me or something, and by five days I was higher than a kite.''

Although formerly skeptical, Alan is now convinced that light has a real biological effect on him and is not just a placebo. He has been asked to stop using the lights on a number of occasions as part of the research program, and he has become depressed each time. When he restarts light treatments, he has observed that the effects are not immediate; it takes a day or two before he begins to feel good again. If he uses them for too long, he gets a tingling feeling in his hands and feet, and becomes "wired" and overactive.

Alan has been using the lights for the past four years. He has special sets at work, where he has no windows, and at home. Since starting light treatment he has functioned well at his job and has worked consistently. Financially, it's made a big difference for him to be working twelve months a year instead of nine. He has been able to establish friendships and hold on to them "without having to start over again in the spring because I've insulted people or disappointed them or just felt too bad to have anything to do with them." He spends time on hobbies he enjoys, such as carpentry. Curiously, he has not been troubled by manic symptoms in the summer, probably because his light environment is more constant across the seasons. Because Alan's mood is more even all year round, he finds life easier and less unpredictable. He has become more optimistic and has been able to enter into more stable, long-term relationships.

We now recognize that most people experience some changes in mood and behavior in conjunction with the seasons. These vary widely across the population. At one end of the spectrum are those who experience hardly any changes at all. At the other end are those, like Peggy and Alan, whose lives are severely disrupted by the influence of the seasons on their mood and behavior. Neal's life has been less severely disrupted. He has been lethargic, sad, withdrawn, and unproductive during the winter, but he has never been unable to function either at work or socially, nor has he ever felt suicidal. All three of these people would qualify for a diagnosis of SAD, based on the severity of their symptoms.

Angela's winter problems fall on the milder side of the spectrum of seasonal change. They have never led her to seek medical attention, nor has she been conspicuously depressed. However, the lethargy and dullness she experiences during the winter have interfered with her ability to function as a creative writer. She is not severely affected enough to qualify for a diagnosis of SAD, but could rather be described as suffering from the "winter blues" or, as it is more technically termed, "subsyndromal SAD."

Despite diagnostic differences, all of these people benefited from therapy with bright light. Peggy and Alan received this in a formal treatment setting, whereas Neal and Angela undertook treatment on their own. Both Neal and Angela believe that they made mistakes as a result of not having had their treatment properly supervised. In Neal's case, he used the lights for too many hours each day. As a result he felt "wired"—excessively activated and uncharacteristically irritable. Through trial and error he finally found out how much light he needed. In Angela's case, she did not realize that she should sit within three feet of the fixture and thus did not experience the full benefit of the light for some time.

The four people described in this section are very different individuals, united by one particular trait—their marked physical and emotional responses to the changing seasons. Although their symptoms will sound familiar to all SAD sufferers, individual experiences are colored to a large degree by a person's particular personality and life situation. The following chapter will show you how to evaluate your own degree of seasonality, and whether you might stand to benefit from light therapy.

3

How Seasonal Are You?

"It is certainly very cold," said Peggotty.
"Everybody must feel it so."
"I feel it more than other people," said
Mrs. Gummidge.
        —*Charles Dickens,* David Copperfield

In the charming exchange from *David Copperfield* quoted above, both characters are correct, at least to some degree. While all people have some reaction, both physical and emotional, to extreme seasonal or climatic changes, some people really do experience them more severely than others. Such sensitivity is often experienced as a change in mood and behavior. As I have noted, seasonality exists as a spectrum within the population. Patients with SAD find themselves on the extreme end of it, whereas others have extremely low degrees of seasonality. The purpose of this chapter is to help you evaluate how seasonal you are, what your pattern of seasonality is, and how it compares to those with diagnosed cases of SAD or the winter blues.

My colleagues and I at the National Institute of Mental Health set out some years ago to develop a scale to measure an individual's seasonality. Questions from this scale, called the Seasonal Pattern Assessment Questionnaire (SPAQ) are shown below. The SPAQ has been found to be a valid way of measuring seasonality in many different populations. Although a person's seasonality is to some degree inherent, it also depends on where he or she lives. For example, someone who shows marked seasonality in Alaska may show none in Hawaii. In order for

32

you to obtain a stable and accurate assessment, it is necessary for you to think back over a period of time—say, three years—when you have lived continuously in one climatic region. Since seasonality can change over time, and the most recent years are generally clearest in one's memory, think of the most recent three years during which you have lived consistently in one area when considering the questions below.

INSTRUCTIONS FOR COMPLETING THE SEASONAL PATTERN ASSESSMENT QUESTIONNAIRE (SPAQ)

The purpose of this questionnaire is to find out how your mood and behavior change over time. Please fill in all relevant circles. Note: Answer according to *your* experience—not that of others you may have observed.

How to Score the SPAQ

1. Your pattern of seasonality: You can determine your pattern of seasonality by examining your answers to question 1, which asks during which months of the year you feel best and worst, eat most and least, gain and lose the most weight, sleep most and least, and socialize most and least. In practice, we generally evaluate the pattern of seasonality only according to when you feel best and worst. Answers to the other parts of this question provide us with additional information regarding some other typical symptoms of SAD.

If you feel worst in December, January, or February, you have a winter seasonal pattern.
If you feel worst in July or August, you have a summer seasonal pattern.
If you feel worst at both of the above times, you have a summer-winter pattern.
If there is no time of year when you generally feel best or worst, you have a nonseasonal pattern.

Questionnaire for Evaluating Your Degree of Seasonality (Modified from the Seasonal Pattern Assessment Questionnaire —SPAQ, of Rosenthal, Bradt and Wehr).

The purpose of this form is to find out how your mood and behavior change over time. Please fill in all the relevant circles. Note: We are interested in your experience; not others you may have observed.

1. In the following questions, fill in circles for all applicable months. This may be a single month ●, a cluster of months, E.G., ●●●, or any other grouping.
   At what time of year do you . . .

	J F M A M J J A S O N D	
A. Feel best	O O O O O O O O O O O O	O
B. Tend to gain most weight	O O O O O O O O O O O O	O
C. Socialize most	O O O O O O O O O O O O	O
D. Sleep least	O O O O O O O O O O O O	O
E. Eat most	O O O O O O O O O O O O	O
F. Lose most weight	O O O O O O O O O O O O	OR O
G. Socialize least	O O O O O O O O O O O O	O
H. Feel worst	O O O O O O O O O O O O	O
I. Eat least	O O O O O O O O O O O O	O
J. Sleep most	O O O O O O O O O O O O	O

   No particular month(s) stand out as extreme on a regular basis

2. To what degree do the following change with the seasons?
   (ONE CIRCLE ONLY FOR EACH QUESTION)

	0 NO CHANGE	1 SLIGHT CHANGE	2 MODERATE CHANGE	3 MARKED CHANGE	4 EXTREMELY MARKED CHANGE
A. Sleep length	O	O	O	O	O
B. Social activity	O	O	O	O	O
C. Mood (overall feeling of well being)	O	O	O	O	O
D. Weight	O	O	O	O	O
E. Appetite	O	O	O	O	O
F. Energy level	O	O	O	O	O

3. If you experience changes with the seasons, do you feel that these are a problem for you? . . . . O No
                                                                                                              O Yes

	MILD	MODERATE	MARKED	SEVERE	DISABLING
If yes, is this problem	O	O	O	O	O

4. By how much does your weight fluctuate during the course of the year?
   - O 0–3 lbs.
   - O 4–7 lbs.
   - O 8–11 lbs.
   - O 12–15 lbs.
   - O 16–20 lbs.
   - O Over 20 lbs.

5. Approximately how many hours of each 24-hour day do you sleep during each season? (Include naps)

   Hours slept per day / OVER 18 HOURS

O WINTER (Dec 21–Mar 20)	0 1 2 3 4 5 6 7 8 9 10 11 12 13 14 15 16 17 18	O
O SPRING (Mar 21–June 20)	0 1 2 3 4 5 6 7 8 9 10 11 12 13 14 15 16 17 18	O
O SUMMER (June 21–Sept 20)	0 1 2 3 4 5 6 7 8 9 10 11 12 13 14 15 16 17 18	O
O FALL (Sept 21–Dec 20)	0 1 2 3 4 5 6 7 8 9 10 11 12 13 14 15 16 17 18	O

6. Do you notice a change in food preference during the different seasons? . . . . O No
                                                                                                      O Yes

   Please specify:
   _____
   _____
   _____

There are other less common seasonal patterns. For example, some people feel worst in the spring; others in spring and fall.

2. *Your degree of seasonality:* You can determine your degree of seasonality by examining your answers to question 2, which asks to what degree you experience seasonal changes in six different functions: a) sleep length, b) social activity, c) mood (overall feeling of well-being), d) weight, e) appetite, and f) energy level.

Each of these functions should be scored according to the five possible levels of severity. Score each item as follows:

No change	0 points
Slight change	1 point
Moderate change	2 points
Marked change	3 points
Extremely marked change	4 points

In order to calculate your level of seasonality, add up your scores for all six items, thereby deriving your overall seasonality score.

3. *Are seasonal changes a problem for you and, if so, to what degree:* This information is derived from question 3. If seasonal changes are a problem for you, you may regard them as mild, moderate, marked, severe, or disabling.

4. *Other information derived from the SPAQ: not for scoring purposes:* Answers to questions 4, 5, and 6 provide information about the actual number of pounds you gain and lose during the year, the number of hours you sleep during different seasons, and whether you have any change in food preference through the year. Although these questions are not taken into account for scoring purposes, they are of interest to clinicians and researchers who treat SAD, and may be of interest to you as well. For example, we have found that patients with SAD report sleeping an average of two-and-a-half hours more in winter than in summer. Corresponding figures for people with the winter blues and the general population in the northeastern United States are 1.7 hours and 0.7 hours respectively.

How to Interpret Your Scores on the SPAQ

1. Your pattern of seasonality: Almost half of all people in the northern United States report that they feel worst during the winter, and can be said to have a winter pattern of seasonality. This pattern is more marked among people who live in the higher latitudes. For example, a higher percentage of people dislike winter in New Hampshire (42° north) than in Sarasota, Florida (27° north). On the other hand, as one examines locations closer to the equator, more people say that they dislike the summer. By the time one reaches Sarasota, Florida, more people report disliking the summer than the winter, presumably because of the heat and humidity. This information is derived from surveys in which the SPAQ was used as part of a collaboration between the NIMH, the New York State Psychiatric Institute, and the Psychiatric Institutes of America.

Most winter types report eating most, sleeping most, and gaining the most weight in the winter months and, conversely, eating and sleeping least, and losing weight, during the summer months. They also find it easiest to socialize during the summer. Although they often join in the round of parties that takes place at Christmas, they find it hard to muster up the spontaneous pleasure of summer get-togethers, where they feel a true desire to mix with people. Rather, winter celebrations often take on the quality of a chore, a command performance, asked of people who would much rather be left alone with a dish of sweets. Indeed, people with SAD often report a strong preference for sweets and starches during the winter months—an exaggeration of an eating trend observed in the general population. People also commonly report preferring "heavy" foods—stews and casseroles—during the winter months, whereas salads, fresh fruit and vegetables, and protein-rich foods are preferred in the summer months.

Summer types, by definition, mark the summer months as the time when they feel worst. Some of them like the winter months best, but others—the summer-winter types—also mark January and February as months when they feel bad. This last group may only enjoy the spring and fall. People who dislike summer may tend to socialize least at that time. Unlike winter types, they often do not overeat, oversleep, and gain weight during the time of year when they feel the worst. Instead, they tend to eat less, lose weight, and sleep less. As more people learn to control their winter symptoms by modifying their environmental light, and as the world's climate heats up as a result of the greenhouse effect, I would predict that the percentage of those who dislike summer will increase and the percentage of those who dislike winter will decrease.

Some people report very few seasonal changes at all. These people will generally mark most of the items in question 2 as not changing with the seasons. They often have a hard time understanding why their more seasonal friends and relatives are making such a fuss about the cold or heat, the humidity or cloudiness. They may be tempted to see these exaggerated responses as character defects. These non-seasonal people should understand that they are blessed with a constitution well-insulated against seasonal changes, and that this is a biological gift not a moral virtue.

The pattern of seasonal behavior changes seen in SAD patients— sleeping and eating more and gaining weight in the winter—are also seen in the general population. What distinguishes people with SAD and the winter blues from the general population is the overall seasonality score, which is greater in the first two groups than in the general population.

2. *Your overall seasonality score:* Since there are six items on which this score is based, and you can obtain a score of zero to four on each item, the overall seasonality score has a possible range of 0 to 24. The behaviors that make up this score—sleep length, social activity, mood, weight, appetite, and energy level—vary seasonally, particularly in SAD patients, but also in those less severely affected and in the general population. The extent to which they vary is reflected in the overall seasonality score.

An average overall score ranges from 4 to 7 points. If your score is 8 to 11, you may fall into the category of subsyndromal Seasonal Affective Disorder, also known as the "winter blues" or "February blahs"; and if your score is 11 or more, you may well suffer from Seasonal Affective Disorder (SAD). More specific guidelines to help you evaluate whether you may be suffering from these conditions are outlined below (see table 1). People with higher seasonality scores are more likely to regard the changing seasons as a problem (see question 3); tend to show greater changes in weight and in the number of hours they sleep per day during different seasons (see questions 4 and 5); and are more likely to report a seasonal change in food preference (see question 6).

The seasonality score may change over time, and also according to where you live. For example, someone who has difficulty with the winter is likely to have a higher seasonality score when living farther from the equator. The reverse is true for someone with a summer problem.

According to a population study conducted by Dr. Siegfried Kasper and colleagues in the Seasonal Studies Program at the NIMH women in their late thirties are likely to have the highest seasonality scores, and these scores tend to decrease as they get older. There is less evidence that the seasonality score changes with age in men.

We still do not understand why certain people are more seasonal than others, although a tendency to develop SAD does seem to run in families. It is possible that the genetic vulnerability to seasonality may be expressed as an abnormality in visual information processing or in certain light-sensitive areas of the brain.

3. Are seasonal changes a problem for you and, if so, to what degree: The answer to this question should be related to your overall seasonality score. The higher your score, the more likely it is that the changing seasons are a problem for you. Almost all people accepted into the NIMH programs as either SAD or subsyndromal SAD patients rated their seasonal changes as being at least a mild problem. Approximately 25 percent of the general population surveyed in the northern United States report that the changing seasons are a problem for them. Most of these complain of winter rather than summer difficulties, and could benefit by increasing their environmental light exposure during the winter months.

The section that follows should help you evaluate whether you suffer from one of the two conditions that have been found to respond to bright environmental light: SAD and the winter blues. It is important to remember, however, that the SPAQ has been developed as an instrument for population surveys, as well as to screen patients in a clinical setting. No one should depend upon the test results alone as a guide to diagnosis. If, after completing this questionnaire, you think you may have a significant problem with the changing seasons, I would encourage you to follow up by scheduling a detailed clinical evaluation. Guidelines are provided on the following pages to help you decide when it may be appropriate to consult a doctor.

ESTIMATING WHETHER YOU ARE SUFFERING FROM SAD OR THE WINTER BLUES ON THE BASIS OF THE SPAQ

Your answers to questions 1–3 on the SPAQ can give you a rough idea as to whether you have suffered from SAD or the winter blues. Remember that these two conditions are not clearly demarcated from each other. A person may have the winter blues when living in one type of climate (say, southern California) but this may develop into full-blown SAD after moving north (say, to Michigan). The same person may be free of all symptoms after relocating permanently to an equatorial climate, such as the Galapagos Islands. Guidelines for making diagnoses of SAD and the winter blues are provided in the following table:

Table 1: Diagnosing SAD and the Winter Blues on the Basis of the SPAQ

	SAD	Winter Blues
Question 1		
Seasonal Pattern: During which months do you feel worst?	winter type (Feel worst in months between December and February.)	winter type (Feel worst in months between December and February.)
Question 2		
Overall Seasonality Score: To what degree do the following change with the seasons: sleep length; social activity; mood; weight; appetite; and energy level? (Obtain score as indicated above)	11 or more	8–10

	SAD	Winter Blues
Question 3		
Are seasonal changes in mood and behavior a problem for you? If yes, is the problem mild, moderate, marked, severe, or disabling?	Yes, at least moderate	At least mild, but you may answer "no"

In providing diagnostic guidelines, based on a questionnaire, we decided on cutoff scores which include most people who have the condition in question, and exclude most people who do not have the condition. The guidelines outlined in the above table tend to be a little on the strict side, especially for diagnosing the winter blues. In other words, studies have shown that some people may not meet SPAQ criteria for these conditions, but may be found to have SAD or the winter blues on the basis of clinical evaluation. Those people with SAD will generally, at the very least, meet SPAQ criteria for the winter blues. Some people with the winter blues, however, may not qualify for any diagnosis, according to the above SPAQ criteria. People tend to rate themselves differently—more or less strictly—which may account for some of the discrepancies between self-rating and clinical evaluation. If your diagnosis, based on your SPAQ responses, differs from your perception of yourself as someone with SAD or the winter blues, remember that the SPAQ is only a guide, not a hard-and-fast diagnostic test. The following table shows how clinicians go about making the diagnoses of SAD and the winter blues, and may provide you with further insight into whether you may be suffering from one of these conditions.

Table 2: Clinical Guide to Distinguishing SAD from the Winter Blues

	SAD	Winter Blues
Winter changes last at least four weeks	Yes	Yes
Regular winter problems (at least two consecutive years)	Yes	Yes
Interferes with function (work or interpersonal)	To a significant degree (productivity decreases markedly; marked loss of interest or pleasure; withdrawal from friends and family; conspicuous changes in energy, sleeping, or weight)	To a mild degree (less creative; slightly less productive; less enthusiastic about life; less enthusiastic about socializing; slight decrease in energy or bothersome weight gain)
Have seen doctor or therapist about winter problem (or others have suggested it)	Yes	No
Have felt really down or depressed in winter for at least two weeks	Yes	No

The Implications of Your SPAQ Results

The main practical value of knowing how seasonal you are and what your pattern is relates to how likely you are to benefit from increasing the level of light in your living environment. Many research studies have shown that most people with marked winter difficulties—those suffering from SAD—will benefit from enhancing their environmental lighting. Recent studies have shown that the same is true for those suffering from milder winter changes—the "winter blues." (see chapter 4). On the other hand, in a series of studies at the NIMH, we have shown that people with little or no seasonal change are unlikely to benefit from light therapy when it is administered in the same way in which it has been given to SAD patients. In fact, some people have even found that light therapy makes them feel uncomfortable!

When to Seek Medical Advice

It is likely that in the future, more and more people will become aware of comparatively minor, subtle seasonal difficulties and will attempt to modify their environmental lighting to cope with them. You should definitely seek medical help if:

1. Your functioning is impaired to a significant degree. For example, if you develop problems at work, including:

- difficulty completing tasks that you could previously manage
- difficulty getting to work on time on a regular basis
- marked reduction in your ability to think and concentrate

The problem can also occur in your personal life. For example, you may feel that you want to be left alone and withdraw significantly, which can cause difficulties with friends or family. Your spouse or partner may feel that you are distant and unavailable.

You should also suspect that your ability to function is slipping if you begin to fall behind with bills and other necessary chores.

2. You experience significant feelings of depression. This includes:

- regularly feeling sad or having crying spells
- feeling that life is not worthwhile, or wishing you would not wake up in the morning
- thinking negative thoughts about yourself—that you are a bad person, incompetent, unreliable, an impostor—which would not really apply to you at other times of the year
- finding yourself feeling guilty much of the time
- feeling pessimistic about the future

3. Your physical functions are markedly disturbed during the winter. For example:

- you require several more hours of sleep per day, or have great difficulty waking up in the morning
- you would like to lie about for much of the day
- you feel you have no control over your eating and weight

All of these symptoms are indications that you should have the situation checked out by a qualified professional. If light therapy is required, a qualified professional should supervise the treatment. People with mild winter changes may choose instead to increase the lighting in their homes or workplaces. This topic is discussed in greater detail in the section on light therapy.

Besides the seasonal changes noted above, some people react strongly to a variety of climatic conditions. Most people enjoy sunny days and dislike gray, cloudy days; most prefer dry to humid weather. The difference between seasonal types is primarily in the degree to which they dislike certain types of weather or climate. Winter types strongly prefer long, sunny days and abhor short, dark ones. Summer types, on the other hand, strongly dislike the heat, and greatly prefer cool weather.

Obviously, there are external factors that can produce changes in mood or physical symptoms on a seasonal basis that do not imply SAD. For example, people with allergies have trouble during certain seasons. Pollen appears in high concentrations at different times of the year, and your specific allergy may determine when you are most miserable. I mention this mainly to point out that if a problem occurs seasonally, that simply provides a clue that some seasonally changing variable may be causing distress or difficulty. This might include a psychological or work-related factor. For example, an accountant may be most stressed at tax season, and an air-conditioning salesman during the summer. In all of these cases, the changing seasons are like some giant shapesorter, sorting out different types of people according to their specific biological or occupational vulnerabilities.

Seasonality As a Dimension of Human Experience

Through most of this section, I have considered seasonality insofar as it indicates illness and needs to be reversed. I believe it is important that we do not regard seasonality only as a disease—as one might regard diabetes or asthma. Especially in its less marked degrees, seasonality provides us with a shifting way of experiencing our world—a richness and color that most people would not wish to do without. There is evidence that some artistic and creative people experience marked shifts in moods and energy with the changing seasons, and many of them regard these as necessary or integral to their work. But even in those of us not given to creative work, the internal shifts associated with the changing seasons may be a source of joy and inspiration. If this is the case, there is clearly no reason to alter them. But if the effects of certain seasons create more pain and havoc than fulfillment, the good news is that there is now a way to alleviate them.

4

SAD: An Owner's and Parent's Manual

What are the risk factors that predispose people to getting SAD? What do we know about the biological and physiological basis of the various symptoms? What is it like to have the winter blues, as opposed to full-fledged SAD? How does SAD manifest in children and adolescents? How common is the problem? These are some of the most frequently asked questions about SAD. Many of them have been addressed to some degree already, but for those who want a fuller understanding of the subject, here are some of the answers, based on my clinical experience and the latest research.

WHAT PREDISPOSES PEOPLE TO GETTING SAD?

The symptoms of SAD result from factors in the environment that act upon a vulnerable individual, resulting in the problems already described. What is it about certain people that makes them vulnerable to these environmental effects? Which environmental effects are important?

45

If we can find out those influences that are important in producing the symptoms of SAD, then perhaps we can modify them. That line of thinking was the key to recognizing the critical role of light deprivation in the development of winter depressive symptoms, and to the use of light in reversing these symptoms. Both clinician and patient should be continually vigilant toward fluctuations in harmful environmental influences, such as light deprivation, even after these have been initially identified. It is surprising how often such a simple explanation for clinical deterioration can escape even an experienced clinician or a sophisticated patient. For example, one patient with identified SAD begins to feel badly during the bright summer weather. At first, neither the patient nor his therapist realizes that this is happening because he is spending most of the day developing film in a darkroom. Among the other environmental influences that should be considered in understanding the development of symptoms in SAD patients are psychological and interpersonal stresses.

The three keys to the development of depression in SAD are:

- Inherent vulnerability
- Light deprivation
- Stress

Inherent Vulnerability

Although SAD affects all types of people, women are most vulnerable, and the twenties through the forties seem to be prime time for this problem. SAD runs in families, and most patients have at least one close relative with a history of depression (often SAD) at some time in the past. An example of familial transmission is described below by a woman in Tennessee, who has had a long history of SAD. She notes: "We have identified [my SAD] as coming to me through my paternal grandmother, being carried by her seven sons, and showing up as active illness in the females of my generation."

Are certain ethnic groups more likely to suffer from SAD? This frequently asked question is often inspired by the idea that SAD may have evolved as an adaptive mechanism—a condition that conferred a survival advantage on the sufferer. Perhaps among those in the far north, where winter conditions are harsh and food is especially scarce during the cold months, it was advantageous to be inactive, overeat, store body fat, and withdraw during winter. Maybe the symptoms of SAD had an energy-conserving function, like the hibernation of bears. If this were the case, perhaps you would find more SAD in those of Scandinavian origin—the blond-haired and blue-eyed among us—rather than in the dark-skinned people who hail from Africa and the shores of the Mediterranean. So far there is no evidence that this is the case, and I have seen SAD patients from a broad variety of ethnic backgrounds.

This theory about the energy-conserving functions of SAD might also be used to explain the preponderance of women patients. In primitive societies, it might have been adaptive for the women, who stayed at home, pregnant or breast-feeding or raising children, to evolve such energy-conserving behaviors, while the men—the hunter-gatherers—needed to have a ready supply of energy all year round in order to carry out their functions. Once again, there is no direct evidence for such speculations; in fact, the NIMH group has shown that patients with SAD actually tend to have a higher resting metabolic rate (the rate which people burn up calories when they are at rest) than their normal, nonseasonal counterparts.

So we really don't know why women are more vulnerable to SAD. It could be due to hormonal differences, but that is not a very satisfying explanation. A better answer awaits further research, as does an answer to the genetic basis for this disorder. Is there a gene—or a collection of genes—for unusual sensitivity to the presence or absence of environmental light? Probably, but we don't know where among the spaghettilike tangle of our chromosomes it might reside. However, it is quite possible that such a gene or genes will be discovered in the next decade. An answer may come from the same type of research that recently led to the discovery of at least two distinct genetic markers for manic-depression. Finding such a genetic marker means knowing the general vicinity of the gene in question, if not its exact location. Using large families in which there was an abundant history of manic-depression, two separate groups of researchers recently came up with two different genetic markers, one on chromosome eleven, near the gene for insulin, and one on the X, or sex chromosome. The first discovery came from research conducted among the Old Order Amish in Pennsylvania, and the second from research on Israeli families from the Jerusalem area.

Environmental Considerations

The most important environmental factor to consider when a patient with SAD becomes depressed is light deprivation, in all its forms. Many people experience feelings of low energy and sadness similar to those that SAD patients report in the winter months, as a result of light deprivation, no matter at what time of year this may occur. A change in latitude is a frequent cause of light deprivation, eliciting winter depressions which may not previously have been a problem. For example, a young physician who moved from Texas to New York City and became depressed the following winter might have been suffering from light deprivation and SAD, rather than from problems of adjustment to big-city life. The following letter provides a good description of how one middle-aged woman looks back on her experiences at different latitudes:

> The last two winters have been miseries of depression for me. About February I begin to regain hope as spring approaches (in Florida), and I am truly euphoric by May. Yet even now, as I revel in July's bright days and in my own comfortable stability, I am inwardly dreading next winter.
>
> I grew up in Canada, and of course it is worse there—it depresses me even to visit there now. But even in Florida there is a different quality to the daylight in winter: it seems as though it takes something really wonderful to make me happy during the winter, whereas in summer it takes something pretty bad to make me sad.

Another unsuspected cause of light deprivation may be a move from a brighter to a darker home. For example, a thirty-year-old secretary who moved from her twentieth-floor apartment, where the sun streamed in every morning, into a basement one, suffered the effects of diminished environmental light and became depressed. Along similar lines, a student from Minnesota writes:

I have often wondered over the past several years why it is that when I go home I lose all energy and have a strong desire to sleep. This occurs all year round for me, although it is more pronounced during the winter months. My house is exposed to very little direct sunlight and is quite gloomy. I have also noticed that when I go and stay at a certain friend's house that is exposed to a lot of sunlight, my mood lightens drastically.

People are particularly susceptible to moving into dark places in the summer, when the prospective home may seem quite adequately illuminated, and the memories of SAD may be far away.

Moves from a well-lit to a darker workplace can create similar problems. One schoolteacher from Minneapolis writes: "In many of our area schools, windows are being closed over to conserve energy, bringing the effect of winter darkness all year round. No wonder I found my classroom depressing after the windows were sheeted up; it was darker." In recent years there has been a tremendous increase in windowless buildings, apparently designed in response to concerns about energy conservation. Even in offices with windows, the glass is often coated with a light-absorbing substance—again in an attempt to conserve energy. Unfortunately, electrical energy is conserved at the expense of human energy, at least in those who suffer from SAD.

Apart from changes in season, latitude, and indoor lighting environment, certain weather patterns, regardless of when they occur, may deprive us of light. It is fascinating to sit each week in the seasonal disorders clinic and listen to patients as they come in, one after the other, each a living weather vane. If there has been a sunny streak, all will be fine. If there has been a long spell of cloudy days, all will be amiss. Small inconveniences will feel like major disruptions and there will be an abundance of symptoms, both physical and psychological. These symptoms may occur even in the summer if there has been a string of rainy days. Conversely, a clear snap in the winter may result in unseasonable remissions.

A woman who writes to me from the Northeast clearly associates light deprivation rather than season with her symptoms: "On gray or stormy days (no matter the season!) I become very depressed. The longer the duration of this weather, the lower I feel. As soon as the sun appears, my mood drastically improves. I do not like a dark environment and will seek out bright areas. Dark rooms are oppressive to me.''

I have received several letters from San Francisco, where fog abounds and obliterates the sunlight in many areas of the city. One street may be foggy, while over the next hill it may be sunny. Apparently the price of real estate depends in part on these patterns of sunlight and fog, and given the powerful effect that light can have on mood, this is not surprising. For individuals who live and work in fog-ridden pockets, it might as well be winter all year round. One self-diagnosed "sun worshiper" wrote to me:

> I live in the coastal region of San Francisco where it is often foggy, overcast, and windy. I often feel depressed about the lack of sun in our area. While this depression is not strong enough to be incapacitating, it does make me irritable and somewhat of a "complainer." My husband simply cannot understand my feelings. When we spend a day or two in an area such as Sacramento, where the temperatures remain in the hundreds during most of the summer, I feel alive. But my husband can hardly wait to get back to San Francisco, to what he and many others refer to as the "naturally air-conditioned city." It is encouraging to find support for my theory that fog, wind, and cold can get some people down while others can thrive on it.

Light deprivation is a major problem in the northernmost countries, although these have been surprisingly slow to recognize SAD as a clinical problem. Nonetheless, there are local names for the condition. For example, in Iceland, the condition of *skamdegisfunglindi,* or short-days depression, was described in medieval epics. In Tromsö, a Norwegian city 125 miles north of the Arctic Circle, all manner of ills are blamed on the *mørketiden,* or murky days—those forty-nine days of total darkness around the winter solstice (see chapter 13).

An unusual cause for the emergence of SAD symptoms came to my attention recently when I was consulted by an engineer in his early sixties, who had developed SAD some three years earlier. It is rather extraordinary for a man of that age to develop such symptoms out of the blue, and I quizzed him about all the usual triggering factors. Had he moved north recently, changed homes or his working environment? "No," he answered. It was only toward the end of the consultation that it emerged that he had injured one eye about four years previously and a cataract had grown across the lens. This greatly decreased the amount of light entering the eye and had apparently pushed him over his threshold of vulnerability for SAD.

No studies have yet been performed on the rate of SAD among the visually impaired. Such research would certainly be worthwhile, for the more we understand about the many different effects of environmental light on brain function, the more likely it seems that in understanding and treating the blind, we will need to take into account not only their loss of vision, but also the loss of these other light-related functions.

Stress in SAD

Light deprivation is not the only environmental factor that can trigger feelings of depression in the winter. Stressful events may also contribute to them. For example, a young sales manager had a sales conference scheduled in January, just at a time when the extra hours of work and preparation required for this major event were most difficult for him. During previous winters he had felt quite well, experiencing only mild drops in his energy and productivity. But this time, the high level of stress and the demands of his work, coming in the middle of the winter, combined to precipitate him into the depths of a depression.

A young mother with SAD was required to start a stressful new job during December. Although she was normally a quick study, she was unable to learn the necessary skills and also juggle the requirements of running a household and coordinating her day-care arrangements. She became progressively more depressed, and when she was able to analyze the difficulties, she concluded that she would have been able to handle all those stresses during the summer, or the household and family ones during the winter, but the combination of stresses, occurring in winter, rendered her unable to function adequately either at work or at home.

THE SYMPTOMS OF SAD

SAD As an Energy Crisis

"Jenny," a middle-aged housewife, makes the point succinctly: "I don't really feel depressed. I just feel like all my systems have been turned off for the winter. I feel leaden and heavy and just want to lie about all the time. It's only when I am expected to do something out of the ordinary, and I realize I cannot do it, that I feel my mood being pulled down."

Jenny's description provides us with an important clue to the understanding of SAD, and of depression in general. Many of the symptoms of depression involve physical functions: sleeping, eating, activity levels, sex drive. Disturbances in these functions produce physical symptoms, and their presence is an important clue that someone is suffering from a clinical depression, and not just ordinary sadness. Often, in fact, the sadness and gloom that we associate with depression are not the most prominent part of the general picture. So important are the physical symptoms that modern diagnostic systems do not permit the diagnosis of depression if there has not been a history of at least some physical symptoms.

Almost all people with SAD have problems with their energy level, and they often express it in similar ways. Here are a few of their voices:

"The fatigue is agony. I feel I have to drag myself from one place to the next."

"Everything seems like more of a chore in the wintertime."

"I have to use all my willpower just to get up in the morning, go to work, be pleasant to people, pay my bills, and put my dishes in the dishwasher."

Changes in Eating, Sleeping, and Sex Drive

Most people with SAD eat more in the winter and report a change in their food preference from the salads, fruits, and other light fare of summer to high-carbohydrate meals: breads, pasta, potatoes, sugary foods. Many have told me that eating carbohydrates actually makes them feel better, more energetic. "Laura," a musician in her forties, describes her seasonal change in eating patterns:

> By September and October, I feel like I am constantly feeding and gnawing. My winter diet consists mainly of pastas, macaroni and cheese, rice casseroles, and chicken and mushroom soup—heavy, heavy food. Things that take a long time to cook so you smell them. Stews and pot roast with potatoes and gravy . . . lots of gravy on everything. And dessert—heavy dessert.

Two research groups have actually tried to record the eating habits of people with SAD at different times of year. Dr. Judith Wurtman at MIT and Dr. Anna Wirz-Justice in Basel, Switzerland have confirmed that the increase in carbohydrate consumption reported by so many patients does, in fact, occur. This pattern seems to be an exaggeration of the eating patterns in the population as a whole. One study performed in the cafeteria of the National Institutes of Health found that people eat more carbohydrates in winter and more salads in summer. Recently, the same patterns were reported in a population study in Montgomery County, Maryland.

Surprisingly, people with SAD report that eating carbohydrates seems to give them *more* energy, because research with people who don't have SAD shows just the opposite. Drs. Bonnie Spring and Harris Lieberman both showed that carbohydrates actually make nondepressed people feel more drowsy. In an NIMH study, my colleagues and I gave high-carbohydrate meals (six big cookies) and high-protein meals (a plate of turkey salad) to people with SAD and nonseasonal people. We found that the patients had been correct in their reports, for the high-carbohydrate meal did indeed make the SAD group feel more energetic, whereas the nonseasonal group felt more fatigued. This would suggest that there is a basic difference in the brain chemistry of seasonal and nonseasonal individuals, resulting in this difference in response to carbohydrates.

We don't yet know what this biochemical difference is, but studies of serotonin, a nerve chemical messenger that is of widespread importance in brain functioning, may provide some answers. Drs. John Fernstrom and Richard Wurtman showed that in animals, carbohydrates increase the production of serotonin in the brain. Further studies show that this mechanism may also be important in humans. One reason why patients with SAD may crave carbohydrates and consume them in excessive quantities may be an instinct to correct an abnormality in their brain serotonin concentrations.

Considering the change in diet and the low level of activity that occur in the winter in SAD, it is not surprising that patients tend to gain weight, often quite dramatically. One physician with SAD tells me that his winter trousers are two sizes larger than his summer ones, and that is not unusual. I have seen people gain up to forty pounds in the winter and lose it all the following summer. Unfortunately, some people do not lose it all, and become steadily heavier from year to year.

People with SAD complain as much about changes in their sleep patterns as they do about their eating. Common problems are difficulty getting up in the morning, making it to work on time, and getting the children off on time. They generally sleep more but don't feel refreshed on waking. Sleep is often interrupted and "low quality." Laura, the musician mentioned above, recalls seasonal changes in sleep patterns from her school days:

> I can remember being unable to get up in the morning during the winter as I was growing up, during high school, junior high. My mother would scream at me to get up and get ready for school. I would drag myself up. In contrast, during the spring, I would go out in the yard every morning before school started and look for a flower to wear in my hair or in my buttonhole. Obviously, I had to get up early enough to go and get the flower, and have the desire to do that.
>
> In winter, I'd have a terrible time staying awake. . . . I used to work in the cafeteria, and I would get these baking powder biscuits at dinner. You could take home whatever was left over after dinner. So I would take a pile of these biscuits and a Coke. If you put a bite of biscuit and a sip of Coke in your mouth it reacts and fizzes—that was how I stayed awake to

study in the evening after I would get back. I gained a lot of weight, but in the summer the weight would come off—without dieting.

Flora, an editor in her forties, describes somewhat different sleep patterns:

> I'm tired all the time during my depressions, but I do have a little trouble going to sleep, so I'll read in bed for a long time. I never knew how often I woke up in the middle of the night until I started keeping track of it, but untreated, that's what I do. Then I would find it impossible to get up in the morning and would sleep through the alarm clock. Once, in college, I slept through a fire drill, which made my dorm mates very angry. The bell was right outside my room, and they all went out in the cold and stood there. But since I didn't go out, they had to repeat the fire drill. . . . This was in the winter.

Studies performed at the NIMH actually show differences between the way people with SAD and nonseasonals sleep at different times of the year. In the winter, people with SAD sleep longer, as measured by electrical recordings of their brain wave activity. They also have a decrease in a type of deep sleep called slow-wave sleep. The decrease in this component of sleep, as well as the tendency to more sleep disruptions in SAD patients during the wintertime, may account for their daytime drowsiness, despite their increased nighttime sleep.

In most people with SAD, sex drive decreases markedly during the winter. Many people report not wanting to be touched or to exert themselves in any way, but rather to curl up and be left alone. I have heard many reports of women who wear long flannel nighties to bed during the winter. While these garments are worn mainly for warmth and comfort, they send out a strong signal to the partner that the SAD victim has little interest in sex. Of course, marked changes in sex drive affect not only the person who experiences them, but her partner as well. The partner can easily feel rejected by the lack of sexual interest shown by the person with SAD. When spring and summer arrive and the SAD patient's sexual interest picks up again, the couple will have to adjust to the new equilibrium, which is often difficult. The patient with SAD, forgetting that she has been uninterested in sex for several months, may be surprised at the aloofness of her partner. The partner, having felt rejected or, at the very least, frustrated during the winter months, may eye the renewed sexual interest with suspicion or anger. An understanding that marked shifts in sexual interest are a common feature of SAD—together with communication between the partners about this problem—can greatly ease the tensions that tend to result.

"Sylvia" and "Jack" are a middle-aged couple who have had to learn to deal with Sylvia's seasonal changes over their twenty years of marriage. Their sex life suffers in the winter when Sylvia just wants to be left alone. She retires to bed before Jack does, and by the time he gets there, she's asleep. He has learned to let her sleep at those times because, as she puts it, "I wouldn't be much fun if he woke me up." For the rest of the year the couple enjoys an active and satisfying sex life.

Although Sylvia and Jack have made a good accommodation to her seasonal changes, not all couples manage as well. One young professional couple, "Jeff" and "Elaine," had a satisfactory sex life except during the summer, when Elaine would become very highly energized, physically and sexually. She would want to make love more often than Jeff did. He became increasingly upset at his inability to keep up with her sex drive, felt like a failure for being unable to satisfy her, and withdrew from her. This, in turn, caused her to feel rejected, and she confronted him with her anger and hurt feelings. An understanding of the biological processes involved in these behavior changes can be very helpful to couples where one of the partners is seasonal and the other is not.

The effect of SAD on relationships is not confined to the sexual arena. People with SAD often just want to curl up in a secluded place and be left alone. A woman who may be a social butterfly in the summer often wants no company in the winter. Conversations are avoided and invitations turned down. Anything that requires expending the energy involved in social contact is experienced as an overwhelming demand, to be avoided if at all possible. Many people with SAD compare themselves to hibernating bears. Although this is not scientifically a sound comparison, it accurately conveys the feeling of wanting to be left alone.

As one might expect, there are considerable social costs to such behavior. Friends become annoyed. Marriages come under strain, as the spouse experiences withdrawal and distancing on the part of the seasonal person. Lovers are lost, although at the time this may be experienced as a relief, since it results in a welcome decrease in personal and sexual demands. I know many seasonal people who have consistently started relationships in spring and summer, but failed to keep them through the winter.

Cognitive Problems

As the seasonal people you have already met in this book will testify, problems in thinking are among the most troublesome symptoms of SAD. Generally, concentration and information processing are things we do automatically. It is only when we are unable to do these things that we really notice them. I am sure you can remember a time when you were not thinking properly—for example, when you were tired. That is how people with SAD often feel during the winter months. They tend to have problems thinking clearly and quickly. It's very difficult, if not impossible, for them to summon up the information and knowledge needed for their work—or even casual conversations. They are not able to keep up with what is going on around them or what needs to be done.

A scene from Chaplin's *Modern Times* comes to mind. A factory worker is working away quite well on an assembly line when suddenly, the conveyor belt begins to move faster. The worker rallies in an attempt to keep up with the increased challenge, but eventually, the rate at which he is called upon to perform is accelerated so rapidly that it is impossible for him to continue. This provides a wonderful vehicle for Chaplin's madcap antics. In reality, however, the feeling of having information coming at you faster than you can handle is an overwhelming, and even frightening, experience.

In SAD, the ability to concentrate and process information varies greatly over the course of the year. In summer it's a snap; everything goes "click, click, click" and gets done. In winter it's a drag, with minor tasks taking on major proportions. I have heard many patients say, "I begin to make stupid mistakes in the fall."

These mistakes can become apparent even in the performance of relatively simple tasks. Routine chores such as doing the shopping or cooking a meal involve several steps that need to be performed in a certain sequence. People with SAD often feel unable to focus on the task, to remember all its different parts and to carry them out in the correct sequence. Patients often say, "I just can't get my act together. Simple things seem so difficult." In all the patients profiled in chapter 2, a combination of low energy, low motivation, and especially, difficulty in thinking impaired their ability to function at work, which was a major complaint.

Many business executives and professionals with SAD complain that during the winter they are unable to take the necessary steps to handle the tasks that await them. Instead they hide behind their office doors, shuffling papers around on their desks, creating the appearance of getting work done. Secretaries and assistants, who aren't fortunate enough to have personal offices in which to hide, often call in sick and say they have the flu, a more acceptable excuse than depression.

Tasks involving logic are often especially difficult, but some people even complain of difficulties in estimating distances. One woman reported that while driving during the winter, she had a hard time estimating the distance between her car and the one in front of her. A young tree surgeon with SAD found it hard to estimate the length of a branch he was sawing off, and injured himself as a result.

Dr. John Docherty, who has had extensive experience with SAD in Boston and New Hampshire, has estimated the frequency of the different work-related problems encountered by his patients with SAD. They are, in order of frequency: decreased concentration, productivity, interest, and creativity; inability to complete tasks; increased interpersonal difficulties in the workplace; increased absences from work, and simply stopping work. Quite a staggering list of problems.

One exciting new research development in the area of information processing has been reported by Dr. Connie Duncan and her colleagues at the NIMH, who have measured the brain wave pattern responses to visual stimuli. A certain part of the brain wave response corresponds to a person's ability to attend to a stimulus. These researchers have shown that this part of the brain wave increases in strength in patients with SAD after they have been successfully treated with light therapy. This change occurs at the same time as people begin to feel better and their ability to think improves. It has been very reassuring for our patients to realize that their ability to think can be objectively measured and shown to change after light therapy. It helps them to recognize that they are suffering from a problem in brain function and that their cognitive difficulties are not their fault.

Mood Problems

As I mentioned earlier, many people with winter problems may feel physical changes long before any feelings of sadness occur. Some people may experience only physical changes with the changing seasons and never feel depressed. These people are comparatively lucky because the emotional aspects of depression are among the most painful experiences known to man.

"John" is an engineer who has just turned fifty. He is a handsome man, with gray hair and blue eyes. He sits in my office, trying to control himself, as he has always been told he should do. But the depression breaks through his mask and the tears begin to roll down his cheeks. He says he feels sad but doesn't know why. Life has no meaning for him anymore. His wife, children, and job have all ceased to give him any pleasure. He feels he is just a burden to his family and that they would be better off without him. He feels guilty—he has let them down, been a bad father and husband. He thinks back on his childhood and feels that even then he failed to come through for his parents when they needed him. He goes to work each day wracked with anxiety—small problems become overwhelming. How will he get it all done? Perhaps the best thing would be to end it all, but that is against his religion. He contemplates a spot on the freeway where the road veers sharply to the right, and there is a steep decline to the left. Sometimes he thinks about driving his car over the edge if the pain gets too bad.

John expresses feelings that are typical of depressed people and, indeed, he is severely depressed. His thoughts—that he is a failure as a father, husband, and worker—are not shared by his children, his wife, and his supervisor, all of whom feel he is caring, devoted, and hardworking. They can legitimately be regarded as distortions of reality, though they certainly feel real to him. A serious symptom of severe depression is losing touch with reality.

A college student in her late twenties described the loss of perspective that occurs in depression: "A patient with diabetes knows that his pancreas is disordered, and that's not so hard to understand. But when you're depressed, your mind and heart and soul are disordered—everything that makes you a human being—and that's not so simple to understand, especially when you are in the middle of it."

The anxiety that John reports often occurs in depression, and treatment often helps it, as well as the sadness. People with SAD also complain of being snappy, irritable, and unpleasant toward others.

Depressed people—including those with SAD—often distort reality by blaming themselves unfairly. Another type of cognitive distortion that may occur involves blaming others—or one's life circumstances—for problems that are really the result of SAD. A woman might say, for example, "My marriage is going wrong because my husband is inconsiderate and too demanding," while the major reason may be that she is depressed and unable to meet his needs. Another might say, "This job is not right for me. It's causing me distress and feelings of failure." While a difficult job can aggravate the symptoms of SAD, the main cause of the problem at work may be the SAD itself. I often counsel patients not to make important decisions while they are depressed if they can possibly avoid doing so. Decisions made hastily by a depressed person are often the result of mistakenly attributing one's problems to one's life circumstances, and they are often regretted later. The best way for a depressed person to handle problematic life circumstances, either at work or at home, is to have the depression treated first, and then to decide on the best course of action.

PHYSICAL ILLNESSES AND SAD

People with SAD may suffer all sorts of physical problems during the winter months, from backaches, muscle aches, and headaches, to different types of infections. Many people with SAD feel as though they have suffered from the flu all winter long. We don't really know whether having SAD or being depressed actually makes you more likely to get the flu or whether it just feels worse to be sick when you are already suffering from SAD. Dr. Robert Skwerer and his colleagues at the NIMH have shown that patients with SAD have certain abnormalities in their immune functioning, so it is quite conceivable that they are more susceptible to infections. The idea that the mind or brain exerts an influence on our immune system is gaining increasing acceptance in scientific circles and is an exciting new area of developing research.

PREMENSTRUAL DIFFICULTIES

At least half of all menstruating women with SAD also have emotional and physical problems related to their periods, usually in the week before it begins. This is called premenstrual syndrome (PMS) and much has been written on the subject. Some women experience these symptoms all year round, but most severely in the winter. Others have PMS only in the winter. Many women say that during their premenstrual period they feel a bit like they do when they have SAD.

"Sharon" is a housewife in her early thirties and the mother of two teenagers. She is aware of eating too much, craving sweets and starchy foods, gaining weight, and sleeping more during the four or five days before her menstrual period. She tends to retain fluid, and her rings feel tight on her fingers around that time. She also has abdominal cramps. But most distressing to her and her family is her irritability at those times. She will tend to pick fights with her husband, with whom she normally gets along rather well. This was especially bad before they recognized the cyclicity of their arguments and their biological origin. Now they have learned to beware during the week before her period and have resolved to postpone all contentious topics until after it has passed. Even her children have learned to tread carefully during those premenstrual days. Irritability is more typical of PMS than of SAD, where people more commonly feel lethargic and sluggish. One woman pointed this out to me in colorful terms when she noted: "My premenstrual problem is like a black cloud hanging over me; the winter problem is more like being in a blue funk—it's a condition inside of me that I walk around with."

Not every episode of PMS is necessarily the same. During some cycles a period may arrive unexpectedly without any symptoms of PMS. Yet at other times, unpredictably, these difficulties may be rather severe. In a similar fashion, the severity of episodes of SAD may also vary from cycle to cycle, from one year to the next.

HUNGER FOR LIGHT

Even before any formal studies of light therapy had been performed, some patients had made a connection between light and mood. For example, one woman would routinely sit in front of her plant lights because she found she felt better there. Another would wander through brightly lit supermarkets at night, while a third would seek out the photocopying room because it was well-lit. It is common for people with SAD to want to turn on all the lights in the house during the dark winter days. One middle-aged woman was nicknamed "Lights" by her husband because of this habit. For some women, the wish to turn on all the lights in the house has led to arguments about the high cost of electricity from husbands who have not understood the biological nature of their wives' need.

In their search for light, some people have instinctively chosen winter vacations in the south, year after year. Others have relocated permanently. In many instances, the people involved may not have realized how medically important it was for them to move—they may just have done so instinctively. Not all patients with SAD have made the association between their symptoms and the amount of available environmental light. Some have reacted by lying down in darkened rooms, thereby inadvertently making their problems worse.

In general, attempts to enhance one's environmental lighting are useful for patients with SAD.

SELF-TREATMENT WITH DRUGS: ALCOHOL, CAFFEINE, NICOTINE, AND OTHERS

Stay me with flagons, comfort me with apples
For I am sick of love.
—*Song of Songs*

Since biblical times, people have realized the mood-altering effects of food and wine. In an attempt to feel better, depressed people often resort to commonly available drugs, some of which may compound the problem. I have already discussed the use of sugar and starches as mood regulators by people with SAD, but obviously, the effects of food go beyond its carbohydrate content. Many people specifically crave chocolate, perhaps seeking the combination of sugar and caffeine that it contains. Others crave stews, pastas, "heavy" and "crunchy" foods. One woman with SAD actually craved broccoli in the wintertime. We cannot explain these idiosyncratic choices, but it is possible that these cravings may represent the physiological need for a particular nutrient. Gratifying that need may result in an improved sense of well-being.

Caffeine is a mood-altering drug that often appeals to people who feel sluggish, lethargic, and unable to get anything accomplished. Flora, mentioned above, recalls her caffeine addiction during her depressed times:

> I used to drink eight, ten, or twelve mugs—tremendous amounts—of coffee steadily all day: espresso, made by drip method. At times the amount of coffee it took to keep me going was enough to upset my stomach.

Caffeine is such a widely available and accepted stimulant that patients with SAD naturally gravitate toward the coffeepot or the teakettle. When these are not available, caffeinated sodas are a common substitute. People often drink many more cups of tea or coffee in the winter than in the summer. Although the immediate stimulant effects of caffeine can be quite useful in certain circumstances, it also has distinct problems and limitations. These are becoming more widely appreciated, as evidenced by the growing number of calls for decaffeinated coffee. Besides indigestion and abdominal cramps, caffeine can cause jitteriness, palpitations, and insomnia. In addition, people frequently become tolerant of its effects, so they may have to drink increasing amounts to get the same energy boost. Nevertheless, the problems associated with caffeine should not be overstated: some people drink it with impunity and for them, a few cups of tea or coffee a day may be helpful. I should remind those who want to stop drinking tea or coffee that abrupt discontinuation of caffeine can cause withdrawal symptoms, which include sluggishness and headaches.

Alcohol is another substance to which depressed people at times resort—"drowning their sorrows in drink," as the saying goes. One patient who comes to mind is John, the engineer in his early fifties, mentioned above. During the fall and winter he feels increasingly depressed as he becomes less able to function effectively at work. His regular routine of exercising usually falters at this time and he tends to drink to obliterate his painful feelings of failure. Not surprisingly, the heavy drinking becomes a problem in its own right, and causes him further difficulties at work and at home. Drinking too much alcohol can, of course, cause many problems, a detailed description of which goes beyond the scope of this book. Suffice it to say that excessive alcohol use can be physically harmful, disrupt relationships, kill others (as in driving while intoxicated), and ruin the life of the addicted individual.

I have also seen people turn to marijuana in the wintertime. One young man—a tennis instructor greatly concerned with his physical health—turns to marijuana each winter, despite his awareness of its potential physical dangers. He is an enthusiastic and upbeat person in the summer, sought out by friends and employees for his support, understanding, and counsel, but he feels desolate and bleak in the wintertime.

Life loses all of its charms and nothing seems to give him any pleasure. At these times he smokes marijuana to escape into a haze in which his daily cares seem far removed. He does not feel happy with this solution to his problems and is eager for alternative approaches.

Even smoking tobacco may seem more appealing in the winter. One physician in his mid-forties, who hardly needs any lectures on the harmfulness of tobacco, takes up smoking during the winter, even though he has given it up the previous spring.

So it is that many people seek refuge from the pain of SAD in commonly available substances. Some, like pasta and cookies, may be innocuous unless eaten to great excess. Others, like alcohol, can be extremely destructive, creating problems that far exceed those for which it is consumed. Why some people resort to alcohol, while others resort to cookies or chocolates, is not understood at all. It may be a feature of our peculiar individual biochemical makeup, or a result of what we were conditioned to associate with comfort from childhood. For example, one friend of mine recalls being comforted with sips of brandy when she woke up at night as a child feeling sick. In other families, ice cream or candy may be the standard remedy. In general, these "drug" solutions are regarded as unsatisfactory by those who adopt them. For better solutions, I refer you to part 2 on treatments for SAD.

OTHER CONDITIONS THAT MAY RESEMBLE SAD

In medicine, it is always important to question a diagnosis. Could you have a condition other than the one you suspect? In evaluating whether someone is suffering from SAD, we need to consider other conditions that produce similar symptoms, such as lethargy, overeating, carbohydrate craving, weight gain, and depression. Many physical illnesses can cause lethargy and depression, which is why it is important for people who think they are suffering from this condition to be thoroughly examined by a physician. However, it is unusual for other conditions to appear in the winter and leave in the summer, year after year. Even so, it is better to be on the safe side and have a physical examination and the necessary blood tests, since you could have another illness as well as SAD.

Specific illnesses that need to be considered are:

1. Underactive thyroid function (hypothyroidism): In this condition, people feel sluggish and cannot tolerate the cold weather. The thyroid gland, situated centrally in the front of the neck, is responsible for producing hormones that regulate the rate of metabolism. Underactivity of the thyroid can usually be treated simply by taking thyroid hormone in the form of pills.

2. Low blood sugar (hypoglycemia): People with this condition feel weak and light-headed at times, usually one to two hours after a meal. At times they may feel very hungry and crave sweets. This condition can usually be treated by dietary regulation. People with hypoglycemia should avoid foods containing high concentrations of sugar in forms that are rapidly absorbed into the system. Examples of these "simple" carbohydrates are candies and other very sweet things. Instead, people with this condition should eat combinations of proteins and complex carbohydrates, such as fruit, rice, and sugar-free cereals.

3. Chronic viral illnesses: SAD symptoms can resemble those of the Epstein-Barr (E-B) virus (which is responsible for infectious mononucleosis) or even the flu. Some people are susceptible to viral conditions, which may be most prevalent during the winter. It is not uncommon for people to feel lethargic and debilitated for some time after a bad attack of flu. Similarly, the E-B virus, which has attracted a fair amount of media attention recently, may cause long-term lethargy and fatigue.

Unfortunately, chronic viral illnesses are very difficult to diagnose precisely and there are no specific treatments for them. Blood tests showing antibodies against the E-B virus simply indicate that a person has been infected in the past—not that the virus is necessarily responsible for the present symptoms. Luckily, however, most cases of chronic E-B virus infection get better with time.

Although viral conditions may masquerade as SAD, the occurrence winter after winter of typical SAD symptoms, which improve in spring and summer, points strongly toward SAD. In any event, since the presence of viral infections is difficult to document and there are no specific treatments for them, and since there are specific treatments for SAD, it usually makes sense to treat the problem as SAD.

SAD IN CHILDREN

Recently, a middle-aged woman walked into the NIMH clinical center and asked me if I knew of any articles on SAD in children. I said I did indeed have an article, and wondered why she was interested in the subject. "My son asked me to stop by and find out more about the condition," she said. "He thinks he has it." It emerged that her twelve-year-old son had seen a television program on the subject and had identified with the patients.

I was reminded of "Jason," another smart twelve-year-old, who had seen both of his parents suffering from SAD and being treated with light therapy. That winter he approached his father, saying that he thought he was also suffering from SAD, as he had noticed that he was eating more candies. His father dismissed this observation with a psychological explanation—the boy was clearly identifying with his parents, and what child doesn't eat too much candy? But Jason, normally a fine student, began to have increasing difficulties with his schoolwork. One day his father, finding him dozing over his homework, asked him again what the problem was. "Dad, I think it's the winter," Jason replied. And he was right. Light therapy has since reversed the problem almost entirely.

Jason is something of an exception in his diagnostic abilities. Many children with SAD do not understand what is wrong. Often they are not even aware that the change is internal, but blame it instead on the world around them, which they experience as having turned cruel and uncaring. Teachers have become excessively strict and parents unfairly demanding. Many adults similarly misperceive the source of their SAD symptoms and seek external explanations to account for the dramatic difference in the way they feel when they are depressed.

I first started looking for children and adolescents with SAD because about one-third of our adult patients reported symptoms going back to these early years. In addition, many of the adult patients reported similar symptoms in their children, which is not surprising, considering the high familial incidence of the disorder. SAD in children has many similarities to the adult form—for example, there is often difficulty waking up on time in the morning and accomplishing tasks, particularly schoolwork.

One difference is that children appear to show more irritability during their winter depressions than do adults.

Dr. William Sonis at the University of Pennsylvania is currently studying children with seasonal difficulties. In his experience, seasonal problems are not uncommon in the general population. In a survey of schoolchildren in Minnesota, he found that one in twenty children experienced highly seasonal changes that interfered with their functioning. Two percent of these children reported depression associated with these symptoms. Most patients with childhood SAD first come in for treatment when they are about fifteen or sixteen, having experienced an average of six winters of symptoms. There are several reasons why it takes so long for children to get diagnosed. First, some of the symptoms of SAD fit the stereotype of what people might expect to find in adolescence, such as lethargy, irritability, and lack of motivation. According to Sonis, this stereotype is a myth that has not been borne out by research studies. Second, many physicians are still not aware of SAD, especially in its childhood and adolescent manifestations. It is particularly important to diagnose SAD as soon as possible, since it is eminently responsive to light therapy in children, as in adults. At present, children too often suffer unnecessarily for several winters before getting appropriate help.

Telltale Signs of SAD in Children: A Guide for Parents

The single biggest clue that your child may be suffering from SAD is if he or she develops problems at the same time each year: during the fall and winter. This particular point may be more important than the actual symptoms themselves, which may be atypical in children, and may manifest, for example, as anxiety or school avoidance. More usual signs are:

- Feeling tired and washed out
- Feeling cranky and irritable
- Temper tantrums
- Slipping grades

- Reluctance to undertake chores and other responsibilities not previously regarded as a problem
- Vague physical complaints, such as headaches or abdominal pains
- Marked increase in cravings for "junk food"

Several children with SAD come to mind: "Michael," a twelve-year-old swimming champion, had swim times which invariably deteriorated during the winter and improved during the summer. "Susan," an eight-year-old with long, flowing blond hair and a wistful gaze, had suffered from pronounced seasonal rhythms since infancy. Her parents noticed marked differences between her sleep length during the short summer nights, when she would wake up with the first rays of the sun, and the long winter nights, when she would sleep for hours and hours. Her problems began in nursery school, when teachers noticed that she would withdraw from friends and be uninterested in the usual routine of daily activities during January and February. "Jeannie," a thirteen-year-old, not only had the usual difficulties with schoolwork and social activities in the winter, but became overactive in the summer. At that time her activity level would increase, she would need little sleep, and she would tend to be impulsive and show poor judgment. On one occasion her father found her cavorting about on the roof, enjoying the night air, apparently unaware of the danger of falling.

Attention Deficit Disorder and SAD

A school problem called "attention deficit disorder" may look like SAD in some instances, but it should not appear regularly in fall and winter unless the child has a seasonal problem as well. Indeed, I have encountered patients with both problems. One young girl I treated suffered from attention deficit disorder all year round, for which she was treated with the stimulant, Ritalin. During the winter she experienced typical symptoms of SAD, apparently inherited from her mother, who suffered from similar problems. Thirty minutes of treatment with bright light in the morning reversed all her symptoms and helped her wake up and get to school on time, which had previously been a serious problem for her.

Nonseasonal depression may also occur in children but, by definition, it should occur only in the fall and winter months.

Treatment of Children with SAD

Treatment of SAD—including light therapy—is discussed at length in part 2, and much of that section can be applied to children. A few special considerations include the amount and timing of light. In my experience, children often do well with "pediatric" doses of light—for example, thirty to forty-five minutes in the morning. However, timing of treatments does not appear to be critical in most cases, and Dr. Sonis has found that a few hours of light in the early evening is quite effective and less disruptive to children's schedules.

THE FLIP SIDE OF DEPRESSION: SPRING FEVER

Although many people with SAD feel normally cheerful during the summer months, it is quite common for individuals to report feeling exceptionally energetic and creative at this time. Herb Kern, the first patient with SAD to be treated at the NIMH, was exceptionally productive scientifically during the summer—so much so that his boss was happy to let him cruise through his less productive winter months. Artists and writers may also get most of their creative work done during the summer, and may leave the more humdrum aspects of their work for wintertime.

Such enhanced productivity is not universal for those who develop extra energy in the summer. In some people this acceleration goes too far and may result in major problems—bank accounts overdrawn from excessive spending, difficulties getting along with friends and colleagues, and even trouble with the law. This state is referred to clinically as mania.

An exaggerated sex drive caused by a midsummer high resulted in problems for "Marie," a housewife in her twenties, who was at home with her two young children. Although she was a faithful wife under ordinary circumstances, one summer she could not resist the attentions of a carpenter who was installing bookshelves for her husband. This dalliance caused her a considerable amount of guilt until she understood that her abnormal mood state had disrupted her usual level of responsibility and judgment, while at the same time increasing her libido.

Others may spend large sums of money that they can ill afford on items that, at other times, would seem extravagant. They may show poor judgment in their driving and speed along the highway, assured that their lightning reflexes make them invulnerable to accidents. Or they may suddenly and impetuously decide to undertake some long journey for reasons that to the outsider would seem frivolous.

The degree of acceleration does not have to reach manic proportions in order to be considered a problem by an individual or, more commonly, by the person's partner, friends, and colleagues. Others may frequently complain about not being able to get a word in edgeways, or being interrupted repeatedly during a conversation. This condition, known as hypomania, often impairs efficiency. Although hypomanic people have a great deal of energy, they have so many ideas for projects that they find it difficult to focus on any single one. As a result, their energies are scattered, their attention darts from task to task, and, fueled by grandiosity, they are often left with several unfinished projects at the end of the summer.

Summer Highs: Scenes from a Marriage

Although Jack and Sylvia have some problems with each other when Sylvia is in her "low" winter state, her summer highs present the couple with more serious difficulties. The following excerpts from an interview with the two of them, conducted during the summer, illustrate some of these.

Jack: During her lows Sylvia really gets down. She will say, "I don't know how anyone can love me," or "I'm so slow, I hate myself." And then in the summer, when she gets in the high, she'll say, "Aren't you fortunate to have somebody with my personality?" It's just a complete reversal. I'm amazed—sometimes the highs are more trying than the lows. A day can make a huge difference. In just one day she can come alive.

Most of our arguments come in the early spring, when she comes alive and wants to do all kinds of things. I remember going to Wolf Trap [an open air amphitheater near Washington, D.C.] with some friends; she was so excited that everyone said, "Look at Sylvia, she's so high." She became the focal point of her friends because of her excessive energy. It is difficult for me because Sylvia gets after me to join in on her whirlwind of activities. Just the other day I said to her, "Look, I can't be as high as you unless I take cocaine, and I don't plan to take cocaine." At Wolf Trap she just bounced around—it was unreal. I thought she could fly, and I think Sylvia and all her friends thought she could, too!

Jack documents many incidents that have occurred during the summer as evidence of Sylvia's hypomanic state. She spends money on projects that he regards as unnecessary, but that she feels are interesting or creative. For example, she bought an expensive video camera so that her sons could learn to make films. On another occasion, she bought a pet iguana, capable of growing to a length of eight feet. While Jack regarded the animal as a bizarre nuisance, Sylvia identified with its love for the sun. She remembers, "When he would get out of the house and I couldn't find him, I would wait for the sun to start going down and know that he would be in that one spot in the yard where the sun was still shining."

Although they have generally been able to resolve their financial difficulties amicably, Jack actually suggested taking Sylvia's credit cards away from her during the summer on one occasion. She became extremely angry and threatened to leave him, and he backed down.

They discuss their seasonal problems further:

Sylvia: There's a kind of power struggle that goes on between us because for six months you can just lead me anywhere, and then in the summer, I want to lead. And Jack is not the kind of person who likes a boss.

Jack: In the winter Sylvia would be really down, and I'd feel really sorry for her and try to keep her spirits up. Then in the spring she'd almost turn on me. I almost got the feeling she didn't like the person she was in the winter, and the fact that I cared for that person in the winter was held against me in the spring. And I couldn't believe that. I think to myself, "I've done all kinds of things for you in the winter, driven you around, made excuses for you to your friends, but because you hate that Sylvia, you hate me, too."

Sylvia: Jack's reactions to me have always worried me. I like myself in the spring and summer, but I don't think Jack really enjoys me then.

When asked how she feels about Jack's having helped her and taken care of her during the winter, Sylvia replies: "I don't like to think about it."

"Do you forget it, put it out of your mind?" I ask.

"I certainly do. I want to think about happy things," she replies.

Jack comments: "The heck with that! Next winter I'm going to let her take care of herself."

Both Jack and Sylvia agree that she becomes short-tempered in the summer and is most likely to have run-ins with other people then. On one occasion, when Jack's mother came to visit during the month of May, she and Sylvia had an argument from which Jack says it took his mother two years to recover. As a result, Jack makes sure to keep the two women apart during the summer. Sylvia also has to stay away from meetings at her church then, as she is likely to monopolize them and antagonize some of the other church members with blunt and tactless remarks. She relates this with a certain amount of enjoyment and little evidence of regret.

Although Sylvia's high periods are a source of frustration for Jack, there are aspects of them—the humor, creativity, and liveliness—that he enjoys as much as she does. In the past year or two, however, Sylvia has become worn out during her high periods from lack of sleep and excessive activity. She has been reluctant to take any medications for this, and I have treated her by having her wear dark glasses during the summer days. This treatment has been quite successful, and at times she has even slept with eyeshades on to prevent herself from waking up with the first rays of dawn.

The couple has benefited greatly from marital therapy as well, which has helped them to identify the symptoms of SAD, understand that biological processes are at work, and help them cope with these changes. Jack sums it up: "I think we're like ships passing in the night. We're very seldom at the same level. She's either below me or above, and only momentarily do we see eye to eye."

THE WINTER BLUES OR FEBRUARY BLAHS

Soon after we first encountered patients with SAD, it became clear that there were many people with a milder form of the condition. These people would not generally seek out medical help for their winter difficulties but, when asked specifically about them, would recall that they had some problem each winter—for example, lack of enthusiasm or decreased productivity. In order to study this question, Dr. Siegfried Kasper and I undertook a study of what we called subsyndromal SAD, or the winter blues, at the NIMH. We established criteria for this condition, which are outlined in chapter 3, and set out to find people who met the description.

"Jeff," a typical victim of the winter blues, read the article in the *NIMH Record,* which gave a checklist of symptoms that people with this variant of SAD experience: low energy, difficulty concentrating and getting one's work done, and tiredness; in short, a syndrome that was milder than the depression previously described as responding to light. Jeff is in his mid-forties and is a well-informed mental health professional, but he had never quite recognized the basis of his seasonal problem.

Looking back on his difficulties, it was clear to him that his ability to concentrate would decline each winter. A self-declared workaholic, he was always less productive during the winter months than during the rest of the year. During the winter, he felt tired and attributed it to a lack of sleep, even though he was actually sleeping more than he did during the summer. He had never been formally treated for this winter problem. He treated his low energy level with cups of coffee and found that if he put several very bright lamps on his desk, it helped him concentrate. He also found that if he had to meet a deadline, he could sometimes do so by sleeping from 7:00 P.M. to midnight, and working straight through the night and the following day. Sleep restriction is a known treatment for depression and is discussed later in this book.

Curiosity led Jeff to take part in the NIMH research program—curiosity and a hope that maybe there was an explanation and a simple treatment for his recurrent winter difficulties. He entered the program with great skepticism. His expectations of the effects of the light treatment were very low. But the treatment worked dramatically for him, and he has used bright light at his desk ever since.

Kasper has shown that bright light is effective for most people with the winter blues, which seem to affect at least twice as many people—though not as dramatically—as SAD does. Nevertheless, this milder winter syndrome does interfere with the quality of life in those who suffer from it and decreases their productivity. Since it is easily reversible in most cases, it is important that we identify these people and offer them information and treatment.

Scientists believe that SAD and the winter blues are two broad categories of problematic seasonal change to which many people are susceptible. Although some clearly fall into one category or another on the basis of the severity of their winter problems, many fall into a gray zone between the two. The important point is that bright light can help those in either category. The distinction between the two is that those who are depressed should seek out professional help and receive light treatment as part of a comprehensive evaluation and treatment plan. Those who are affected by only mild winter changes may be able to obtain satisfactory relief of symptoms simply by increasing the amount of light in their living and working environments. Guidelines are provided in chapter 3 to help the interested reader decide when a physician should be consulted.

COMMONLY ASKED QUESTIONS ABOUT SAD

1. How common is SAD? How many people suffer from it? Does it get worse the farther north you go?

This question has recently been studied by several researchers, many of whom have used versions of the Seasonal Pattern Assessment Questionnaire, just like the one you may have used to rate your own seasonality. Studies done in several different parts of the United States suggest that the farther north you go, the more common are both SAD and subsyndromal SAD (the winter blues). The table below shows the percent of the population thought to be affected by SAD and subsyndromal SAD at different latitudes.

Estimated Prevalence of SAD and S-SAD at Different Latitudes in the U.S.*

Latitude	States/Cities	SAD (%)	Subsyndromal SAD (%)
45–50°	Washington, Montana, North Dakota, Minnesota, northern Michigan, Maine (Quebec, southern Ontario, Manitoba, Saskatchewan, Alberta, and Columbia)	10.2	20.2
40–45°	Oregon, Idaho, Wyoming, South Dakota, Nebraska, Iowa, northern Indiana, Massachusetts, Ohio, Wisconsin, Pennsylvania, New York, Vermont, New Hampshire, Rhode Island, Connecticut, New Jersey	8.0	17.1

Latitude	States/Cities	SAD (%)	Subsyndromal SAD (%)
35–40°	Northern California, Nevada, Utah, Colorado, Kansas, Oklahoma, Missouri, southern Illinois, Tennessee, Kentucky, West Virginia, Maryland, Delaware, Virginia, Washington, D.C., North Carolina	5.8	13.9
30–35°	Southern California, Arizona, New Mexico, Texas, Arkansas, Louisiana, Mississippi, Alabama, Georgia, South Carolina	3.6	10.6
25–30°	Mexico, south Texas, Florida	1.4	7.5

*This table is based on a collaborative study between the NIMH, Psychiatric Institutes of America, New York State Psychiatric Institute, and Walter Reed Army Institute of Research. The rates at different latitudes were calculated by Dr. Leora N. Rosen, based on only four sites: Nashua, New Hampshire; New York City; Montgomery County, Maryland; and Sarasota, Florida. Generalizing these rates to other parts of the United States and Canada may not be valid.

As one might gather from the above table, the projected rates for SAD and subsyndromal SAD (winter blues) in the United States are high. Our estimate for SAD in the entire U.S. population is 6.1 percent, or 10.8 million people; for subsyndromal SAD, the corresponding figures are 14.3 percent, or 25.3 million people. If one examines the entire population likely to benefit from enhanced environmental lighting—namely, a group consisting of SAD plus subsyndromal SAD subjects—the estimated figures are 20.4 percent of the population of the United States, or 36.1 million people.

These estimates may be a little high for the most northern latitudes, since a recent study in Fairbanks, Alaska (64° north), by Drs. John M. Booker and Carla J. Hellekson, found an 8.9 percent prevalence of SAD and a 19 percent prevalence of the winter blues. Although lower than the figures one would have predicted from the study by Rosen and colleagues, the Alaska study confirms that SAD and the winter blues are extremely common in the North.

Latitudinal Equivalents in Europe

50–55°	The British Isles
45–50°	Northern France, northern Italy, Switzerland, Austria, Romania, northern Yugoslavia, Hungary, Czechoslovakia, northern East Germany
40–45°	Southern France, Yugoslavia, northern Spain, northern Portugal, Albania, Bulgaria
35–40°	Southern Portugal, southern Spain, Greece

2. I have heard that the commonest seasons for suicide are the spring and summer. How does this tie in with SAD occurring in the fall and winter?

This question is answered in greater detail in chapter 5. In most studies there is a peak incidence of suicide in the spring and summer. The reason for this paradox seems to be that those who suffer from SAD and those who are at risk for committing suicide in the summer appear to be two distinct and different groups, with completely different patterns of response to the seasons.

3. Is SAD the same as holiday blues or Christmas depression that we hear so much about?

For therapists in clinical practice it is not unusual to see some feelings of sadness around the time of the holidays. Although this is a time when people are supposed to be happy, and many are, there are some for whom the expected happiness does not arrive. Lonely people, people without family or friends, feel lonelier than ever when they see celebrations going on all around them. It is a time for nostalgia—perhaps for remembering holidays when things were better. It is a time for missing people—perhaps relatives or friends who have passed away during the previous year.

However, this element of sadness is where the resemblance between SAD and the holiday blues stops. When we think of depression as a clinical term, as opposed to the sadness that is a part of our ordinary lives, we think of a sustained state, lasting several weeks, accompanied by physical changes—for example, in eating, sleeping, energy level, and daily functioning. There is no evidence that most people reacting to Christmas or the holidays exhibit this picture, whereas it is typical for SAD patients to show all of these features.

Although a number of studies have looked for the holiday blues by examining, for example, the incidence of visits to the emergency room for psychiatric help, or admissions to psychiatric units during the holiday season, none has been able to find evidence of Christmas depression as a psychiatric entity. In fact, one study showed that presentations to psychiatric emergency rooms decreased in the few days before major holidays and increased in the few days after them. It is as though people did not want to spoil their holiday by going to the emergency room, so they waited until the holiday was over before doing so.

4. What about the possibility that people may regularly feel bad at a certain time of year because something bad once happened at that time of year in the past?

In clinical practice, we certainly see patients who experience symptoms that appear on or around the anniversary of some traumatic event. Freud recognized these and, in his description of Fräulein Elisabeth von R. (1895), he wrote: "This lady celebrated annual festivals of remembrance at the period of her various catastrophes, and on these occasions her vivid visual reproduction and expressions of feeling kept to the date precisely." Longfellow also recognized the "secret anniversaries of the heart, when the full river of feeling overflows." These anniversary reactions tend to be experienced rather specifically around the date of the anniversary and do not typically last for weeks or months, as is the case with SAD.

In many cases of SAD I have seen attempts on the part of the patient or therapist to explain symptoms in terms of some anniversary. For example, patients might say, "I always thought it was because school began at that time of the year," or might recollect a loss that occurred in October or February. For example, one patient with SAD observed that his mother had died in September. His therapist tried to understand his winter problems in terms of the anniversary of this sad event, but the patient experienced this interpretation as unsatisfactory. In my experience, such explanations don't usually stand up to careful scrutiny. If the symptoms of SAD last for five months—almost half the year—it stands to reason that there would have been a high percentage of unpleasant occurrences during those months. In addition, why should an anniversary reaction for something that occurred in January or February begin in September or October? Finally, one would not expect anniversary reactions to respond to treatment with bright light.

5. Are there people who develop symptoms in the evening, when the sun goes down?

Indeed there are. One psychoanalyst recognized this symptom and called it "Hesperian depression" after the Greek goddess of the dusk, Hesperus. Some patients with SAD complain of this problem. For example, one observed that she could not keep working after the sun went down. Another felt unable to make love to her husband except during the day, when the sun was shining.

It's a curious symptom because it suggests an immediate response to the light. This coincides with the experience of some patients using light therapy, in whom I have seen an increase in energy occur even within the first half hour of light treatment.

5

"Summer SAD" and Other Seasonal Afflictions

*Of natures, some are well- or ill-adapted
for summer, and some for winter.*
—*Hippocrates*

THE SUMMERTIME BLUES

Although the commonest form of regular seasonal depression is the winter pattern of SAD, it is by no means the only one. In response to the first newspaper articles on SAD, approximately one in twenty people with seasonal depressions mentioned a pattern of mood change just the opposite of those that had been described in the articles. They regularly became depressed each summer and felt better when fall arrived. Dr. Thomas Wehr personally encountered a few of these patients and became fascinated by this reverse SAD.

One of Dr. Wehr's original summer-SAD patients, "Marge," was a retired government administrator in her mid-sixties when she came to the NIMH for help. She had suffered from regular bouts of depression for the previous forty-five years, but had not recognized that her moodiness, lethargy, and irritability were out of the ordinary until the last fifteen years.

For her, summers were always the worst times, except once when she went on vacation with her family for a few weeks to the Finger Lakes in upper New York State. She recalls swimming two or three times a day, "in that deep, dark, cold water. After a few days of that, my mood lifted and that summer, at least, the depression never came back."

Although she knew her depressions were related to summer, she was never really sure why that was so. Perhaps, she thought, it was related to being on vacation. During the summer she was "too down and lethargic" to think about it, "and when fall came, I felt so much better I didn't bother because I had so many other things to do. When it goes away, you don't expect it to come back. But it always comes back in the spring." When she first saw Dr. Wehr in the summer, she said that her depression had apparently remitted spontaneously a day or two before the consultation. This coincided with an unusual cold front of air that had moved into the Washington, D.C. area, changing its usual sweltering and humid summer days into cool and pleasant ones.

Dr. Wehr postulated that it might be the heat of the summer that was triggering this patient's depressions and that the cool air and her swims in the cold, spring-fed lakes of the north might have exerted a therapeutic influence on her mood. He observed that temperature changes had been suggested as a cause of depression since the time of Aristotle. On the basis of this hypothesis, Dr. Wehr suggested that Marge stay in her air-conditioned apartment for a week and avoid the summer heat completely. She followed his suggestion and showed a markedly positive response to this treatment.

As often happens in clinical work, it took a very interesting, prototypical patient to make researchers wonder exactly what caused these recurrent summer depressions. Marge played this role for summer SAD. Following her successful treatment, Sandy Rovner ran an article in the *Washington Post* in which she described the summer version of SAD, and mentioned that a new research program at the NIMH was looking into the condition. Numerous responses followed, and Dr. Wehr evaluated the histories of these patients.

In general, there are many similarities between people with summer and winter depressions. Most of the patients are women, and feelings of low energy are once again a prominent part of the picture. Many are not aware of experiencing any actual mood changes but, according to Wehr, regard themselves as "being in a holding pattern." They just want to be left alone. As one of Wehr's patients put it, "I'm just not running on all cylinders." Just as for winter depressives, a notable proportion of family members of summer depressives have also suffered from mood disorders.

In contrast to winter-SAD patients, who tend to eat more and crave sweets and starches during depressions, summer sufferers tend to eat less and lose weight. These differences have also been observed by two Australian researchers, Drs. Philip Boyce and Gordon Parker, who sent out questionnaires to those responding to an article in a women's magazine, and similarly received responses from both winter- and summer-SAD patients. Whereas the winter-SAD patients feel physically slowed down during depressions, summer-SAD patients are often agitated. In addition, those with summer SAD express more suicidal ideas than their winter counterparts, and may be at greater risk for harming themselves or taking their own lives. This is in keeping with studies that show that the peak time for suicide in the general population is the spring and early summer.

Summer depressives frequently ascribe their symptoms to the severe heat of summer, whereas winter depressives more often attribute their symptoms to a lack of light—educated perhaps by the publicity surrounding research in this area. Some winter depressives feel that the extreme cold of winter may also play a role in their symptoms, but this possibility has not yet been explored. Studies indicate that most people in the northern United States dislike winter more than summer. When you look as far south as Florida, however, the pattern is reversed and more people dislike the summer. If the greenhouse effect is occurring, as disturbing evidence suggests, and the world is becoming progressively hotter and hotter, summer depressions may become increasingly more common in future.

Curiously, some patients report having both regular summer and winter depressions. For these people spring and fall are the only times when they feel good. Flora, for example, an editor in her mid-forties, recalls winter depressions since age sixteen, which last "from Thanksgiving until the daffodils begin to bloom in April." It's only in the last fifteen years that she has become aware of having summer depressions. Before then she lived in upstate New York, where temperatures do not often go above 85 to 90 degrees—the point at which she has observed that she begins to get "slowed down and stupid and forgetful and depressed.'' Her summer depressions usually last from the middle of June until the middle of September. She has become aware of this because, as a keen gardener, she has noticed that ''I garden pretty seriously through June. Then I look up in September, and the garden is full of weeds.'' In her professional life, she is least proud of the editing she does in the summer.

Flora has noticed many similarities between her summer and winter depressions. She feels lethargic, needs more sleep, craves candy bars, and gains weight in both seasons. She has used light treatment for several winters, but has not had any equivalent treatment for her summer depressions. Indeed, no specific physical treatment has been fully worked out yet for summer depression, though the potential therapeutic value of changing environmental temperature continues to be explored. One difference between the two types of depression that Flora has noted is the rapidity and ease with which they can be reversed. ''During my summer depression, I feel better instantly if I go north. In the winter, on the other hand, if I am separated from my lights, it takes me several days to feel better again after I return to them.''

The winter depressions tend to be longer and deeper for Flora. In the summer, she notes, ''I never get so far from reality that I lose track of how it actually is. I can't always deal with it at that moment, but I don't think that I get really buffaloed, while in the winter I think I actually lose touch with reality; I begin to get kind of paranoid.''

One big problem for people with both summer and winter depressions is that they have to cram as much as possible into the spring and fall. Flora notes that because of her depressions, ''I go through cycles of letting things slide, and then, when I feel better, I scurry around, pay my income taxes and bills, clean my basement and weed my garden, make new friends, and start a whole bunch of projects.''

Gary is another person who has suffered both winter and summer depressions since he was ten years old. A tree surgeon in his early thirties, he loves outdoor activities, particularly rock climbing. In spring and fall he is lean and fit and strong, ''like a horse let out of a starting gate.'' But when winter comes along, he gains up to thirty pounds and feels slowed down and sluggish. ''I can't fight it. It's as if a switch has been thrown. Each time you think you've conquered the beast, the depression starts again.'' Summer sets him back in just the same way, derailing his plans, frustrating the hopes that come with the spring. "You think, 'look how far I've come since winter.' Friends come up and tell me how good my body is looking. And I can feel it. I'm stronger and fitter. Projecting the curve up, I think of how well I can do if it just keeps going that way. Unfortunately, that's usually exactly the time when I begin to get depressed again." Gary did very well with lights last winter. The following summer his usual depression was successfully prevented by his taking the antidepressant, Prozac (see Part 2). Because of his outdoor work, it is impossible for him to avoid the intense heat of a Washington summer.

In my experience, most SAD patients retain the same pattern of seasonal depressions throughout the course of their lives. But I have encountered one patient who started off experiencing depressions only in the winter, and later developed only summer depressions. Some people who have one form of the depression have relatives with the other form, or with depressions that are not seasonal at all. These observations raise questions as to how the different types of depression may be related to one another.

Patients with regular spring depressions seem to be quite rare. One such person whom I have treated did not respond to light therapy, but did well when given appropriate medications.

UNDERSTANDING RECURRENT DEPRESSIONS

How can we understand the recurrences and cycles of mood, energy, and behavior that occur in some individuals? What is the nature of this vulnerability? How is it that different people become depressed at different times of year and in response to different types of stresses and stimuli?

Claude Bernard, a great pioneer in the field of physiology, stressed the concept of constancy of the interior environment. According to this idea, all animals, humans included, are designed in such a way as to keep their internal environments constant. This would include body temperature, the concentrations of bodily chemicals, the rate of metabolism, and all manner of other essential functions. We now know that the internal environment does not really remain constant, but that it varies in a regular and predictable way over the course of the day, the menstrual cycle, and the year. Such predictable internal changes take place despite challenges from our external environment—for example, alterations in temperature and light.

Areas of our brain, most notably our hypothalamus, help us to adjust to these external fluxes, almost as a thermostat in a house helps to keep the indoor temperature constant. In people who are susceptible to seasonal depressions, the capacity to react appropriately to these changes in the environment appears to be impaired. We have not as yet discovered the exact location of this abnormality, but in the case of winter SAD it is quite possible that the problem resides somewhere between the eye and the hypothalamus. In summer-SAD patients the problem presumably resides elsewhere—perhaps in the neuroanatomical pathways involved in the body's response to heat. Clearly, this is the sketchiest of explanations, and further research will be needed to define the abnormal circuitry more precisely.

Some medications seem to correct the regulatory abnormalities in SAD and restore normal functioning, as long as they continue to be used. An exciting new development in the treatment of seasonal depressions, however, involves altering the physical environment in such a way as to induce the brain and body (perhaps via the hypothalamus) to behave normally. Thus, exposure to bright light might correct abnormal responses to light deprivation, and cooling the environment might correct abnormal responses to high temperatures. There are several attractive features of these nonpharmacological approaches. First, one avoids the side effects that often go along with giving medications. Second, one can develop new and better treatments—including medications—by understanding the environmental changes that cause or reverse the symptoms of these conditions. And finally, these treatments are wonderful tools for helping us understand the abnormalities that underlie seasonal depressions.

EFFECTS OF THE SEASONS ON BEHAVIOR IN THE POPULATION

> *For everything there is a season and a time for*
> *every matter under heaven.*
> —*Ecclesiastes 3:1*

When is the peak time for suicide? Not, as one might guess, during the dark and gloomy days of winter—though this was long held to be the case—but rather, during the warm, sunny days of spring and summer. In his classic text, *Suicide: An Essay on Comparative Moral Statistics,* Henry Morselli analyzed data from much of Europe and showed a peak incidence of suicide in the two warm seasons, spring and summer, for almost all countries. He looked to temperature as the cause of these seasonal changes, but failed to find a clear-cut connection between environmental temperature and the incidence of suicide. He concluded that "suicide and madness are not influenced so much by the intense heat of the advanced summer season as by the early spring and summer, which seize upon the organism not yet acclimatized and still under the influence of the cold season." Morselli also recognized a second peak in suicide, in the months of October and November, in the annual curves of some countries.

Emil Durkheim, the famous French sociologist, accepted Morselli's figures but rejected his explanation of them. He pointed out that there was a far better correspondence between length of day and incidence of suicide than between temperature and suicide. In his view, this was a strong argument against a physical environmental explanation for the seasonal variation. Instead, he suggested that this trend was due to differences in the amount of social interaction that occurred during the long days of summer, as opposed to the short days of winter. Why a greater opportunity for social interactions should predispose to suicide, rather than protect against it, is not clear to me, but that was how Durkheim saw it.

The controversy between climatic and sociological explanations for the seasonal variation in suicide was impossible to resolve, in large measure because the information was correlational. Scientists have frequently pointed out that just because two things change together, you cannot assume that one causes the other. Often such associations are the first clue that a cause-and-effect relationship exists, as in the case of smoking and lung cancer but actual experiments are required before such a relationship can be definitively established. Population studies are therefore only able to provide us with clues about the effects of the seasons, and the environment in general, on human behavior, but not with conclusive answers.

More recent studies of seasonal patterns of suicide continue to point to spring and summer as peak seasons, although in many studies, a smaller peak is also apparent in the fall. Dr. Jürgen Aschoff, one of the major figures in rhythm studies in humans, recently reviewed patterns of suicide in Europe and Japan for the past century and related the pattern of seasonal change in different locations to patterns of change in climatic variables, such as temperature and day length. These variables show a minimum seasonal variation just north of the equator along a line that could be considered "the biological equator." Aschoff found a close correlation between the amplitudes of seasonal rhythms of suicide and of two environmental variables: temperature and the number of hours of sunlight per day. In the Northern Hemisphere these rhythms all reach their maximum amplitude at about 40 degrees north. This does not mean that the actual rate of suicide varies with latitude. Rather it is the amplitude of the seasonal rhythms of suicide—the extent to which the rate of suicide varies with the seasons—that is associated with latitude. Aschoff pointed out that the amplitude of the seasonal variation in suicide has decreased over the past century, corresponding to increased industrialization, which may diminish the impact of the changing seasons on our behavior. This difference in the extent to which we are directly exposed to our physical environment may also explain why urban dwellers have shown less seasonal variation in suicide than those in rural areas—an observation that has been made for at least a century.

Despite the increased sophistication of studies such as those conducted by Aschoff, we still don't know for sure why the rate of suicide varies markedly with the seasons. However, recent studies of the effects of such physical factors as light and heat on mood make physical environmental theories more plausible than ever. I should emphasize that even hard-nosed proponents of physical environmental theories, such as Morselli, recognized that suicide is a complex act, occurring in vulnerable individuals for a multitude of reasons. These researchers did us a service, however, in drawing our attention to the role of physical and climatic influences on the tragic—and often preventable—phenomenon of suicide.

THE HEAT AND VIOLENCE CONNECTION

The debate about the nature of the relationship between suicide and the seasons that began over one hundred years ago has been replayed recently in scientific journals and the popular press in relation to the association between the seasons and violence. Two leading researchers in the field, Drs. Richard Michael and Doris Zumpe, published a paper in the *American Journal of Psychiatry* in 1983, called "Sexual Violence in the United States and the Role of Season," in which they analyzed seasonal variations in over fifty thousand rapes in sixteen locations in the United States. They found a seasonal variation, with peak occurrences in July and August. This corresponded closely to seasonal variations in assaults, but not to that for robberies, which peaked in November and December, or for murders, which showed no specific pattern. The timing of the maximum incidence of rape closely paralleled that of the maximum temperature values. These researchers suggested that environmental temperature might influence this seasonal variation by its effect on the secretion of certain hormones. Indeed, the male sex hormone, testosterone, has been shown to have a seasonal rhythm in humans, with a peak in the summer months, and is known to influence aggressive behavior in both humans and animals.

An outcry followed. A strongly worded essay by Stephen J. Gould in *Discover* magazine pointed out the hazards of confusing correlation and causation, and suggested the "more obvious" association between hot days and the opportunity for violence when people are out and about. This argument is reminiscent of Durkheim's sociological explanations. Two prominent psychiatrists wrote a letter to the editor, criticizing Michael and Zumpe for making "statements that appear to embody misperceptions of the experience of sexual violence and that look narrowly at an enormously complicated interaction between biological, psychosocial, and environmental determinants of human behavior." The researchers replied that they were not disputing the importance of all sorts of factors as determinants of rape, but simply drawing attention to the potential importance of temperature, "a factor that has been ignored by science for one hundred years." Indeed, Morselli wrote about the influence of temperature on the seasonal variation of violent crime in the nineteenth century.

Michael and Zumpe, commenting on the outcry produced by their paper, suggested that this came from "all those who believe passionately that men and women should be in total control of their personal destinies and that, if they are not, then it is society that has perverted them." They addressed some of their critics in a follow-up study on domestic violence, a type of behavior where availability of the victim does not vary seasonally in the same way as in community violence. Once again they found a peak incidence of crisis calls to shelters for battered women in the summer months, corresponding closely to the peak environmental temperatures. Besides the excellent work of these researchers, there is substantial scientific literature on the influence of temperature on irritability, which may in turn lead to anger, directed at someone who just happens to be in the way.

It has been my experience that criticism and derision frequently attend any suggestion that human emotions and behavior are influenced by our physical world. Such physical influences are often not regarded as plausible explanations for our actions, since we consider ourselves to be reasonable creatures. In the early years of our research on the seasons we experienced a great deal of derision over SAD and the postulated effect of light on human mood—until our studies were widely replicated by other research groups.

FULL MOONS, AIR IONS, AND EVIL WINDS
_____

Demoniac frenzy, moping melancholy,
And moonstruck madness.
                              —*Milton,* Paradise Lost

The wind's in the east . . . I am always con-
scious of an uncomfortable sensation now and
then when the wind is blowing in the east.
                              Charles Dickens, Bleak House

So central is the influence of the moon in the mythology of madness
that it would hardly be right to omit it from this book. The word *lunacy*
derives from this belief. Yet the actual evidence of its influence on
human behavior and emotions is rather slim. Dr. Arnold Lieber analyzed
the patterns of homicides and aggravated assaults in Dade County,
Florida, and showed that they tended to cluster around the time of the
full moon. Yet others have failed to replicate this work in other parts of
the country. Dr. Charles Mirabile has analyzed medical records at the
Institute of Living in Hartford, Connecticut, and has found a small rise
in paranoid behavior around the time of the full moon. The behavioral
effects of the moon—if indeed they exist—may be due to its light or its
gravitational effects on body fluids. I have occasionally come across
individuals who say they are strongly influenced by the phases of the
moon, but I have never seen this influence convincingly documented in
any particular individual. Until someone is able to do so, the age-old
beliefs in the powers of the moon over mankind will continue to lack a
compelling scientific basis.

The weather has been held to have powerful effects on human functioning since the time of Hippocrates. In his famous works he has an
entire section, "On Airs, Waters, and Places," where he outlines his
beliefs on the importance of our physical environment. He emphasized
the effects of good and bad winds. In a modern text, Dr. Felix Sulsman
writes at length on the effects of weather on humans. He devotes an
entire section to the "medical impact of evil winds." Prominent among
these are warm winds that come down from the mountains—such as the

Santa Ana in California, the foehn in Europe, and the Chinook in Canada. These winds are reported to cause irritability, restlessness, lethargy, depression, and general debility. The foehn has been associated with increased rates of crime, suicide, and traffic accidents. I have already discussed the important effects of heat on emotions and behavior, and as these mountain winds generally raise the environmental temperature abruptly by as much as 15 to 20 degrees Celsius, it is possible that many of their effects may be due to heat alone. However, they do have other meteorological effects as well, including the introduction of air ions, and these charged particles have been shown experimentally to increase irritability in people.

Those who have studied the effects of weather changes on people observe that some individuals are particularly sensitive to these changes. Goethe wrote, "It is a pity that just the excellent personalities suffer most from the adverse effects of the atmosphere." He numbered himself among that unfortunate but privileged group. It does indeed seem as though different people react differently to various weather conditions. I have seen a few people who have reported marked feelings of depression or irritability when the weather changes, particularly when a storm is about to hit.

For one man, whom I shall call "Ahmed," a computer scientist in his early forties, the problem was serious enough to induce him to come from Saudi Arabia to Washington, D.C., for a consultation on his problem. He noticed that just before clouds drifted across the sky, he began to feel weak and depressed. His stomach seemed bloated, and his head felt "blown up." When the weather was stable, he would feel even better than normal—exceedingly energetic and enthusiastic about life. Several members of his family reported almost identical, weather-related symptoms. Because he had suffered from multiple depressions and mild high periods, I suggested that he be treated with lithium carbonate, which is often very helpful for stabilizing such mood fluctuations.

The effects of weather on vulnerable individuals has been a rather neglected area scientifically. Apart from the specific focus on SAD that I have already discussed, little systematic work has been done on other types of climatic influences. The literature is full of assumptions and old nostrums, culled from the classics. It has been widely claimed that some people are able to predict the weather based on its effects on their minds and bodies. This phenomenon is also poorly understood and we are little further along in our understanding of it than the author, John Taylor (1580–1653), who wrote:

> Some men 'gainst Raine doe carry in their backs
> Prognosticating Aching Almanacks.
> Some by painful elbow, hip or knee
> Will shrewdly guesse what weathers like to be.

Recent research bears out Hippocrates's view that, "Of natures, some are well- or ill-adapted for summer, and some for winter." Just as some people are adversely affected by the physical environment in winter—the darkness and cold—others have trouble with heat and humidity. Characteristic patterns of depression may result. The symptoms of winter SAD usually include decreased activity, overeating, oversleeping, and weight gain, whereas the symptoms of summer SAD often include loss of appetite and weight, insomnia, and agitation. It seems as though these two patterns represent extreme manifestations of physical changes seen in a large proportion of the population in these two seasons. Somehow, seasonally depressed people seem less well-insulated against the effects of extreme changes in climate and are unable to function adequately in such conditions. The symptoms of depression result. Fortunately, there are many ways in which the depressed person can find relief from these symptoms. The second part of this book describes how this can be accomplished.

Part 2:

Treatments

*Everybody talks about the weather; but
nobody does anything about it.*
                              —*Charles Dudley Warner*

There are many ways in which our physical environment can influence, for better or worse, the way we feel and act. But what can we do
about it? The most exciting discovery in the field of SAD, or winter
depression, is that the depression can be helped by light therapy, in most
cases. Regular summer depressions, on the other hand, appear to be
influenced more by environmental temperature than by light, and it is
possible that cooling the environment can help a person who gets
depressed during the dog days of summer. Since winter depressions are
more common than summer depressions, and since we know more about
them, most of this section deals with how best to handle the gray days of
winter.

The development of the best treatments for emotional conditions has
been greatly slowed down by professionals who are sure that their
particular theory is the only one that will really cure a problem. Such an
approach closes the therapist's mind toward other possible avenues of
treatment. Many modern therapists have learned to take a more eclectic
approach to treatment and are showing a greater willingness to combine
different types of treatment. Of course, in order to do so, the therapist
either has to be skilled in many different types of treatment, or willing to

refer the patient to somebody else for some specific type of treatment which he is not qualified to administer. In practice, this ideal is often not obtained. The therapist may be ignorant of new developments in one area or another, or may be skeptical of the value of some new treatment, even though he has not really examined the evidence for and against it. This is the therapist's problem, but it also becomes the patient's problem in that he may be delayed in, or prevented from, getting the necessary treatment. This problem is especially likely to occur with newly described conditions, such as SAD, and with newly developed treatments, such as light therapy.

In my experience, a patient can usually tell when a therapist is being defensive about a new type of treatment. The therapist may offer critical or discouraging comments without being able to substantiate them with good reasons. He may "interpret" the wish to seek other treatments as a patient's "resistance" to looking into the true causes of his problems. Patients have the right to have their questions about new types of treatments dealt with on their merits. Their inquiries should be taken seriously by the therapist, who should ask the most relevant questions: is this treatment likely to be helpful for you, and what harm, if any, is associated with it?

One patient I recall, a physician himself, was in traditional psychoanalysis. When he became interested in exploring the possibility of light therapy for himself, his analyst "interpreted" this wish as an attempt to avoid dealing with his underlying unconscious conflicts. Nonetheless, he looked into light therapy and decided to enter the research program at the NIMH. His analyst took a traditional hard-line approach toward the decision and gave him an ultimatum: light therapy or analysis, not both. The patient chose light therapy and has done very well with it. However, the ultimatum induced him to stop his analysis abruptly, which was less than ideal for his general treatment. It is possible for therapists to collaborate successfully in the treatment of a patient, and I have seen many people treated successfully with light therapy in conjunction with other types of therapy, including psychoanalysis.

Any depressed person should obtain the help of a qualified professional, and the person with SAD is no exception. Although it is often easy to diagnose SAD on the basis of a patient's history, there are other conditions that may masquerade as SAD. For example, underactivity of the thyroid, hypoglycemia, and chronic viral illnesses. These problems should be considered and ruled out before SAD is diagnosed. The first treatment tried may not be helpful, and it is important for the patient not to despair, but to try other approaches, instead. It is also possible that the treatment is not being carried out correctly. A professional may be able to detect this and make the necessary suggestions for correcting the problem. Side effects may develop, and an expert may be able to help minimize these.

As the slogan of a well-known discount store goes, "An educated consumer is our best customer," and this applies no less to getting the best type of health care than it does to the purchase of clothing. One of the chief goals of this book is to provide the sort of education that will ensure that those who have difficulties with the seasons get the best type of assistance for it. What follows is a comprehensive picture of the treatment choices available to individuals with seasonal difficulties. I hope that it proves helpful not only to them, but also to their families and friends.

6

Light Therapy:
The Nuts and Bolts

INTRODUCTION

This chapter deals with the practical details of light therapy: how it has been most commonly administered, what effects one can reasonably expect it to have, and the potential problems associated with it. Because light therapy has been around for less than ten years, its technology is still in its infancy, and many changes and advances are sure to take place in the future. But it is exciting and reassuring to think that many hundreds of patients have already been treated safely and effectively with light therapy as it is currently practiced.

HOW LIGHT THERAPY SHOULD BE ADMINISTERED:
A STEP-BY-STEP GUIDE

A word of caution: If you have any eye or skin condition that might be affected by exposure to bright light, be sure to check with your physician before starting light treatment. Examples of conditions that may be made worse by exposure to bright light are macular degeneration—a condition of the retina; or lupus—an immune condition where exposure to sunlight and other bright light may cause rashes to develop.

1. *Obtaining a suitable fixture:* Obtain a light box from a knowledgeable distributor, several of whom are noted in the resource section at the back of the book.

Two types of light fixtures have been widely tested and these are shown in the photos on page 230. Both have been found to be safe and effective. Which of the two types is best for you depends on the type of person you are and on the nature of your seasonal difficulties. You should discuss the matter fully with your therapist before proceeding to make the investment in either type. The information that follows is designed to help you and your therapist reach the best decision for you.

The first type of fixture, which I shall refer to as the conventional type (see photo, page 230, top), is a version that we have used since our first treatment studies for SAD were conducted. It is a metal case, 2 feet by 4 feet, with space to hold six 40-watt fluorescent tubes. The tubes I have generally used are full-spectrum fluorescent lights, though cool-white fluorescents may be just as effective. Behind the tubes is a shiny metal surface, which increases the amount of light reflected into the room. In front of the tubes is a plastic diffusing screen, which spreads the light over an even surface.

The second type of light fixture, which I shall refer to as the tilted fixture, has arrived on the light therapy scene only in the past few years. As you can see by the picture (photo, page 230, bottom), it is not the fixture itself that is so different from the conventional type, but rather the angle and distance at which it is administered. The new type of fixture, which was developed by Dr. Michael Terman and colleagues at the New York State Psychiatric Institute, is also a metal box, which contains cool-white fluorescent light tubes, in this case three U-shaped tubes. By having the light tilted at an angle towards the subject, the light source is brought much closer to the subject's eyes, which increases the intensity of the light reaching the eyes fourfold. It also serves to decrease the glare that occurs with straight-on illumination.

A big advantage of this new type of fixture is that people need to spend much less time in front of the light in order to be successfully treated. Dr. Terman has found that as little as 30 minutes of light treatment in the early morning has a powerful antidepressant effect on most of the SAD patients whom he has studied. Since the tilted fixture uses light tubes that emit minimal ultraviolet light, the risk of potentially harmful effects of ultraviolet radiation to the eyes is greatly reduced. So far, extensive testing has not revealed any harmful effects of the tilted fixture on visual function.

The only potential disadvantage of the tilted fixture is that clinicians have had far less clinical experience with it than with the conventional fixture. It has only been studied thoroughly at one center and further experience will be necessary to confirm its outstanding track record. In contrast, the conventional type of light fixture has been used safely and effectively on many hundreds of patients for several years. Although patients may need to spend more time in front of the light, this is not a problem for some individuals, especially since one can do all sorts of things in front of the lights without loss of efficacy.

If you are the kind of person who likes to go with the latest technology, and if you have very little time to sit in front of the lights, you might prefer to try the tilted fixture. On the other hand, if you prefer more established technology, even if it may prove to be less efficient or effective, the conventional fixture may be for you.

Smaller light boxes are available, and these are especially useful for those who travel frequently or need to move the box from room to room. However, if the mobility of the fixture is less critical, the larger box is preferable. With it, the light is spread out over a greater surface area, which some users find more comfortable. In addition, the safety and efficacy of the larger box are more extensively tested.

Suitable light fixtures, lamps included, currently cost approximately $350 to $500. That may sound like a lot of money, and many handy individuals have considered making their own. In my experience, this has not proven satisfactory for most people. Ordinary fixtures in hardware stores usually are not wired for the right number of lamps, and therefore do not put out enough light. Industrial fixtures, which may be designed for the right number of lamps, may need to be electrically wired. This generally requires an electrician, since amateur wiring can be hazardous. Incorrect fixtures can put out too much light. One patient, an engineer who built his own fixture and supervised his own treatment, ended up with a burn on the surface of his eye. Fortunately, this has not been reported with properly supervised light therapy. Finally, homemade fixtures, if they are made correctly, cost almost as much as the custom-built ones. If you do decide to build your own box, a few words of advice: Build it in the summer, when you are not depressed. Build it exactly according to specifications and be sure to wire it correctly.

Full-spectrum fluorescent lights are slightly different in color from cool-white fluorescents. They contain a little more red and blue and less green and yellow. The result is a purer white, which more closely resembles sunlight. Full-spectrum lights also contain a small amount of ultraviolet (UV) light in the same proportions as sunlight. I should emphasize that full-spectrum fluorescents are very different from the lamps used in tanning salons, which emit such large amounts of UV light that skin and eye damage may result unless they are used sparingly and carefully. The full-spectrum lamps used for SAD have proven quite safe so far, and there are no documented cases of eye or skin damage in patients who have used them for five or six years.

2. *Setting up the lights:* It is important to position them correctly. If you are using the conventional fixture, your face should be directed towards the light. For this reason, the light should be placed at eye level, either horizontally on a desk, table, or other flat surface, or vertically on the floor, in which case it is important to sit in a low chair. It is not necessary to stare at the light or even to glance at it on a regular basis, though it is quite safe to do so. Many people have used the time in front of the lights for reading, craftwork, chores, or watching TV.

If you are using the tilted fixture, the front of the frame should be lined up with the edge of the desk or table at which you are sitting. You need to be able to get your legs underneath the table or else you will not be close enough to the light source. You do not need to stare at the light source at all, but rather look downward towards the desk surface. In doing so, you should receive enough indirect light to produce the desired effect.

3. *Distance from the lights:* It is important to sit at just the right distance from the light because the actual amount that reaches your eye depends on how far away from it your eyes are. If you are using the conventional fixture, you should not sit farther than three feet away from the front of the box while you are having your light treatment. Of course,

at other times of the day, you might choose to use the light box as a source of room lighting and ignore the question of distance. If you are using a conventional fixture and find it is not turning out to be as effective or efficient as you hoped it would, the intensity of the light you receive—and perhaps the effectiveness of the treatment—can be increased by sitting a little closer to the light than three feet. There is no reason to believe that this would be harmful, provided you do not stare at the light for long intervals.

If you are using the tilted fixture, it is important that your forehead be just below the upper portion of the light box, angled towards you. If your head is farther back, the amount of light you receive will fall below the required level. On the other hand, if you lean too far forward, your head will cast a shadow on the desk surface, which will also reduce the light level.

Light intensity is measured in "lux." A bedroom illuminated by a single bedside lamp would have a light level of about 100 lux, whereas a well-lit office interior might give light measurements of 500 to 1,000 lux. The amount of light you should receive at a distance of three feet from a conventional fixture is approximately 2,500 lux, which is the amount that has been shown to be effective in many light treatment studies. The amount of light you should receive if you sit at the appropriate distance and angle in relation to the tilted light is 10,000 lux. Despite the higher intensity of the tilted fixture, it may not appear to be brighter than the conventional fixture because the light reaches the eye more indirectly.

Although the intensities of these fixtures are considerably higher than ordinary indoor lighting, they are far lower than that of outdoor sunlight. For example, 10,000 lux—the light output of the tilted fixture—is the amount of light that would reach your eyes outdoors under clear skies about half an hour after sunrise. Of course, you would receive much more light (approximately 100,000 lux) on a sunny day at the beach.

4. *Time of day and duration of treatment:* This section, involving varying the duration of light treatment, refers to the conventional fixture only. There has been much less clinical experience over extended periods with the tilted fixture, which has generally been used—apparently with considerable success—for only thirty minutes in the morning. I therefore suggest that at this time you should not use the tilted fixture in the

manner described above for more than thirty minutes a day. If, however, you sit approximately three feet away from the tilted fixture, it gives off approximately the same amount of light as the conventional fixture. So, if you have the tilted fixture, the following suggestions, based on my experience with the conventional fixture, would be equally applicable if you sit a few feet away from the edge of the table. Alternatively, you could switch the light level down, using a single lamp. In fact, many people find it most comfortable not to switch off the lights suddenly at the end of a treatment session, but to leave them on for general illumination while moving out of the strict therapeutic range. This may be especially important for the early morning sessions, when it is still dark outdoors. One patient, for example, has observed a sudden plunge in mood when he switches off his lights abruptly.

The actual number of hours of light needed varies from person to person, at different latitudes, and at different times of the year. For example, in the early fall, as people begin to feel the winter syndrome setting in, it may be enough to use the lights for thirty minutes in the morning. As the days get shorter and darker, more light is generally required. A typical person with SAD in the northern United States may start light treatment in mid-September with thirty minutes in the morning and increase it to an hour in October and an hour and a half in November. In December, an hour or two may be added in the evening, and in January and February, a total of six hours or more may be necessary. By late February and early March it is usually possible to decrease the length of time gradually until around mid-April, when it may be fine to stop using the lights altogether.

If you begin treatment in the middle of the winter and are already feeling moderately to markedly depressed, it would be reasonable to start with about four hours of light per day—two in the morning and two in the evening. If that proves to be too much or too little for you, you can easily alter the timing and duration after a week of treatment. For example, if it appears to be working well and you find that the initial dosage of four hours per day is inconvenient, you could reduce it gradually to the minimum effective dose, which may be as little as thirty minutes per day.

There is some controversy over the optimal timing of treatment. In my experience, *the most important factor is for treatment to occur at a convenient time,* given that most people need two to four hours of light per day. Fortunately, for many people, it seems to work well at all different times of day. You can divide the treatment between the morning and the evening; alternatively, you may get all the light you need during the daytime while you are at work. Certain people respond best to light treatment in the morning hours—at which time two hours of treatment may be enough to keep them feeling well all day.

Obviously, *the only way you can find the routine that works best for you is by trial and error.* For example, should you start using two or three hours of light in the evening because that is the most convenient time for you, and you find that it isn't working well, it would be advisable to switch some of the time to the morning before concluding that light treatment is not helpful.

One of the most important factors in determining the amount of light needed for any particular individual at any particular time is the amount of environmental light available, rather than the season of the year. For example, an overcast spell of several days may cause SAD symptoms, even if it occurs in the summer. Several of my colleagues have light boxes in their offices, and when the weather turns gloomy, they switch them on—almost as though they have heard a "SAD warning" announced on the radio. Some people with windowless offices, who work long days without sunlight, may be perennially light-deprived and chronically fatigued and depressed. Not surprisingly, some of these folks use their light boxes all year round—even in the summertime.

A tip for those who have a hard time getting out of bed during the dark days: it is often helpful to have the lights in the bedroom on a timer, set to go on an hour or two before you are due to wake up. Even if you are asleep during those few hours, some of the light will get into your eyes, and waking up and getting out of bed will be easier. This should be regarded as a supplement to, and not a substitute for, light therapy itself, which we believe will work only if the eyes are open during treatments.

5. *Consistency of treatment:* For treatment to remain effective, it must be continued as long as there is a deficiency of environmental light. For example, if a person usually feels the symptoms of SAD between November and March, he or she will have to use the lights on a daily—or almost daily—basis during those months. It is possible to skip a day here or there without suffering a relapse of symptoms, but many people find that if they skip more than one day, they feel their SAD

symptoms creeping—or crashing—back again. As the days become longer and brighter, it is possible to decrease the duration of light treatment and skip more days without adverse consequences. Watch out for the spring, however, when the weather tends to be erratic. Bright sunny days alternate with cloudy and rainy ones. You may think that the problems are over for the season and then crash, back they come. So, keep an eye on the sky before you pack your lights away.

THE EFFECT OF LIGHT TREATMENT ON THE SYMPTOMS OF SAD

Some people feel the effect of light treatment even after their first session. But for most people, the effect takes about two to four days to occur. The first sensations may be physical—a sense of lightening of the body or increased energy. There may be a feeling of "butterflies in the stomach" or "pins and needles" in the hands. In the days that follow, people report that it feels as though some fundamental problem is being corrected; ideally, the symptoms of SAD disappear, one by one. In those people where this effect takes hold completely, the results may seem dramatic, almost a miracle. In others, the result is less complete. Treatment may be helpful, but some difficulties may remain. In a minority of people, the light treatment may not work at all. The good news is that over 80 percent of people with SAD or the winter blues may expect to benefit from light therapy, although it should not be expected to control all the problems associated with winter.

While on light therapy, people typically feel more energetic. Suddenly, chores and daily activities no longer feel like drudgery. Along with a physical sense of lightness, the burden of living, of carrying your body around from place to place, seems to lift, and the overwhelming need to sleep subsides. Suddenly, you feel less driven by cravings for sweets and starches. Cakes and candy bars become resistible. Even dieting seems possible again! Thinking becomes more efficient. No longer does your mind creak along like an old machine in need of oiling. Your computer is up and running again. Computations and calculations are possible and new ideas spring readily to mind. You think of tackling problems in ways that hadn't occurred to you before. Exercise becomes less onerous—no longer does that trip to the gym, that walk, jog, aerobics class, or exercycle seem like a mountainous obstacle. There is once again a wish to communicate: to call friends, write notes, arrange trips to the movies, a ballgame, or the theater. Sex seems not only possible, but even desirable. In short, you feel human again.

TROUBLESHOOTING

The effects of light treatment should be noticeable within four days. What should you do if that does not occur? First, make sure you are using the equipment correctly. Do you have the right sort of fixture? Have you placed it at eye level, no more than three feet away from you? Have you been using the lights long enough? With the conventional fixture, you may need as much as five or six hours of exposure. It may be helpful to take the treatment at a different time of day. If the therapy is still not helping or is only partially helpful, be sure to touch base with your psychiatrist about it.

What should you do if therapy is helpful for a while but becomes less effective with time? Although this may occur, it is rarely because the light has stopped exerting a beneficial effect. In other words, the system rarely becomes so used to light treatment that it no longer responds. Instead, you should examine your life to see if anything has changed in your work, relationships, environment, or in the treatment itself. For example, if life has become more stressful or difficult for any reason, this may aggravate your depressive symptoms to the point that light treatment alone is not able to reverse them. In that case, it is obviously important to attend to what is going on in your life so you can begin to alleviate its effects on your mood. Light treatment that is completely effective in November and December may become only partially effective in the darker days of January and February. In those months, the days are longer but are often cloudier, so there is less light available. In order to combat this climatic change, you may need to increase the amount of light or add some other type of treatment. It is important to check the way you have been doing your treatments. Have you slacked off, skipped days, or cut your treatments short? Are you sitting at an angle that doesn't expose your eyes to the light? One final possibility to bear in mind is that the quality of the light bulbs may have deteriorated. This usually happens only after the first season of use, at which time fluorescent lamps begin to give out less light and may need to be replaced.

SIDE EFFECTS OF TREATMENT

In my experience with hundreds of patients, light therapy is generally very well tolerated, and side effects, when they occur, are generally mild. It is unusual for someone to be unable to use light altogether because of side effects. However, there are some people in whom these may be quite disturbing. The side effects I have encountered most commonly are:

1. Headaches
2. Eyestrain
3. Irritability
4. Overactivity
5. Insomnia
6. Fatigue

If headaches or eyestrain are a problem, I suggest that people restart treatment with a short duration of exposure—for example, fifteen minutes per day—then build up gradually over a week or two to the more usual exposure durations. The problem can also be handled by sitting slightly farther away from the light source until the symptoms subside. Generally, it is possible to move closer to the light box again after several days without having these side effects recur.

People who become irritable during light therapy usually say that they often have the same kind of feeling during the summer. This problem responds well to decreased exposure.

Insomnia occurs especially when the lights are used late at night.

Some people complain that it makes them feel too energized and "wired" to go to sleep. The best way to handle this problem is to shift the treatment to an earlier time of day. If it is not possible to use the lights in the morning hours, however, it may be quite satisfactory to use them earlier in the evening or even during the day.

Fatigue may occur after several days of light therapy, especially if the amount or timing of sleep has been changed in order to accommodate treatment. This problem is usually transient. It may require shifting the time of treatment to allow adequate sleep to occur.

We have not encountered any long-term side effects with the therapy so far, even in patients who have used the lights for several hours per day for five or six years. However, those with eye conditions or sun-sensitive skin should certainly check with the appropriate physicians before using it. Light treatment can be combined safely with almost all medications. Those that predispose to sun-sensitive rashes—and this information is usually obtained from the prescribing physician or from the package insert—may cause similar problems after light therapy. However, it is important to remember that the amount of light coming out of the light box is forty times less than that which comes off a summer sky. I know of no cases of sun-sensitive rashes—and only a few cases of mild sunburn—following even intensive use of light therapy.

PREDICTION OF SUCCESSFUL LIGHT TREATMENT

It is not possible to predict exactly who is most likely to respond to treatment with bright light, but we have a few general pointers that help us. If a depressed person has a seasonal history, it is helpful to know whether changes in environmental light that have occurred during his life have affected his mood. Have symptoms improved when the person has traveled south in the winter? Was there ever a change in mood, for better or worse, when the indoor environment became brighter or dimmer? If the answer to these questions is "yes," that would suggest that the person is more likely to respond to light.

Besides the above clues, there are certain physical symptoms that suggest that a person is likely to respond well to light. These include fatigue, oversleeping, anxiety, variation in level of symptoms throughout the day, and carbohydrate craving. In my experience, the most severely depressed people, who lose sleep, eat less, and lose weight in the winter, tend to do least well with light therapy alone. Nevertheless, if you have a history of seasonal or light-sensitive depression, it is certainly worth trying light treatment, regardless of the clinical picture of the depression.

HOW TO HANDLE OTHERS' REACTIONS

Bringing a large box that emits intense light into an indoor environment is certain to have some impact on those around you. Those patients who have used the light in work or home settings have found that some people are drawn to it and find it pleasant, while others dislike it and find it irritating.

There is obviously a concern that bringing a light into the workplace will label one as unhealthy or peculiar in some way. Reactions of colleagues and employers vary quite a bit in this regard. Generally, the employee has the best sense of how accepting the people at work will be and whether the use of lights there is advisable. Supervisors at a graphic design company or a mental health center will obviously be more understanding and accepting of lights than senior officers at the C.I.A. or the Pentagon, settings where it would clearly be imprudent to bring the box into work. Most people have been surprised at how accepting their colleagues are toward the light box and the underlying condition that its presence implies. Perhaps it is because most people understand that seasons can affect behavior in animals, and the majority of the population experiences some seasonal changes, albeit to a milder degree.

Questions about the lights are best handled in a matter-of-fact way, though one college student I know chose humor instead. When asked by his roommates why he used the lights, he replied that experiments had shown that bright light maintained rats in a constant state of sexual arousal. That usually put an end to the questioning.

Many people have commented that their pets seem to react favorably to the lights. I have been told that cats in particular seem drawn to them and sit mesmerized in front of them. The best pet story I have heard concerned a cat and a parakeet who was able to open his own cage. Ordinarily, when the cat encountered the bird, he would give chase and the parakeet would make a dash for his cage and slam the door shut behind himself. However, when the bright lights were turned on, the parakeet emerged from his cage and strutted in front of them, despite the dangerous proximity of the cat. The cat, for his part, appeared so entranced by the lights that he showed no interest in pursuing the parakeet. (Perhaps we should try out the lights on the lion and the lamb!)

Of greater interest than the reaction of pets to the light fixtures is the reaction of insurance companies. Many people I know have tried to get reimbursed for their light boxes, but very few have succeeded. Clearly, the expense of the light box is medically justifiable, and I have little doubt that insurance companies will come to acknowledge that in time. Meanwhile, it may still be worth having your physician write a letter to your insurance company to substantiate your claim. One that I have used in the past, albeit with limited success, is shown below.

Sample for Insurance Reimbursement

To Whom It May Concern:
This is to Certify that Ms. Jane Smith has been a patient of mine since June 1985. I have treated her for recurrent major depressions (DSM III-R-296.3), with a seasonal pattern. This condition, also known as Seasonal Affective Disorder (SAD), has been shown in many studies in both the United States and Europe to respond to treatment with bright environmental light (phototherapy). Phototherapy is no longer considered experimental, but is a mainstream type of psychiatric treatment, described in the Task Force Report of the American Psychiatric Association: Treatment of Psychiatric Disorders, Vol. 3, pages 1890–1896, A.P.A. Press, 1989. In order to administer phototherapy adequately, a light box, such as the one described on the attached invoice, is required. In Ms. Smith's case, the use of such a light fixture should be regarded as a medical necessity and preferable to other forms of treatment.

FUTURE LIGHT

In the years to come, I anticipate the development of exciting new technology in the area of light delivery. For example, a portable light fixture, the light visor, has been developed at the NIMH by my colleagues, Drs. Thomas Wehr and Stephen Leighton, and myself. The light visor looks like a baseball cap attached to a light source, which hangs over the forehead. Although the visor emits only a small amount of light, the eyes, by virtue of their proximity to the light source, receive more light than they would from a conventional light box. Early studies indicate excellent results with the visor, and its portability allows the patient freedom of movement while receiving treatment. The light visor is not yet commercially available, but plans are underway to make it so in the near future.

To summarize the most important points in this section, light therapy for SAD is best carried out under the supervision of a professional. Standard fixtures made specifically for this purpose generally work best and homemade versions may be ineffective or even dangerous. The optimal duration and timing of light treatment varies from person to person and with climate and season. A good way to begin is to follow the directions above. If they don't work well or prove to be inconvenient, you might experiment with different durations and treatment at different times of day. Even when light therapy is not completely successful, it may provide part of the solution. Other helpful measures are outlined in the sections that follow. The best results may be obtained by combining light therapy with other types of treatment.

7

Beyond Light Therapy: Other Ways to Help Yourself

Although most people with SAD can benefit from light therapy, this is often not a complete solution to the problem. Some difficulties may persist, albeit to a lesser degree. While many people find that light therapy has made an enormous difference in the way they feel, they still don't feel as well in the winter as they do in the summer. Luckily, there are many other ways in which people can help themselves or be helped through winter depression—or indeed, depression at any time of the year.

UNDERSTANDING SAD: THE FIRST STEP

One of the most useful things that the definition of SAD has accomplished is that it provides people who suffer from the condition with a new way of understanding their difficulties. This understanding has developed only in the past few years, so people who have suffered from the condition have long been misunderstood, and have also failed to understand their own difficulties. Classical depressions—the kind that physicians have traditionally recognized as coming from within, and have thus termed "endogenous"—have typically been associated with loss of appetite, weight loss, and insomnia. People who have suffered from this condition have often been completely incapacitated, may have seriously considered taking their own lives, and have often required hospitalization. In contrast to this dramatic picture of classical depression, patients with SAD are usually less severely affected and are able to continue functioning, to some degree, at work or at home, although much less effectively than they do at other times of the year, and they have rarely needed hospitalization. In addition, the pattern of eating and sleeping in SAD patients is frequently different from that seen in the types of depression more easily recognized by physicians. Patients with SAD often tend to eat more, crave carbohydrates, and gain weight during the winter. Their energy level is very low, and they often feel fatigued, physically heavy, and weighed down. They withdraw and want to be left alone.

Since the pattern of symptoms in SAD is as much physical as psychological, patients with this problem have often sought help from family practitioners and internists, rather than psychiatrists or therapists. They have been examined and tested for various medical conditions: underactivity of the thyroid, hypoglycemia, or chronic viral infections, such as the Epstein-Barr virus. When these investigations come back negative, as they generally do, the physician is left without any diagnosis or clear course of treatment to suggest. The physician might honestly declare that he or she does not know what is wrong, or imply that the patient is exaggerating the problem. The patient can easily be left with the impression that because the tests have come back negative, the problem is not real, but imaginary. He may feel responsible for his own predicament. After all, if the doctor can't help, it's up to the patient to find the solution. *It is important to remember that, at present, there is no laboratory test for SAD. The diagnosis is made on the basis of history alone.*

Before the recognition of SAD, psychiatrists also often had trouble understanding what was going on. The patient was not, after all, incapacitated—he could continue to work and function to some degree. They concluded that the problem must therefore be "neurotic"—tied up in various conflicts or due to difficulties adjusting to life stress.

Many of my patients have told me how guilty they have felt about their inability to perform at their usual level, to meet the demands they make on themselves, or those others make, during the winter months. Attempts to explain this disability on the basis of psychological factors—childhood traumas, conflicts, anniversary reactions—have been ineffective, and patients have often viewed their inability to benefit from such treatments as just one more failure. The understanding that seasonal problems are an unusual or exaggerated response to physical and climatic changes makes intuitive sense. After all, plants and animals change with the seasons, so why should humans be different? This idea often relieves the sufferer from feelings of guilt and responsibility for his symptoms and makes seasonal changes in mood and behavior understandable and, therefore, easier to deal with.

The explanation that the exaggerated response to the seasons, and the symptoms that result from it, are due to a disturbance in brain chemistry is an example of the "medical model." According to this model, disturbances of brain function are regarded as comparable to those of any other organ—for example, the pancreas in diabetes. Just as the diabetic does not produce enough insulin, the patient with SAD does not produce the correct chemical response when there is inadequate environmental light. And just as an injection of artificial insulin can control the symptoms of diabetes, so bright light can control the symptoms of SAD. The result of the medical model is that the symptoms of depression are no longer seen as character flaws for which the sufferer is somehow responsible, but rather, as the affliction that they really are. Many people have told me how, before their diagnosis of SAD was made, they felt lazy, bad, or immature. Just knowing that they have an illness which has a name, an explanation, and for which effective treatments exist, is already therapeutic.

There is also considerable comfort in knowing you have control over your life, despite the symptoms of SAD. The availability of light and many other ways to combat symptoms makes you feel less a victim of fate and allows you to take charge of things. People who have been accustomed to functioning at low levels can now plan for year-round productivity. In some instances, this allows people to make certain long-term plans—for example, go to graduate school or start a new business—which would formerly have been unthinkable.

In summary, the benefits of recognizing that one may be suffering from SAD, and that light can have antidepressant effects, go well beyond the immediate relief of symptoms. They alter the way a person thinks about the problem, its future outlook, and the options available, and can therefore be a liberating experience that continues to deliver new rewards over time.

CHANGING THE ENVIRONMENT

More Light

The benefit of increasing environmental light can be obtained not only from formal therapy in front of a light box, but whenever your environment is brighter. Some people have several light boxes in the house, which gives them more exposure without the feeling of being trapped in one location. It is not critical for the extra light to come from special boxes. Enhancing light levels at home or in the workplace may be helpful, even if this is accomplished by installing more lights on the ceiling or placing more lamps in the room.

Modifications of the home to increase indoor light levels may be as simple as trimming hedges around the windows or low-lying branches of trees near the house, or as elaborate as constructing skylights. Using bright colors and surfaces can also be effective. Many of my SAD patients have found attractive ways of accomplishing this. Dark wood paneling can be replaced with light-colored wallpaper. Splashes of yellow and orange on curtains and cushions seem to be popular with some people, while others choose white or off-white carpeting and furnishings. SAD patients buying new homes should pay attention to the size of the windows and the directions that the rooms face.

Exposure to natural light can be both enjoyable and therapeutic. This applies to lunchtime walks on sunny winter days or sunlight reflected from snow. Many people have told me that the brightness of the snow is one of the reasons they enjoy skiing. Some people have chosen to work the evening shift, which allows them to enjoy as much outdoor sunshine as possible. On the other hand, a psychiatrist who has seen many SAD patients in Hawaii, where it is sunny for most of the year, tells me that these people develop symptoms because they are reluctant to go outdoors during the day. He has found that encouraging them to do so can control their depressive symptoms.

Once you pay attention to the amount and quality of your environmental light, you will come up with all kinds of ways to enhance it, which will help you feel more comfortable and cheerful.

The Value of Warmth

Many patients have told me that warmth, in conjunction with light, seems to be helpful in combating the symptoms of SAD. They have reported feeling better when they turn up the thermostat, use electric blankets, and drink warm beverages. While this strategy lacks scientific backing, it may help and can't hurt. Among animals, environmental temperature is an important influence on seasonal rhythms, and often operates in conjunction with environmental light.

Winter Vacations

Bright light and warm temperatures can be pleasantly combined in the form of a winter vacation in the south. Many of my patients have learned that if they have a choice, it's better to take vacations in the winter than in the summer. Two weeks in a sunny climate in January can effectively interrupt the worst stretch of the winter. I am reminded of a television commercial in which a somber-looking man stands on the beach in Jamaica on day one of his vacation, looks a little more cheerful on day two, and is positively blissful by day three. For the SAD sufferer, this is truth in advertising! People seem to feel better in this natural sunlight than they do up north, even with light therapy. As an alternative to popular seaside resorts, some of my patients have undertaken adventurous trips—to Antarctica (where the days are very long when it's winter in the Northern Hemisphere) or the Galapagos Islands, for example—with similarly beneficial results. Unfortunately, the beneficial results are usually short-lived, and after returning from vacation, the usual regimen of light therapy must be resumed. Some people find that the sudden exposure to intense sunlight in the middle of winter can make them feel overstimulated, as they are in summer. It is important to watch out for this possibility and monitor your exposure to sunlight accordingly.

Relocation

Several of my patients have chosen a more dramatic solution than those outlined above—to move permanently to places with sunnier climates. Generally, they have been pleased with these moves. They feel more energetic and their energy level is more evenly distributed year-round. Of course, there are many factors other than climate that have to be taken into account when one relocates. One must decide whether relinquishing all the benefits of one's current life-style—the proximity of friends and family, job and cultural amenities—will be repaid by life in a sunnier climate. Clearly, the pros and cons of such a move have to be carefully weighed. Before embarking on such a move, the following considerations should be taken into account:

- How well can the SAD symptoms be controlled by light therapy and other means?
- Will you really feel better during the winter in the new climate? One way to test this is to visit the place during the winter before making a commitment to move.
- What are the exact weather conditions in the place in question? For example, even though a place may be located in the south, local weather conditions may cause clouds to obscure the light for much of the winter.

• What is the summer like in the new place and how do you respond to heat and humidity? Be careful that a move doesn't result in exchanging one climatic problem for another.

DIET AND EXERCISE

There is growing evidence that regular aerobic exercise has a beneficial effect on mood control in those who suffer from depression in general. In SAD, where the exercise may mean increasing your exposure to bright light, either outdoors or on a stationary bicycle in front of a light box, the antidepressant effect can be even greater. Typically, if exercise alone is chosen as the mode of treatment, people often do not have enough willpower to continue it through the winter months. However, the combination of exercise and light therapy may work better than either treatment alone. Exercise, of course, has the added virtue of reducing weight, or at least preventing the much-dreaded winter weight gain.

Most patients with SAD can derive some benefit from exercise. The most important factor in finding the best regime for you is to choose something you enjoy. This could be brisk walking, swimming, jogging, cycling (moving or stationary), cross-country skiing, or aerobic dancing. If you enjoy it, you are much more likely to stick with it. If you choose the exercise on the basis of its aerobic properties or therapeutic value and don't enjoy it, it's unlikely to work out over the long haul. Finding a friend who also wants to exercise can be a valuable support, and you can bolster one another's motivation during the dark days.

Ravenous hunger, cravings for sweets and starches, and weight gain are among the more distressing symptoms of SAD for many people. I am often asked by patients how this unfortunate tendency can be kept to a minimum. Although light therapy tends to decrease appetite and lessen weight gain, it is often only partially effective in this regard, and exercise alone is not usually sufficient to control one's weight. There is no getting away from the fact that diet has to be taken into account as well. There are certain general dietary principles that can help keep weight gain to a minimum and, in more successful cases, I have actually seen some SAD patients lose weight in the winter. Some general principles of diet for winter weight control, as well as sample menus and recipes, are provided in the resource section of this book.

The Importance of Carbohydrates

Most people tend to eat more carbohydrates in the winter than in the summer, and show the opposite seasonal pattern for protein intake. Patients with SAD show this tendency to an exaggerated degree and may actually binge on sweets and starches. These binges can wreak havoc with any attempt at weight control. My colleagues and I at the NIMH have found that carbohydrate-rich meals actually make SAD patients feel energized, whereas they make non-SAD people feel sedated. Since draggy, low-energy feelings are a major problem for people with SAD, it is easy to understand why many of them gravitate to foods that make them feel more energetic, especially if they have work to do.

Diets fall into different categories. Two types commonly used are low-calorie and high-protein. Low-calorie diets may allow a fairly high proportion of calories to come from carbohydrates, whereas high-protein diets are very liberal with protein and, to some extent, with fat, but very stingy with carbohydrates. The reasoning behind these high-protein diets— the Scarsdale Diet, for example—is that carbohydrates are necessary for the metabolism of protein and fat. If you starve the system of carbohydrates, you can eat large amounts of protein and fat but, since you will be unable to metabolize it all, you will excrete a lot of the calories in the urine in the form of a substance called ketone bodies.

In the experience of Dr. Judith Wurtman, who has worked specifically with overweight people who crave carbohydrates, high-protein diets invariably increase cravings for carbohydrates, which eventually become so great that the diet fails. This has also been my experience with SAD patients. On the other hand, when spring and summer arrive, and the craving for carbohydrates decreases, it may be quite possible for the SAD person to go on the Scarsdale Diet or some equivalent carbohydrate-restricted regimen, and shed pounds without difficulty. In this section, however, I will focus on diets for the winter, when carbohydrate cravings rage and weight control is at its most difficult.

One way in which carbohydrates may affect the way we feel is by changing the nerve chemicals, or neurotransmitters, in our brain. Serotonin is one of the neurotransmitters that may be abnormal during the winter in patients with SAD. Drs. John Fernstrom and Richard Wurtman have shown that carbohydrates in the diet shift the distribution of amino acids (the building blocks of proteins) in the blood in such a way as to promote the entry of the amino acid, tryptophan, into the brain. Tryptophan is the substance from which serotonin is synthesized. These researchers have shown that dietary carbohydrates can actually increase serotonin synthesis in the brains of animals. It is quite possible that, by eating carbohydrates, we may also increase the serotonin content in our brains. For people who do not have enough serotonin—and SAD people may fall into this category—dietary carbohydrates may thus have a normalizing effect on the way we feel by altering brain serotonin metabolism.

The menus in the resource section are designed so that calories are maintained within a certain limit and ample carbohydrate-rich foods are provided. I have specifically allowed for three snacks per day, apart from the meals. This should help ease the cravings over the most difficult times of the day. These times vary from person to person, so decide which three times of the day you feel hungriest and most in need of a snack, and allocate the snacks to those times.

Complex versus Simple Carbohydrates

Different types of carbohydrates are absorbed from the bowel and converted into glucose in the blood at different rates. Carbohydrates with a high content of simple sugars, such as candies, pure sugar, and honey, are known as *simple carbohydrates*. Starches, on the other hand, such as those found in cereals and legumes, are made of sugar molecules, bound together in complex arrangements. They are therefore absorbed more slowly and are known as *complex carbohydrates*. Sugar has been accused of many crimes—for example, making hyperactive children feel worse—but few of these allegations have stood up to scrutiny in the strict court of scientific research. However, many dietitians and dieters continue to feel convinced that the pure sugars spell trouble. The transient sugar "rush" can be followed by a letdown, which can send the victim straight back to the cookie jar. At the very least, pure sugar, added to food, supplies calories without any nutritional value. Thus, the menus provided focus on complex carbohydrates and foods that are absorbed relatively slowly.

Fiber

The virtues of dietary fiber have been widely stressed, and rightly so. In experimental animals, the same number of calories, administered with fiber, cause less weight gain than if the fiber is omitted. Fiber has also been associated with a decreased rate of bowel cancer. You will find that the menus and recipes provided are relatively high in fiber. It occurs naturally in cereals— most notably bran—vegetables, and fruit.

STRESS MANAGEMENT

If you are a seasonal person, you have the advantage of being able to predict that at some times of the year your energy level will be low and you may find it difficult to accomplish certain tasks, whereas at other times of the year, it will be high and you may be able to tackle all sorts of things. You can use this information to regulate your stress level throughout the year. Some stresses are unpredictable and cannot be planned, but many can be anticipated. These include purchasing a new house, moving, starting a new job, beginning a major undertaking, and many other projects that we impose upon ourselves.

Many people use the summer months for the creative aspects of their work, and the winter months to consolidate and work on more humdrum tasks. Our original seasonal patient, Herb Kern, followed this pattern. An engineer for Bell Laboratories, he conceived his best ideas and conducted his most exciting experiments in the summer, then wrote up his data—a more routine task—in the winter months. There is evidence that some famous composers, most notably Handel and Mahler, were seasonal and did most of their composing in the summer months.

On a less lofty level, there are all sorts of ways in which you can reduce stress in your own life. Be careful not to take on too many commitments during the summer months, when you are feeling good and expansive, to prevent yourself from becoming overwhelmed during the winter. Undertake difficult projects at that time of year when you feel best. For example, if you find entertaining difficult during the winter months, and have social obligations, perhaps you would be better off tackling them in the summer. By the time winter rolls around, you will then feel free to entertain only if you really wish to do so.

Anticipate those predictable burdens that come up in the winter and try to handle them in advance. These may include such chores as Christmas or Hanukkah shopping, which could be done before the seasonal low sets in. This has the added benefit of allowing you to avoid crowds of last-minute shoppers. You can even wrap gifts, buy your cards, and address the envelopes well ahead of time. If you want to write that long note to people with whom you communicate perhaps only once a year, a letter in late August might serve just as well to catch them up on the news as would one in December. Such advance planning can go a long way toward taking the burden out of the holidays, and allowing you to enjoy the social aspects of the season without feeling overwhelmed by the duties that go along with them.

Other ways of preparing for the winter may include cooking large batches of your favorite food and freezing it in small portions, stored in containers that can go straight into the microwave. This can be done both at the beginning of the winter and on weekends during the winter, minimizing the amount of cooking you have to do during the week. If you work during the day, you may find it helpful to eat your major meal at lunchtime, thereby saving yourself from having to cook it when you get home at the end of a long day. Anticipate your clothing needs before winter sets in. The last thing that most people feel like doing when they are depressed is going clothes shopping and having to look at themselves in all those mirrors.

Paying for help and services can be a wise use of money in the wintertime. You can use some of that money you are not spending for the socializing and shopping you do in the summer to pay others to help you with difficult chores. Such solutions might include taking your clothes to the laundry, hiring a cleaning service, and buying take-out dinners. Mothers can have a particularly hard time meeting the demands of small children when they are feeling depressed, and paying for extra child- or home care can provide a great deal of relief. If you have some money to spare, think of ways in which you may be able to solve a problem by hiring someone else to do chores, such as grocery shopping and housekeeping. You may find yourself coming up with some rather creative solutions.

Sometimes feelings of guilt can be an obstacle to your getting the help you need. In order to feel comfortable paying for services you may feel you should be providing, remind yourself that you are not being lazy, neglectful, and all the other derisive adjectives that depressed people are so good at using on themselves. Reduced levels of energy and motivation, and inability to cope are key symptoms of depression. Even though you may be doing many things to reduce these symptoms, these measures may not be completely effective. It is therefore very important to reduce your stresses and commitments, and if paying others to help out is financially possible, it is worth it for your mental health.

Getting help can also save money in the long run. By paying someone to take care of certain chores, a seasonal person may have more time and energy to devote to his or her job, thereby managing to hold on to it. Overloading one's boat with too many things may cause it to capsize. For example, it is false economy to skimp on help with chores if one's job is at stake.

A major problem for depressed people is concentrating and remembering things. Many seasonal people have developed methods of coping with these difficulties. One woman I know has developed some tricks to help her remember things in the winter. For example, she keeps a very careful calendar, writing everything down, and doesn't assume that she will remember things that she would recall easily in the summertime. She cross-indexes the people she relies on for help of various kinds under a section "H" for "Help." This section includes addresses and phone numbers of plumbers, workmen, and even her doctors, whose names she often forgets in the winter. She leaves notes for herself on the back door, where she will see them as she goes out of the house, and writes notes to herself late at night about what she needs to do the following morning. She also notes down other information, such as friends' birthdays and directions to people's homes.

SLEEP RESTRICTION

One surprising way to handle the sluggishness associated with SAD is to sleep less. This may seem odd, since we usually think of sleep as refreshing and providing extra energy, but it may actually increase depression. Robert Burton, in his classic *Anatomy of Melancholy*, noted that:

> "sleep . . . may do more harm than good in that phlegmatick, swinish, cold, and sluggish melancholy. . . . It dulls the spirits, if overmuch, and . . . fills the head full of gross humours, causeth distillations, rheums, great stores of excrements in the brain and in all other parts."

Some modern researchers agree with Burton's sentiments and have shown that sleep deprivation can have antidepressant effects. Forcing yourself to wake up at seven or eight in the morning instead of ten or eleven may have a salutary effect on your mood and energy level.

As far as stress management is concerned, the bottom line is: *nurture your resources and use your creativity to find shortcuts and ways to conserve your energy to help keep you going through the down season.* There must be all sorts of other strategies for minimizing stress, which I have not as yet come across—see if you can discover some new ones yourself.

ACCEPTANCE

Sometimes, even with the best therapy, mood control is not perfect. As long as the lows are not too low or too long, a measure of acceptance can sometimes be very therapeutic. I only counsel acceptance after every reasonable means to counteract depressive symptoms has been tried. For example, I have one patient whose moods have not been successfully controlled, despite all manner of treatments. Bright light is helpful to her, but only to a modest degree. We meet at intervals, discuss possible approaches, and evaluate new ideas for treatment as they come up. But she has reached a degree of acceptance of her condition and is not willing to try new approaches that appear to hold little advantage over those she has tried before. I support her acceptance while we both search for a better long-term solution.

Acceptance often comes slowly, bit by bit, rather than all at once. There is a great temptation each year, as spring arrives, to think that the problem is over, only to have it reappear again the following fall. I have seen many reactions to this familiar experience. For example, one woman I know has had SAD for the past fifteen years. It was first diagnosed six years ago and she has been treated with light therapy, antidepressant medications, and psychotherapy, with considerable success. Her depressions no longer disable her as they used to, but she is still less energetic, enthusiastic, and effective in the winter than in the summer. Last winter, for the first time, she felt enraged at the limitations the condition imposes on her, the way in which her life seems to flip-flop between feeling good and feeling depressed every six months. This anger is one more phase in her slow journey toward acceptance.

It can be useful to regard some degree of fluctuation in energy, mood, and ability to function as part of the ordinary ebb and flow of life. This idea is often in opposition to our ideal for ourselves. Many of us expect to function happily and at peak levels at all times. By expecting this, we often place unreasonable demands on ourselves, which it would require machinelike efficiency to carry out. A great measure of contentment can be attained by accepting the inevitable. This is perhaps more in keeping with Eastern than Western thinking. For example, the ancient Chinese script, the *Nei Ching*, advises people to behave in certain specific ways during each season, recommending, for example, that during winter people should go to bed early and get up late in the morning. The message there is to yield to the physical and emotional changes that come with the changing seasons, rather than to oppose them. After you have done all you can to reverse the unpleasant and disabling symptoms of SAD, that is not bad advice. But *before* resigning yourself to your problems, there are certain specific types of treatment that should be tried—most notably, medications and psychotherapy. These treatments are discussed in the sections that follow.

There are many different types of approaches you can take to help yourself cope with winter depression or, for that matter, any type of depression. A first step requires the recognition that the difficulties associated with depression—low energy level, pessimism, lack of motivation, low self-esteem, and withdrawal, to name just a few—are symptoms of an illness, not flaws in your character. They require understanding, not judgment and condemnation, and the first person who needs to understand them is the depressed patient. This is helpful in itself. In addition, for seasonal depressives, changing the environment may be quite beneficial. Brighten your living and work areas, travel to sunny places in the winter, or, if all else fails, relocate permanently to a better climate. Exercise moderately and regularly in a way you find enjoyable. Find a companion to join you, and help each other stick to your routine. Diet sensibly. Don't deprive yourself of carbohydrates, and snack regularly but judiciously at those times of day when you are hungriest. Limit your stresses. Don't make commitments during your summer highs that you are unable to keep in the winter. Anticipate predictable chores and use your creativity to figure out solutions to them ahead of time. Finally, *accept* that which you cannot change. Life has its ups and downs, and no one understands that better than the SAD patient.

It is ironic that many of the suggestions offered in this section have been known for centuries. In fact, the physician A. Cornelius Celsus gave the following advice to melancholics during the reign of the Roman emperor, Tiberius:

> Live in rooms full of light
> Avoid heavy food
> Be moderate in the drinking of wine

Take massage, baths, exercise, and gymnastics
Fight insomnia with gentle rocking or the sound of running water
Change surroundings and take long journeys
Strictly avoid frightening ideas
Indulge in cheerful conversation and amusements
Listen to music

8

Psychotherapy and SAD

For many people with seasonal difficulties, psychotherapy has proven to be invaluable. Indeed, most of the seasonal people I have described in this book have received psychotherapy at some time in their lives, and most have found it to be beneficial. For example, one woman in her fifties recently sought psychotherapy to cope with the aftermath of a divorce; for one young man, therapy was valuable in dealing with difficulties that arose at work. Others have found it extremely helpful in understanding and coming to terms with events that happened in their childhood, but which continue to exert a detrimental influence on their adult lives. However, not everyone with a seasonal problem needs or will benefit from psychotherapy. How do you decide when therapy is necessary?

Having made the decision to enter therapy, what sort should you seek? There are dozens of different types. Which ones will work best? And how do you find and choose a therapist—someone in whom you can put your trust? You generally tell your therapist your deepest and most private thoughts. How do you know whether you can trust him to treat these precious thoughts and feelings with respect? How do you know whether he is competent; that he will understand your problem and know the appropriate thing to say or do about it?

Once in therapy, how do you manage to integrate psychotherapy with light therapy or antidepressant medications? How do you know whether the therapy is working? All these are difficult questions, yet they are often foremost in the minds of those in search of some form of psychological help. I shall attempt to answer them below.

WHEN SHOULD YOU CONSIDER ENTERING THERAPY?

Suppose you suffer from winter depressions. We now know that these are often due to light deficiency. Let us therefore assume that you seek out a therapist qualified to advise you on light therapy, undergo the treatment, and find that this takes care of many, if not all, of your symptoms. In addition, you follow all the advice outlined above. We can consider two opposite outcomes, though, of course, there are many gradations in between. In the one outcome you feel good. Finally, you have an explanation for all these seasonal difficulties and, moreover, you have a way of treating and controlling them. This frees you to get on with your life, to love and to work, as Freud would say, and also to enjoy yourself. Your relationships grow stronger and more fulfilling; you are successful at work. You are justifiably proud of your accomplishments and enjoy the fruits of your labor. And you even find some free time to do whatever it is that you enjoy the most. Do you need psychotherapy? Of course not.

Now, let us imagine a different scenario. Your seasonal symptoms have responded. You no longer sink to the depths of depression, familiar to you for so many years. All should be well, but it is not. Something is amiss. Perhaps you feel stuck where you are. You have been following certain routines and activities that once were fulfilling but now aren't. Some change is necessary, but nothing suggests itself to you. Persisting in the same course gets you nowhere in this mission. At this point, psychotherapy can be beneficial. It can help you define the problem and search within yourself for solutions that may be very difficult to find on your own.

I am reminded of a fly, trying to escape from a room by banging against a window. He does not realize that the door behind him is open. He can see the world he longs for stretched out in front of him, but his ignorance dooms him to bang his head repeatedly against the windowpane. Fruitless, repetitive behavior of this kind is commonly found in people, too, and can be helped by psychotherapy. The example of a woman who gets into a series of relationships with men who mistreat her has become almost a cliché in recent years. However, like all clichés, this one is grounded in reality, and the pattern is all too familiar. So is the situation of the man (or woman) who repeatedly fails, just when success appears to be within reach. It has often been said that the neurotic does not remember, he repeats; and most clinicians have seen this pattern many times.

Freud provided insights into the compulsion to repeat, tracing it back to childhood events. An image that comes to us from our age of computers is that some bug has been incorporated into the software which causes the program to make the same error again and again. Following this analogy a little further, insight-oriented psychotherapy can be seen as an attempt to track down the problem in the software and reprogram it to succeed, rather than to fail. Returning to the vignette of the fly and the windowpane, we can compare the process of psychotherapy to showing the fly that there is another way out of the room—through the open door. A wonderful, therapeutic sense of freedom accompanies a new way of seeing a problem and new strategies for dealing with it.

One type of programming error that is frequently responsible for unhappiness involves our self-esteem. In growing up we may have incorporated incorrect or derogatory images and opinions of ourselves into the software of our brains, and these may continue to haunt us into adult life. Apart from our upbringing and early childhood experiences, there are other influences that shape our self-esteem from both the outside world and our own internal experiences. For example, suffering from repeated depressions—long stretches of time when one is unable to function properly—can have long-term detrimental effects on one's self-esteem and self-image. Even after these depressions are treated, self-esteem problems may persist, and may require psychotherapy in order to be properly resolved.

Many examples of people with self-esteem problems come to mind.

"Melissa," an artist in her early forties, is a case in point. Intelligent, talented, attractive, and with a charming personality, she nonetheless grew up believing that she should aspire to be an empty-headed blonde. According to the voices of her upbringing, women were supposed to be pretty but vacuous, available to support the men in their lives. Signs of burgeoning talent were viewed as danger signals, which might scare off eligible men. Women were meant to conceal their talent and intelligence and to draw men out. After graduating from high school, Melissa went on to get a degree in counseling, choosing this more "appropriate" profession over the artistic areas that were her real love. Two marriages followed, which were unhappy, except that the second one resulted in a lovely daughter. After entering the seasonal program at the NIMH and having her winter depression treated with light therapy, Melissa entered into psychotherapy. In the course of therapy she was able to understand how she had been programmed to believe she had to become someone at odds with the person she really wanted to be. Therefore, no matter what she did, or how successful she was at it, it didn't feel right to her. She was a fine mother, a talented artist, a good friend to many, and a delightful person, but it still didn't feel right. She was not fulfilling those early programs and her parents' expectations of her. Once she understood this in therapy, she was able to change her expectations of herself and recognize that these new expectations, which were quite compatible with what she truly wanted to do, were legitimate. Psychotherapy has been a liberating experience for her. Whereas light reversed the symptoms of her winter depression, something that no amount of psychotherapy would have been able to do, psychotherapy helped her understand and come to terms with problems from her past—something that no amount of light therapy, by itself, would have been able to accomplish.

Melissa's story is one of many. I have frequently seen such successful and liberating effects of good psychotherapy. Her story also shows how well psychotherapy and other forms of therapy can work together. If there are significant problems of the sort outlined above, which persist after treatment with light therapy or medications, psychotherapy should be strongly considered.

TYPES OF THERAPY

There are many different types of therapy available and, depending on where you live, therapists may be more or less abundant. How does the consumer choose? Some of the more commonly practiced types of therapy are summarized below. More detailed information can be found by consulting the references in the reading list in the back of the book. I should emphasize that most skilled therapists combine elements derived from different schools of therapy, much as a skilled chef would combine different ingredients to prepare a gourmet meal. I am generally quite suspicious of people who believe that only one narrow school of thought carries the key to curing all psychological problems. People are far too diverse and complicated for such simple solutions.

Elements common to all therapies are understanding, support, and provision of hope. These elements are critical. It is very important for a depressed person to feel understood by someone who has seen other depressed people and has helped them through their illness to recovery; to know that there is someone out there who understands how bad depression can get; who is available through the dark days. Depression is a condition where hope is lacking. The present seems bleak; the future even bleaker. These are symptoms of the illness, rather than a realistic appraisal of the situation and its prospects. The therapist needs to make this clear to the patient, as well as to explain why there is good reason to be hopeful, and indeed there is. Depression is almost always reversible. Beyond these general points, there are certain specific types of therapy.

Cognitive Therapy

This brand of therapy, developed by Dr. Aaron Beck, is quite helpful in SAD. It is based on the idea that a depressed person's thinking is distorted, and that this, in turn, leads to depression. During one SAD patient's depressed periods, she would feel stupid, even though she had tested very well in school and had all sorts of academic laurels to her credit. When she became depressed, she believed she was a fraud, and that teachers had given her good grades because they liked her, not because she had deserved them. Depressed people often describe themselves as frauds who have managed to trick people into thinking that they are smart or talented, but who eventually will be exposed and shown up for the incompetent individuals they believe they are.

According to the principles of cognitive therapy, depressed feelings result from distorted thoughts. Pointing this distorted thinking out to the depressed individual often helps the depressed feelings go away. So the following imaginary conversation might take place between the patient and her therapist in a therapy session:

Patient: I am a fraud; I didn't deserve all those prizes.

Therapist: If you are a fraud, how did you manage to trick so many people?

Patient: I'm just crafty. Mom always told me I used to try to get away with things.

Therapist: But you have tricked so many different people over so many years. Is it not possible that you were not tricking them after all; that their perceptions were accurate and that now you are tricking yourself into believing that you do not have the talents that must have been necessary in order to win those prizes?

Patient: Yes, but I feel incompetent. I can't do anything properly.

Therapist: Well, let's review what you've done this past week and check whether your perception is correct in this regard.

The therapist then reviews the week and it soon becomes clear that the patient has done many things quite competently. Perhaps she has not met her own high expectations at every turn, but the outcome is quite acceptable. And anyway, how could anyone perform at peak level every single week, during all seasons? The therapist invites the patient to examine systematically all these distortions and, in so doing, can help her change them, which may result in a lessening of her depressed feelings.

In dealing with people who have SAD, part of cognitive therapy involves pointing out that many of the difficulties they experience are symptoms of their seasonal condition; that these symptoms have an explanation; that they can be reversed, and do not reflect character flaws. Depressed people find all sorts of insults to hurl at themselves—incompetent, lazy, bad, immature, deserving of punishment, to name just a few. The depressed person is generally very unfair to him- or herself, and part of the therapist's role is to point this out.

To the credit of those working in the field of cognitive therapy, they have actually studied this treatment scientifically and have demonstrated its effectiveness with certain depressed patients. Such systematic studies have not been performed for many other types of therapy.

Behavior Therapy

In this form of therapy, as its name implies, the focus is on behavior. Its theoretical origins come from work on learning. Like Pavlov's dogs, we have been conditioned to respond in certain ways as a result of the experiences we have had. In some cases, these learned behaviors may actually make our problems worse. For example, as a result of feeling repeatedly depressed, a person may avoid getting together with people and may become socially isolated. Such isolation will deprive him of the pleasures and satisfactions that may come from human interactions, which may well make the symptoms of depression worse.

In treating a patient, the therapist might focus on maladaptive behaviors, such as not calling friends or allowing bills and other chores to pile up until they feel overwhelming. It's up to the therapist to help the patient face and tackle these tasks. Behaviors regarded by both patient and therapist as constructive or positive are rewarded. For example, a patient and therapist may construct a program where the patient goes shopping for a long-desired item as a reward for taking care of the bills. There are all sorts of variations on this theme. Behavior therapy can be particularly helpful for individuals who are phobic of certain situations—for example, flying, taking elevators, or being in crowds. The patient is gradually encouraged to confront these situations in an attempt to make them less anxiety-provoking.

Behavior therapy is sometimes combined with cognitive therapy and the patient may be given "homework" assignments, which are aimed at dealing with both behavioral problems and cognitive distortions. Such cognitive problems may inhibit actions that could make one feel better. For example, someone looking for work might think, "I'm not good enough for that job, so there's no point in my applying for it." A man who is interested in a woman might think, "She'll never accept my invitation; I may as well not ask her." By helping the patient to face these fears and negative thoughts, which are often not founded on fact, the therapist encourages the patient to take some risks and to do things that might make him or her feel better. A great deal can be accomplished by combining cognitive and behavior therapy.

Insight-Oriented Therapy

This type of therapy was first proposed by Freud, who advocated the value of obtaining insight into our unconscious processes. Although this type of therapy is extremely difficult to study scientifically in such a way that meets the rigorous requirements of modern clinical research, it is the experience of trained observers that insight-oriented therapy can be extremely helpful.

My own experience has convinced me of the value of this type of psychotherapy, although I did not always believe it to be so. In my medical training in South Africa, Freud and insight-oriented therapy were held in low esteem, and it was only after I had encountered some outstanding psychotherapy supervisors at the New York State Psychiatric Institute that I realized how wrong my medical school teachers had been. I have seen people benefit tremendously from psychotherapy—not just from having someone to talk to, but as a result of specific insight into their problems. This insight is carefully shared with patients, who are encouraged to use it and thereby reach a new and more useful understanding of their problems.

Many of my patients with SAD have benefited greatly from insight-oriented psychotherapy. For example, one woman in her mid-forties went into psychotherapy to help her resolve the guilt she felt at having been the only healthy child out of six siblings. A middle-aged man with SAD struggled for years on his Ph.D. thesis but was unable to complete it, not because of any intellectual limitation, but because it raised anxiety in him about competing with his father, who had been much less successful than he had. Such examples are numerous, but the point is simple: lights and medications do not solve all the psychological problems in all cases of SAD. Some people may find psychotherapy, in conjunction with these other treatments, to be extremely useful. However, psychotherapy is not necessary for everybody. If light treatment or antidepressant medications leave a person feeling happy, fulfilled, and free to live as he or she chooses, there is no need for psychotherapy.

Like all effective treatments, psychotherapy is not without hazards. Probing around in a person's past and stirring up buried secrets, while extremely helpful in some cases, is not universally so. Psychotherapy can amplify feelings of depression and anxiety, and should only be performed by a skilled and properly trained therapist. That person should also be familiar with the biological treatments of depression so that the patient is not allowed to spin his or her wheels discussing childhood conflicts while a raging depression goes untreated. This latter situation remains unfortunately all too uncommon.

CHOOSING A PSYCHOTHERAPIST

It is extremely important that you choose your therapist carefully. It is surprising to think that the same person who might take several days researching a car purchase—consulting consumer reports and friends, going to several dealers, and test-driving cars—might head straight for the Yellow Pages to find a therapist. A therapist is someone with whom you need to be able to share your most important personal secrets. That person's judgment, training, and suitability for *you* should be the primary basis for your choice. How do you find such a person?

I believe that recommendations from other professionals are the best guide. Find a well-respected mental health professional—a medical doctor, psychologist, or social worker. Explain to this person, briefly, the type of problem you are dealing with. Then ask his or her opinion as to who might be suitable for you. If possible, I would encourage you to ask more than one professional, to see whether the same name appears on more than one list. That is how I found my own analyst. I asked two psychiatrists whom I respected for a list of five analysts, and one particular name appeared on both lists. Once you have obtained one or two names, set up an appointment to interview the therapist. He or she should, of course, ask you questions about your problem. Consider whether the questions are on target. Does the therapist appear to be exploring the problem thoroughly, asking about it from different angles? Does he seem to understand what you are saying—not just intellectually, but also emotionally? Does he appear to be empathic—on the same wavelength as you are? These early impressions are important, and should be taken into consideration in making your decision.

You are certainly entitled to ask questions of the therapist. What is his background and training? Does he subscribe to any particular school of therapy? If these questions are asked in an ordinary, matter-of-fact manner, they should be met with ordinary, matter-of-fact replies. Any defensiveness about the replies, questions in response to the questions, such as, "Why do you want to know," or interpretations, such as, "It seems as though you suspect my competency," might reasonably raise your suspicion about the security of the therapist.

At the end of the initial consultation, the therapist should provide a formulation of the problem—a diagnosis and some clarification of the issues—as well as specific recommendations about treatment. Sometimes, however, if the situation appears to be complicated, more than one meeting might be necessary before the therapist is ready to provide a formulation and recommendations. It's important for you to consider this formulation and these recommendations as just *one* way to see the problem. There may be other ways to see it, as well, and you may wish to seek other opinions before making up your mind about which therapist you want to see. I recall in the first session with my own analyst, he said in his final formulation, "We could go on and meet several times, and I could collect more and more information. But I can see that the issues you have discussed with me are amenable to analysis and I would be pleased to undertake it with you. The only question that remains is whether you wish to consult other analysts before you make up your mind as to whether this makes sense to you." I was impressed by his independence, by the fact that he was making my options clear to me, unlike a salesman who wants you to sign on the line there and then. I responded that I too could go on seeing people indefinitely, gathering information before I made up my mind, but that I had been pleased with the way the consultation had gone and would be pleased to start working with him. I did not regret my decision.

These early impressions and experiences are particularly important. Later on, when the therapy is underway, all sorts of feelings might arise toward the therapist. Many of these are based not so much on what the therapist does, but on experiences that we have had earlier in our lives. This is the so-called transference, described first by Freud—the process whereby feelings toward important people in our lives are transferred to the therapist or analyst, who has actually done nothing to elicit them. At such a point in therapy one might be inclined to leave, in order to run away from these new insights and discoveries. That is generally a time not to act on one's impulses and instincts, but rather to persist and see what one can discover. If these feelings persist for too long, however, a consultation with another therapist might be advisable.

9

Antidepressant Medications

INTRODUCTION

The administration of antidepressant medications is a subtle art. Prescribing them is not quite the same as prescribing laxatives or blood pressure pills. Antidepressants can—and should—change the way you feel, the way you see your world and yourself. Proper use of them requires close communication between doctor and patient. The psychiatrist should help the patient interpret the internal changes that are taking place and use this information to choose the right medication or combination of medications, and the best dosage. It's a tricky business and should be undertaken only by someone who knows what he or she is doing.

There are all sorts of reasonable concerns that arise in taking antidepressant medications. All your life you have been counseled to avoid and suspect drugs that make you feel good. Now, along comes a doctor who tells you that it's the very thing to do. Will the drugs harm you? Will you feel too good and get hooked on them? If you feel better, is it a result of the pills rather than your own efforts? You may always have

141

been told to take responsibility for your life, to examine the roots of your problems and solve them from the ground up. Now someone is telling you not to worry about roots and origins. Just take the pills and you'll feel better. Can it be so simple?

The following deals with many of the common concerns that people have about taking antidepressant medications. For those who have already decided to take these medications or are currently being treated with them, there is also a section on the most commonly used drugs, their advantages and side effects.

COMMON CONCERNS ABOUT TAKING ANTIDEPRESSANT MEDICATIONS

The thought of taking a mood-altering drug often triggers associations with drug peddlers, to whom we have been advised to "just say no." So why should we react differently toward a doctor who suggests that we take antidepressant medications? There are several important differences between these two scenarios. Recreational drugs are taken in an uncontrolled way to change the mood of the moment, thus providing an immediate "high." These drugs are addictive, and withdrawal often results in serious symptoms, including crashing depressions. Antidepressant drugs do not generally cause an immediate "high," nor can they be regarded as addictive. With recreational drugs, one often needs increasing amounts to get the same mood-altering effect; not so with antidepressants. Since their introduction over thirty years ago, they have been shown to be highly effective in providing long-term relief for the symptoms of depression.

Some people may feel that taking an antidepressant is the easy way out, evading the responsibility for finding the root of the problem and solving it. This idea stems from the assumption that somehow the depression is the patient's fault, a result of something he or she has done. This concern is especially common because one of the symptoms of depression is to feel excessively responsible for your situation. It is therefore logical to think that you should be able to fix it yourself. However, most experts now agree that clinical depression is due to a biochemical abnormality with a genetic basis. Two recent studies have confirmed this belief by finding areas on chromosomes where the genes for some forms of depression are located.

If depression is genetic and biochemical, how can it be the patient's fault? And why shouldn't you treat the problem as you would any other medical illness? If you had diabetes, for example, would you consider giving yourself daily insulin injections to be comparable to shooting up regularly with heroin? Or, for that matter, would you think that you were responsible for the problem in your pancreas and that you should figure out a way to fix it yourself?

Many patients are afraid that when they take antidepressant medications, they will lose control of themselves or their thinking. They are concerned that by taking these medications they will become different and lose their identity. In addressing this concern, it is important to realize that a person feels different about himself when depressed, as compared with when he feels well. Which of these two sets of perceptions is the real person—the sad and weary soul who feels that he has never done anything worthwhile and doesn't deserve anything; or the fundamentally healthy and intact individual, who happens to be suffering a temporary setback? One of the most painful things about depression is that it changes a person's self-image. In my experience, when a patient has been effectively treated with antidepressants, the result is much closer to the "self" that the person would prefer to be, than the depressed individual he was before.

One reason it is difficult for patients to accept the medical model of depression is that there is no good laboratory test for it. This is where a comparison to diabetes or high blood pressure falls short. In diabetes, high levels of glucose are present in the urine and the blood. This can be detected simply by dipping a stick into urine and watching the chemicals on the tip change color. In a case of high blood pressure, the abnormal numbers can simply be read off the blood pressure machine. But in a case of depression, laboratory tests generally come back negative. In the past decade there was excitement about some hormonal tests for depression, but after an initial wave of enthusiasm, these proved undependable. So what remains to the diagnostician is the patient's account of his or her story; accounts by the patient's relatives; a track record of the damage caused by the illness, such as failing grades, poor job performance, and unsuccessful relationships; and how the patient actually looks. At first glance, this may seem like slim evidence on which to make the diagnosis of a psychiatric disorder and an insufficient basis for prescribing antidepressant medications. However, the trained clinician is generally able to diagnose depression easily and reliably. Sometimes just a glance across the waiting room, the angle of a person's gait, or a few sentences articulated over the telephone are enough to give the clinician a good idea of how a depressed person is doing. The brain is an elusive organ to study. Its processes have not as yet yielded their secrets to modern technology in the same way as the pancreas, heart, kidney, and liver. But in attempting to study the brain, we are at an advantage over students of those other organs in that a person can directly report on events going on within the mind. Feelings, thoughts, sensations, and impulses all reflect underlying brain processes. These experiences can be communicated to the clinician and monitored over time. In my experience, these clues provide sufficient evidence for the diagnosis and treatment of most cases of depression.

Many people are concerned about how long they will have to remain on medications. This is easier to predict for patients with SAD than for those with other forms of depression because SAD is usually a self-limiting condition. When summer comes, symptoms generally resolve. In some cases, however, medications may be helpful even in the summertime. Another concern that I have heard from time to time is a fear that antidepressant medications will cause some permanent change or damage to the person who takes them. Fortunately, chronic side effects are rare and there is no evidence whatsoever that any long-term damage to the brain occurs.

SIDE EFFECTS OF MEDICATIONS

Concerns about side effects are common and valid. People vary greatly in their propensity to develop side effects. On one end of the spectrum is the individual who has none at all; on the other end is the person who develops them toward a host of different antidepressants at dosages so low that no effect is possible. Because of this wide variability, many psychiatrists choose to start with low dosages of the medication of choice and to build up after seeing how well the patient tolerates it.

The specific side effects of antidepressant medications differ from drug to drug and are discussed at greater length under each specific heading. In general, however, common side effects include sedation, weight gain, dizziness, and a cluster of symptoms known as anticholinergic side effects. This last group reflects the tendency of many antidepressants to block the effects of a certain part of our nervous system called the cholinergic system. This system is responsible for keeping the surfaces of membranes moist, causing the muscular walls of tubular organs, such as the bowels, to contract smoothly, and opening up sphincter muscles, which serve as valves—for example, in releasing urine. When these functions are blocked, the resulting side effects include dry mouth, blurred vision, constipation, and difficulty in passing urine.

THE PROS AND CONS OF USING ANTIDEPRESSANT MEDICATIONS

In deciding how we wish to lead our lives, we are continuously doing cost-benefit analyses, which is another way of saying that we weigh the pros and cons and make our choices accordingly. Most of these analyses are so routine that we are barely aware that they are taking place. Is the risk of having a car accident worth the potential benefits of going to the supermarket to do the shopping? Is the risk of a plane crash worth the benefits of a Caribbean vacation? And so on. Sometimes, when the decision is of unusual magnitude, we become more aware of the cost-benefit analysis that is taking place.

A cost-benefit analysis should certainly be undertaken every time medications are used. What good is this medication likely to do? What harm might result? In the case of antidepressant medications, this analysis should be a shared process between patient and therapist, perhaps to an even greater degree than for other forms of medicine. The reason for this is that many of the symptoms of depression, such as sadness, guilt, and low self-worth, are hidden, and known only to the patient. The same applies for side effects. The psychiatrist largely depends on the patient's evaluation of how bad both symptoms and side effects are. In addition, since the patient has to live with both the symptoms of the illness and the side effects of the medicine, it seems only fair that he should have the major say in whether he should be on the medications or not.

So where does the psychiatrist fit into the picture? He or she is the expert on both the illness and the medications, having seen other cases before, and how they have responded to different types of antidepressants. However, the psychiatrist cannot know for sure how a drug will work in any particular case. It is necessary to educate the patient about the nature of the illness, the available treatment options, and their potential benefits and possible risks. The psychiatrist should summarize his or her experience with both the drug and the illness, and show how it pertains to the patient's particular situation. The patient, in turn, should share his hopes, fears, and previous experiences with medications. Together, they should balance the pros and cons. Through such a dialogue, the best decision is likely to be made.

Although most medications can cause a wide array of side effects, many of these are extremely unusual. In my own practice, I tend to discuss the commonest side effects of a particular medication and note that other side effects may occur. I also recommend that my patients ask their pharmacist for the medication package insert. If while on medications you should develop any physical or psychological changes that have not been fully discussed, or about which you feel concerned, you should not hesitate to contact your psychiatrist by phone, rather than wait for the next session.

Some people are assisted in making decisions by considering the worst-case scenario. What is the worst thing that can happen if a patient does or does not take a medication? The answer is the same in either case—the course of action can be fatal. In very rare instances a person may have an allergic or exaggerated reaction to a medication, which could prove fatal. This is possible, incidentally, with any medication, including over-the-counter preparations. In certain situations, however, depression may also prove fatal, and I'm not referring only to suicide. There are studies that show that the incidence of sickness and death rate is higher in depressed patients than in the rest of the population. A depressed person may be distracted or uninterested in the world and may be more likely to walk across a street carelessly or to use an electrical appliance without taking all the necessary safeguards. A depressed person may neglect his or her health; for example, a woman may not get regular gynecological checkups or may ignore a breast lump that she finds. So depression is really not a trivial, innocuous illness.

However, since these worst-case scenarios are rather rare, they should generally be given rather limited weight in the cost-benefit analysis, just as the risk of a fatal accident is not generally regarded as an important reason for not going to the supermarket. Those outcomes that are far commoner should be given greater weight

In general, it has been my experience that the cost-benefit analysis greatly favors the use of antidepressant medications, especially when depression is moderate to severe, the individual is relatively healthy, and when nonmedical alternatives (such as light therapy) seem unlikely to do the job by themselves. In addition, people with seasonal depressions seem to respond well to medications, and I cannot think of one patient who was not able to be helped to some degree by a combination of light and antidepressant medication. On the other hand, if depressions can be treated successfully without medications, this course is generally preferable.

MEDICATIONS COMMONLY USED IN SAD

I want to emphasize that antidepressants should be administered only by qualified professionals. The patient's efforts would be well spent in locating and consulting such a professional. Once the doctor has been chosen, the patient should generally defer to his judgment about which medicine is best for a particular clinical situation. However, the patient is entitled to an explanation of why that particular drug has been selected and a discussion of its advantages and disadvantages compared with other possibilities. The discussion in this section is intended to inform you about some of the most useful medications available for the treatment of SAD, in particular, and depression, in general. However, the decision to administer antidepressants and the choice of medication should only be made by a licensed professional who has had a chance to interview and examine the patient in question.

There are many different types of medications available for treating depression. The choice of which drug to use first is an educated guess, based on the clinical picture of the patient and the therapeutic and side-effect profile of the medication. Because there is no scientific method at this time for reliably predicting the best antidepressants for particular patients, administering them often proceeds by trial and error. If the first choice doesn't work, the next should be tried. I have seen some patients who have tried many different drugs without success and then finally hit on the right one. It's a bit like having a large bunch of keys and trying each in turn until you find the one that turns a lock. But once the lock turns, the door opens, and new vistas appear. So it is for the depressed patient who finally feels better and is able to enjoy life once again. It may be helpful to bear this image in mind if the first or second antidepressant fails to deliver its promised effect; otherwise, it is easy to become discouraged and give up prematurely when the next key on the bunch may be the right one.

All antidepressants take time to work. At least two weeks should be allowed after the medication has been administered *in sufficient dosage* before a judgment about its effectiveness can be made. Because of the wide variation in susceptibility to side effects, psychiatrists often choose to start a medication at a low dose and increase gradually. This precaution obviously increases the time before the medicine can have its full effect. Therefore, in severely depressed people, it may be desirable to start at a higher dose and increase more rapidly. One minor problem with starting at a low dosage is that the final one may appear to be huge compared to the initial one, whereas in fact it was the initial one that was very small.

Although antidepressant medications may be used instead of light therapy in some patients with SAD, they are usually used to supplement it. Light therapy may be only partially effective in eradicating the symptoms of SAD, and this partial effect may be enhanced by medications. In addition, if light therapy is used in conjunction with antidepressants, it is often possible to get by with smaller doses and correspondingly fewer side effects. It is often necessary to adjust the dosage with the changing seasons—increasing it as the days become shorter and darker, and decreasing it as the days become longer and brighter.

Desipramine and Imipramine: Old Faithfuls

(Trade Names: Desipramine = Norpramin, Pertofrane; Imipramine = Tofranil)

I call these drugs "Old Faithfuls" because they have been around for a long time, but they continue to be useful weapons in our arsenal against depression. They are generally well tolerated and quite effective. I know of several patients with SAD who have responded well to them. Side effects are generally quite tolerable with desipramine. It may make some people feel energized or "wired," and others a little sedated. Anticholinergic side effects (dry mouth, constipation, blurred vision) are relatively mild. Pulse rate and sweating may increase, and dizziness may be experienced upon standing. These side effects may be inconvenient but are rarely dangerous. Imipramine tends to be a little more sedating than desipramine and generally causes more anticholinergic side effects.

These two drugs are members of a larger family, known as the tricyclic antidepressants. Other members of the tricyclic family are also often prescribed for depression. Amitriptyline, also known as Elavil or Endep, which is commonly prescribed, is very sedating and very anticholinergic and often causes more side effects than the other tricyclics. I rarely use it as a first-line drug in treating depression because of this. Doxepin, also known as Sinequan or Adapin, is another tricyclic that I don't use as a first-line drug because it, too, is sedating and has prominent anticholinergic effects. Sometimes these sedative properties can be used to advantage in people with insomnia. Most SAD patients, however, have just the opposite problem—they sleep too much. The last thing they generally need is something that is going to make them even sleepier.

Fluoxetine (Prozac): An Exciting New Drug

This new antidepressant may turn out to be the drug of choice for the treatment of SAD. The only reason I have listed it second rather than first is that it is relatively new on the U.S. market. This drug acts mainly on the serotonin system in the brain which, we think, is abnormal in SAD. The serotonin system is also an important regulator of several other functions, including eating and sleeping. Unlike the other antidepressants, which have been reported to cause weight gain, Prozac has actually been found to produce weight loss in many patients. It is also not generally sedating (it may actually be activating), and is low in the anticholinergic side effects, such as dry mouth and constipation, that can be so troublesome with other antidepressants. Some of the commoner side effects of this drug are nausea (which can best be avoided by taking it with food), anxiety, and insomnia.

I have seen outstanding results with Prozac in SAD so far. I was recently reviewing the patients after a SAD clinic and so many of them had been successfully treated with Prozac that we jokingly suggested renaming the place the "Prozac clinic." The drug seems to be extremely well tolerated and low in side effects, and one pill in the morning is usually all that is needed. We are hoping that these effects hold up over time and that there is not some hidden danger to the drug that has yet to emerge.

One of the most interesting things reported to me by a patient on Prozac was a vivid accentuation of certain sensory experiences powerfully associated with childhood memories. For example, when on the medication he would walk into a house, smell food, and become overwhelmed by memories of his grandmother's delicious cooking many years before. On another occasion he was trampling over some fallen leaves and was vividly reminded of an enjoyable camping trip he had undertaken as a boy. It is possible that fluctuations in his brain serotonin system, induced by the Prozac, sensitized him to recall these vivid and enjoyable childhood memories when presented with a cue from the present, such as cooking food or fallen leaves. Perhaps we might call this type of response the "madeleine effect," named after the pastry, a madeleine, that Proust describes in *Remembrance of Things Past*. When, as an adult, the hero of the novel bit into the madeleine, soaked with tea, the memories of his childhood came flooding back to him. Our modern counterpart to Proust's hero did well on Prozac, which prevented his SAD symptoms from developing. We know that the seasons are associated both with powerful memories of things past and with changes in brain serotonin systems. Shifts and fluxes in serotonin systems may also account for the symptoms of SAD, the antidepressant effects of light (and Prozac), and the "madeleine effect."

Trazodone (Desyrel)

This drug, relatively new to the U.S. market, is structurally different from the tricyclics, but shares some of their properties. It seemed particularly attractive for the treatment of SAD patients because, like Prozac, it works on the serotonin system. For this reason I have prescribed trazodone for a number of patients when light therapy alone has not been sufficient, and have been pleased at the favorable outcome.

It is surprising to me that Desyrel has been so well tolerated by, and effective for, the people to whom I have given it, since my experience with it in nonseasonal depressions has been mixed. I have generally not found it to be completely effective when given by itself, but helpful when administered along with another antidepressant. In addition, some people complain that trazodone is very sedating and causes weight gain.

The Monoamine Oxidase Inhibitors (MAOIs)

Specific MAOIs: Phenelzine = Nardil; Tranylcypromine = Parnate; Isocarboxazid = Marplan.

The MAOIs have a long and checkered history in the United States. They were the first drugs found to be effective in treating depression, and they were discovered serendipitously. Patients with tuberculosis, who happened to be depressed, became less so when given an anti-TB drug related to the MAOIs. This observation led to the development of other, more effective MAOIs. In my experience it is unusual to have to prescribe the MAOIs in patients with SAD. They generally respond well to the drugs noted above, which are safer and cause fewer side effects.

The MAOIs inhibit the enzyme, monoamine oxidase (MAO), which is found in both the brain and the bowels. It is thought that this action might be responsible for their antidepressant effects. MAO (pronounced M-A-O, not like the Chinese leader) breaks down substances called biogenic amines, of which norepinephrine and serotonin are two examples. By inhibiting the enzyme, the MAOIs promote the buildup of monoamines in the brain. It has been suggested that depression may be due to a functional deficiency of these biogenic amines and that perhaps, by causing these amines to accumulate in the brain, the MAOIs might exert their antidepressant action.

The MAO enzyme is also produced in the bowel, where it has the important function of breaking down certain substances in food that, if absorbed, can be harmful. These substances are present in yellow cheeses, red wines, liver, and all broken-down proteins (such as marinated meats, pickled fish, and any food that is partly spoiled). *All these foods should be strictly avoided in patients on MAOIs.* There are also certain drugs, most notably over-the-counter cold preparations and diet pills, that should not be taken in combination with MAOIs. If a patient who is taking MAOIs should happen to take some of these over-the-counter medications, or should eat one of the forbidden foods noted above, a serious and rapid rise in blood pressure may result. This particular hazard, known as a hypertensive crisis, should be thoroughly discussed with your psychiatrist, who should provide both verbal and written instructions about the precautions necessary to avoid it, and the steps to be taken should it arise.

Unfortunately, the hypertensive crisis mentioned above is not the only difficulty one can encounter when using the MAOIs. Other bothersome side effects include insomnia, daytime drowsiness, weight gain, and decreased sexual pleasure.

So why use these drugs at all? Because they can be extraordinarily effective in some people, who may experience virtually no side effects while taking them. Many people have been greatly helped by them, and for this reason, they have once again emerged as useful tools in the treatment of depression. In deciding to use the MAOIs, a cost-benefit analysis must be carefully made by both psychiatrist and patient, who should take into account the availability of alternative, safer medications, as well as all the necessary information about the patient's medical background.

Lithium Carbonate

Originally used as an antimanic agent, lithium carbonate has been recognized as a versatile mood-regulating medication. It can be used as a general mood leveler, to inhibit the development of both manic and depressive episodes, as well as an antidepressant. It can be used either alone or in combination with any of the antidepressants mentioned above.

The idea of taking lithium is very scary to many people. Perhaps they associate it with extremely disturbed people whose behavior is out of control, or regard it as dangerous. But, in fact, lithium is frequently a very helpful and well-tolerated drug in the treatment of depression in general. In my experience, however, it is not especially valuable in the treatment of the typical winter depressions of SAD. It does not usually, by itself, appear to exert a powerful antidepressant effect. In addition, the medications mentioned above generally work quite well in SAD without lithium.

Common side effects include increased thirst, increased urine volume, and hand tremors. Some nausea and abdominal discomfort may be experienced, but these are often transient and may be minimized by taking the medication with meals. Other side effects include weight gain, memory difficulties, and skin rashes. It is usual to have blood levels of the lithium checked at intervals because if they are too high, symptoms of toxicity may result. These include nausea and diarrhea, vomiting, markedly increased tremor, and coordination difficulties. These should be rare, however, if the drug is properly monitored. If toxicity occurs, the patient should drink plenty of fluid and contact his psychiatrist immediately or go to an emergency room. Long-term side effects, in the form of kidney or thyroid problems, may occur. Fortunately, kidney damage is rare. Interference with thyroid function is somewhat more common, but can easily be treated with oral replacement of thyroid hormone.

Many people have concerns about being on antidepressant medications, and these concerns should be fully discussed with the psychiatrist. Once they are carefully explored, and answers to some of the more common questions are provided, the medications become more acceptable and less scary to most patients. In all cases of depression, the psychiatrist and patient should measure the benefits of taking the antidepressant and balance these against the potential side effects. There are many different types of medications. The choice of a specific drug is an educated guess, and several may need to be prescribed before the best one, or combination, is found. These drugs should be prescribed by skilled and qualified psychiatrists who have a specific knowledge of the patient. The outlines provided above are just descriptions of what these drugs commonly do and my own experience with them; they are not intended as recommendations. It's important to remember that antidepressants frequently work well in conjunction with light therapy in SAD patients, allowing smaller doses of medications to be used.

10

"How Can I Help?": Advice for Family and Friends

It is good to know that other people—friends and family—can be a terrific source of comfort and support to someone with SAD. This section is addressed to the family and friends of seasonal patients, in an attempt to help you be a comfort.

THINGS TO DO

1. *Understand the problem.* Recognize that the seasonal mood problem is a real affliction. This may be hard to appreciate. After all, the person looks okay. There are no obvious wounds or abnormalities. All the tests have come back normal. So what is the fuss about? It is especially difficult for people who have never themselves been depressed to understand what it feels like. Even people who experience mild seasonal changes, which are at worst a nuisance, have a hard time understanding how disabled people with SAD can actually feel. More mildly afflicted friends and relatives sometimes feel that they also have to

contend with the same sort of difficulties. Yet they pick themselves up and get on with their lives, so why can't the SAD person do the same? It is important to realize that severity makes a big difference. Depressed people have major difficulties functioning. I would encourage friends and relatives of the seasonal person to read some of the stories in the earlier part of the book to gain insight into how disabling the problem can be.

It can be helpful to think of SAD as similar, in certain critical ways, to a physical illness. The example of diabetes often comes to mind. It is a condition in which the pancreas does not make enough insulin, which results in an abnormality of glucose metabolism. We do not know what the underlying abnormality is in SAD, but I would wager that it resides somewhere in the brain, where some chemical process does not function normally, resulting in all the symptoms of the condition. Somehow, light that enters via the eyes plays an important role in this key chemical process. During the short, dark days of winter, when there is not enough light in the environment, the brain chemical abnormality becomes manifest in the form of SAD symptoms. Bright light reverses the symptoms, presumably by correcting the underlying abnormality. If your friend or relative had diabetes, you would understand that insulin shots and a special diet were necessary to help control the condition. Similarly, your friend or relative with SAD needs extra light and can benefit tremendously from your support. You can help, for example, by keeping your friend or relative company while he or she is sitting in front of the lights.

Once you understand the mood and energy problems of SAD, you will be able to handle them better. If your spouse falls behind in paying the bills or carrying out various chores when winter arrives, it will be much easier for you to put up with the resulting inconvenience if you recognize that you are probably dealing with SAD symptoms rather than laziness. If you want to find out more about the condition and its treatments, you may find parts of this book helpful. Another way to learn about SAD is by joining a recently formed nationwide support group, open to patients and other interested people, called NOSAD (National Organization for Seasonal Affective Disorder). Further information about this organization can be obtained by writing to: NOSAD, P. O. Box 40133, Washington, D.C. 20016.

2. *Just be there*. Don't feel you have to do anything specific. Your

undemanding presence and company will be experienced as soothing and helpful. Even though the seasonal person may appear withdrawn and unfriendly, he or she will often appreciate having company. As one patient I know puts it, "I want my friends to tolerate me sitting solemnly in a corner reading a magazine. I like people to be around but not asking very much of me, because I don't have very much to give." Another patient echoes this need for understanding, noting that when you are depressed, "you get into a place where it's hard for a person to relate to you unless he really cares about you, has known you for a while, and understands your seasonality." She recognizes that "people don't like their friends to change. It's hard for the people you live with," but she requests of her friends that they do not expect her to be "bubbly and full of myself like I am in the summer . . . just accept me the way I am."

3. *Encourage the seasonal person*. Remind him that this is a passing phase, that he has not always felt this way, and can and will feel better again. A person who is lethargic and uninspired during the depths of the winter may be kind, friendly, charming, or witty at other times of the year. Remind him about the good times. When you're depressed, it's easy to forget that they ever happened.

It's important for a friend or relative to bear in mind that when someone is depressed, everything that he or she has been told about depression—for example, that it is a legitimate and transient illness—is easily forgotten. At such a time the friend or relative, who understands what is happening, can help tremendously simply by saying, "Hey, you're forgetting, this is your winter problem. It will pass."

4. *Help with simple things*. Sometimes even shopping or laundry can feel like a huge chore to the depressed person. Offers on the part of friends and family to help out with these will generally be greatly appreciated. One of the earliest members of our seasonal program worked out such an arrangement with her family. They had a system of rotating household chores, so that each family member would do a certain one for a given week. Some of them, such as tidying up the house, were easier, whereas others, such as cleaning the bathrooms, were more difficult. During the winter, the children understood that their mother was not able to tackle the more difficult chores and all agreed that she should be exempt from bathroom duty during those months.

The best way to find out what help is needed is to ask. Examples are:

going to the grocery store for a friend; fixing breakfast for your wife or helping her get the kids off to school while she sits in front of her lights; sitting and talking to a friend or loved one while he does the laundry or pays the bills; helping him or her wake up in the morning (which is so difficult for a person with SAD). All these things will be remembered and rewarded by a deepening and strengthening of your relationship.

These are some of the things that friends can do. They don't take a lot of effort, but they do make a big difference.

5. *Try to understand the seasonal person when he or she is in the other (hypomanic) phase.* Sometimes it's difficult to understand the high side of SAD as well. Someone who has been hibernating all winter and suddenly springs into action with more energy than anyone else may be hard to take. As one patient puts it, "I think it's easier to love someone who's down and depressed and hurting in some way. But please remember to love her when she's happy and successful as well." It may also be helpful to point out *tactfully* that the seasonal person is going a bit fast for you and most other people, and that it may be useful to get some help to slow down a bit. Wearing dark glasses during daylight hours may help people slow down at such times if they are too "wired."

When people are a bit high, they can become argumentative. The friend or relative exposed to such querulousness would do well to choose carefully what issues are discussed. The husband of one of my seasonal patients, who has learned the value of this strategy over the years, avoids confronting his wife on minor issues. He observes, "If we have a conflict, it's going to be over something worthwhile."

If the patient is showing poor judgment, impulsiveness, or doesn't sleep, he should be encouraged (or taken) to see his psychiatrist.

THINGS TO AVOID

1. *Don't judge and criticize.* The seasonal person is already feeling bad about not functioning up to his normal standards, and letting friends and family down. Very often he is his own harshest critic, measuring his own

actions and finding them wanting. To have these criticisms confirmed by someone he loves and respects can be extremely painful, may further undermine his self-esteem, and could enhance feelings of depression and worthlessness. A tendency to judge and criticize the seasonal person is very understandable, but it stems from a fundamental misinterpretation of his behavior. It is based on the misconception that the seasonal person is willfully declining to do certain things, such as meet social obligations or follow through on commitments, or, at the very least, that he is being self-indulgent, weak-willed, and giving in to things.

The critical friend or family member may well think back on some difficult or unpleasant thing that he had to do in the past and may feel a little self-righteous about it. Resist that temptation. Everyone is different. You may be able to overcome feelings of lassitude, fatigue, and lack of motivation, but this may not be possible for your seasonal friend or family member. It may be helpful for you to think back to some time when you were feeling weak, tired, or out of sorts, perhaps due to a physical condition, such as an infection or operation. Imagine how you would have felt to be criticized at such a time for not meeting your obligations with sufficient energy or enthusiasm.

One young man who has been in and out of seasonal depressions for the past several years still finds it difficult to convince his friends that he has been suffering from an illness. They continue to regard his months of withdrawal and impaired functioning as a character disturbance, or failure of will. As a result of this, he is beginning to reevaluate these friendships, and wonders whether he might not be better off to choose friends with a greater capacity to understand and tolerate differences in behavior, as well as an ability to care, even when he is not functioning at peak level.

2. *Don't take the seasonal person's withdrawal personally.* You should not assume that he or she is mad at you or uninterested in being friends with you. One patient thinks back on friends who have called her during her down times and said, "Well, I've called you the last three times. Do you really want to be friends anymore?" She observes, "That kind of situation seems to pop up all the time in the winter. I understand that other people need certain things from a friendship, but it comes at a time when even getting up to answer the phone is a major effort—who is it going to be, what do I have to talk about now? The best kind of friend is

someone who is willing to keep calling you and to keep saying 'Do you feel like doing anything?' I'm not saying that friends should baby you, nor do they have to sit there and hold your hand. It's very simple: just accept someone who is in a different place." The same person recalls hurtful conversations with friends who have not understood her difficulty. "They say, 'Oh, yeah, here you go again,' and it's sort of mocking. They just don't understand."

If you, the friend or family member, do not understand the nature of the problem, you are likely to feel rejected when the seasonal person doesn't return your telephone call or doesn't call you for a few months. You may think it is because he doesn't like you or doesn't value you. If you make these assumptions, it is understandable that you would feel hurt and angry. It is a mistake, however, to assume that the seasonal person doesn't care about the friendship, and it is likely to cause you to become more demanding, insistent, or rejecting. By reacting in these ways, you put pressure on the seasonal person to do the very thing he finds most difficult when he is feeling depressed—namely, to initiate and maintain social interactions. Confronting the seasonal person with his inability to do so adds to his feelings of failure. Once again, understanding the nature of the problem will cushion you against taking the seasonal person's behavior too personally and will pour balm rather than salt on the injured relationship.

3. *Don't assume that it is your responsibility to make the seasonal person feel fine*. It's not likely to work and you will probably end up feeling frustrated and irritated at your failure. When you feel responsible for bringing a person out of a depression and you have failed to do so, you are likely to feel guilty and angry. You have sunk so much energy into trying to reverse the situation that you may be inclined to see the depressed person as having caused you to fail. You will then be more likely to blame him for making you feel that way. You might interpret your failure as a willful attempt on his part to resist all help, or feel inclined to say that, if he is not willing to accept your helping hand, he deserves to remain in a slump. As I have noted already, anger tends to get turned on the depressed person just when he feels least capable of coping with even the most ordinary things in life, let alone problems with a dear friend or relative. The key to not getting angry is understanding the problem and not feeling responsible for fixing it. But do remem-

ber that simple things, such as being there for your friend or family member, can make an enormous difference, even if the person is not able to show it right away. Your mere undemanding presence can be a comfort; your encouragement and nondepressed perspective can provide crucial support; and help with the simple chores of everyday life will be greatly appreciated.

11

Research on SAD and Light Therapy

INTRODUCTION

Since the description of SAD as a condition and the first controlled study of light therapy for SAD were only published in 1984, research into these areas is still in its infancy. The purpose of this section is to provide the reader with a brief overview of some of the major lines of investigation currently being explored.

SAD AS A DISORDER

The validity of SAD as a distinct psychiatric disorder was recently given the blessing of the American Psychiatric Association in its diagnostic manual, the DSM-III-R, which has included a version of the seasonal syndrome among the traditionally accepted psychiatric conditions. This acceptance came after several studies found that patients with

SAD have certain features that make them different from other depressed patients. These include: the predictable seasonality of their moods, their sensitivity to environmental light, and their favorable response to bright light therapy, which has not been nearly so well documented in nonseasonally depressed patients. There are, however, still many unanswered questions about how SAD patients differ from other depressed people, and these remain the subject of ongoing research.

CONTROLLED STUDIES OF LIGHT TREATMENT

In a controlled study, researchers compare treatments that differ from each other by only one factor—that which is thought to be of key significance in the effect. For example, in the early controlled studies of light therapy for SAD, my colleagues and I at the NIMH compared bright with dim environmental light. The factor being tested in those studies was the intensity of the light. We predicted that the bright light would be effective, and the dim light ineffective in treating SAD, and this prediction was borne out by the results of three separate studies.

There are, of course, special problems associated with designing well-controlled studies of light treatment. One problem is the placebo effect, the bane of the clinical researcher. If a person expects that a treatment will be helpful, then the treatment may help for psychological reasons rather than because it contains some special active ingredient. We wondered whether this might explain the efficacy of bright light in SAD, and others asked the same question. By now, however, the antidepressant effects of light have been so well documented (in about forty controlled studies, by my latest count) by so many different research groups in the United States and Europe, that it seems certain that these effects are due to an active biological principle, and not just a placebo effect.

Besides the placebo effect, another factor that we had to consider in interpreting our early results was sleep deprivation. We knew that by itself, it can have antidepressant effects, and wondered whether this might be the explanation for our early success with morning light treatment. Subsequent studies showed that although sleep deprivation might itself have antidepressant effects in SAD, the light treatment worked well even when there was no sleep deprivation at all. Thus, the two treatments appeared to work in different ways.

Once there was general consensus that light is effective in treating SAD, controlled studies focused on finding out what aspects of the treatment are important in achieving its antidepressant effects. As noted above, brightness was the first variable considered. Timing came next. Did it matter what time of day light was administered? There has been some controversy in this area, as the results of studies have differed. The balance of evidence suggests that light treatment in the morning is superior to evening treatments for many patients. Some patients, however, both in controlled studies and in clinical practice, have shown fine antidepressant responses to light administered in the evening and even during the day.

The duration of treatment is another variable that has been studied by several groups. Up to a certain point there seems to be some relationship between duration and response. For example, one study in Alaska found that one or two hours of bright light were both superior to thirty minutes of treatment, but there was no discernible difference between one and two hours. It is highly likely that individuals require different durations and that these depend on latitude, climate, and time of year. In addition, at the higher intensity of the more recently developed tilted fixture (10,000 lux), patients seem to respond to treatments of shorter durations than are necessary with the conventional (2500 lux) fixture.

Early in the course of our studies, we wondered whether the antidepressant effects of light in SAD were mediated through the eyes or the skin. In a study performed at the NIMH we compared two treatments in the same patients: exposure of the eyes to bright light versus exposure of the skin. We found that the eye exposure was clearly superior, strongly suggesting that the antidepressant effects of light are mediated via the eyes.

The color or spectrum of light necessary to achieve an antidepressant effect is another variable of interest to researchers. Are all the different colors that constitute white light necessary for the antidepressant effects? Are some colors more effective than others? Is the small amount of ultraviolet present in full-spectrum light an important contributor to the effects? As yet, we have no clear-cut answer to any of these questions.

Several researchers have used light sources with minimal amounts of UV rays in treating SAD patients and have obtained excellent results. This casts doubt on the idea that UV rays are necessary for the antidepressant effects of light therapy. Instead, it appears to be light in the visible range that is important for its beneficial effects in SAD.

In a recent NIMH study, Dr. Dan Oren and colleagues compared the effects of red and green fluorescent light and found that the green light had superior antidepressant effects. While this finding does not have any immediate practical applications, an understanding of the wavelengths or colors involved in the effects of light therapy may provide insights into which light-sensitive receptors in the retina are important in mediating the therapeutic effects.

THE ANATOMY OF LIGHT

If we consider that the portal of entry of the antidepressant effect of light is the eyes, then what are the anatomical pathways within the nervous system along which this effect might be transmitted? Light waves that strike the retina are converted into nerve impulses that pass toward the brain along tracts of nerve fibers. One tract directly connects the retina to the hypothalamus, a central way station in the brain that is responsible for controlling many vital functions, including sleeping, eating, temperature regulation, sex drive, and mood—in other words, the very functions that are disturbed in depressed patients. It seems highly likely that depressed patients have some biochemical abnormality in the hypothalamus. In the case of seasonal depression, this abnormality becomes manifest when there is not enough environmental light. Conversely, bright environmental light is capable of reversing these abnormalities. It would seem plausible to suggest that the nerve impulses coming from the retina to the hypothalamus in response to bright light correct the biochemical abnormality present in the hypothalamus in patients with SAD.

BIOCHEMICAL AND OTHER ABNORMALITIES IN SAD

What sort of biochemical abnormality in the hypothalamus might be responsible for the symptoms of SAD? There are many possibilities, but we do not yet know which biochemical systems are disturbed. Of all the possibilities, the neurochemical systems that seem particularly promising are those networks of nerve fibers and terminals that produce and release two chemicals, serotonin and dopamine, substances responsible for passing electrical signals from one nerve cell to another.

A study of human postmortem brain specimens has shown that serotonin concentrations in the hypothalamus decrease to their lowest levels in the winter. Deficiencies in the serotonin system have long been postulated to cause depression. Dietary carbohydrates appear to enhance serotonin synthesis in the brain. It is possible that the craving for, and binging on, sweets and starches, so commonly seen in patients with SAD, may represent a behavioral attempt to rectify a serotonin deficiency in the brain. NIMH studies, directed by Dr. Frederick Jacobsen, have found abnormal behavioral and hormonal responses to a drug that stimulates serotonin systems in patients with SAD, and these responses are, at least in part, normalized by bright light treatment. Dr. Dermot O'Rourke and colleagues at MIT have shown antidepressant effects in SAD patients treated with D-fenfluramine, a drug that stimulates the serotonin system, but which is at present available only to researchers. Fluoxetine (Prozac), an antidepressant that we have found to be so effective in SAD, is thought to work mainly via the serotonin system.

Dr. Richard Depue and colleagues at the University of Minnesota in Minneapolis have suggested that abnormalities in the systems involving the neurotransmitter, dopamine, may be fundamental to the symptoms of SAD. These researchers have conducted a series of studies, which have shown abnormalities in the rate of eyeblinks, in temperature regulation, and in the secretion of the pituitary hormone, prolactin, all of which are strongly influenced by dopamine secretion. Some of these abnormalities are reversed by effective light treatment. Of possible relevance to the dopamine-SAD theory is the presence of dopamine in the retina, which is released in response to light. It is conceivable that abnormal dopamine functioning in the retina might account for the unusual responses of SAD patients to light.

We wondered whether patients with SAD might be less sensitive to environmental light than normal subjects, which could explain why they need more light in the winter. In a recent NIMH study Dr. Dan Oren found that the reverse may be true. Patients with SAD were actually able to detect dim light in a darkened room more rapidly than their normal counterparts! Such increased sensitivity to environmental light is in accordance with my clinical observations that SAD patients are unusually sensitive to the quality of their light environment. Scientifically, however, the paradox of a group of patients who are more sensitive than normal to environmental light, yet need more light than normal, remains unresolved.

It is difficult to study the functioning of the human brain directly. Shrouded by membranes in a tough bony case, infinitely complex, the seat of the mind and therefore to some degree inviolate, the brain keeps its secrets well hidden. Although modern technology is very gradually learning to decipher these secrets, we still have to content ourselves largely with studying peripheral body fluids—blood and urine. These are poor reflections of the brain's subtle processes, but often they are all we have. Although there is no blood test that enables us to make the clinical diagnosis of SAD, several abnormalities in blood hormones have been found, some of which can be normalized by light therapy. For example, Dr. Jean Joseph-Vanderpool and colleagues at the NIMH have recently shown that an abnormality in a major hormonal system involved in responding to stress is present in patients with SAD, and it can be corrected by successful light treatment.

Dr. Alfred Lewy has found that the timing of daily (circadian) rhythms is abnormal in SAD and that effective light treatment normalizes their timing. He has hypothesized that these abnormal rhythms may be instrumental in producing the symptoms of SAD and this theory has attracted considerable interest. There is also evidence that patients with SAD may have abnormalities in information processing and even in immune functioning. These can be measured by special techniques, and effective light treatment has been shown to normalize them.

In summary, although bright light has been found to be effective in the treatment of SAD, no one knows for sure how it works. Although light has been shown to have many biological effects, it is not clear which of these is important in mediating its antidepressant effects.

Although many biological abnormalities have been found in patients with SAD, they are not distinctive enough to constitute a useful diagnostic test. In addition, we do not know whether any of these abnormalities actually plays a role in producing the symptoms of SAD.

WHO BENEFITS FROM LIGHT?

Besides patients with SAD, who else may respond to light? Dr. Siegfried Kasper at the NIMH showed that people with mild winter difficulties benefit from bright light treatment. Individuals without such winter problems do not. In other words, light is not a general euphoriant, like cocaine, but rather a specific antidepressant that reverses symptoms in certain individuals.

Many people with eating disorders, such as bulimia, appear to have problems during the winter similar to those reported by SAD patients. The pattern of binge eating that is typical of bulimia often becomes worse in winter, and ongoing studies are examining whether bright light treatments may help.

One important question is whether patients whose depressions are not seasonal in their distribution can also benefit from light treatment. Although this question has not been nearly as widely researched as has light therapy for SAD, Dr. Daniel F. Kripke, a pioneer in the field of circadian rhythms and mood disorders, has been working in this area for several years. In fact, Dr. Kripke and his colleagues in San Diego conducted their first controlled study of light treatment in non-seasonally depressed patients even before the first NIMH-controlled light treatment study in SAD was performed. In their latest study these researchers have shown that three hours of bright white light in the evening has an antidepressant effect significantly greater than a dim red light control treatment. Although the degree of improvement seen was more modest than that found in SAD patients, further studies are clearly warranted to define the scope of light's antidepressant potential in non-seasonal depression.

Dr. Barbara Parry in San Diego has shown that a few hours of bright light in the evening can reverse the symptoms of premenstrual syndrome even in women whose PMS is not specifically seasonal. In Norway, a condition of midwinter insomnia has been described, which seems to be quite different from SAD, but which may also be helped by bright light treatment.

The capacity of bright light to shift the timing of daily (circadian) rhythms has been used to good effect in people who cannot get to sleep till very late at night and cannot wake up at conventional hours in the morning. A few weeks of bright light treatment (together with the use of dark goggles in the evening) has successfully corrected this abnormal pattern of sleeping and waking. Early studies have shown that judiciously timed bright light and dark goggles may also be helpful in speeding up the recovery from jet lag.

Emboldened by the powerful effects of bright light treatment in the conditions mentioned above, researchers are currently evaluating its potential value in a variety of other conditions. Early evidence suggests that bright light may ease the symptoms of withdrawal from alcohol dependency and perhaps even from cocaine addiction. The rapidly growing Society for Light Treatment and Biological Rhythms (SLTBR)—see Resource Section for further information—is evidence of the excitement about this new area of research. The next decade promises many new insights and developments and I await these with eager anticipation.

Part 3:

Celebrating the Seasons

12

A Brief History
of Seasonal Time

So far, I have discussed the seasons in terms of the discomfort and disability they can cause, and have considered light largely as a medication. These aspects, however, are only a small part of the ways in which light and the seasons affect the mind. The seasons provided an impetus for the development of our solar calendar and helped us come to terms, both intellectually and emotionally, with the passing of time. The fluxes in mood, energy, and vitality that may be experienced with the changing seasons have infused many people with a creative energy that has been the source of many of their finest achievements. These internal changes, coinciding as they do with those in the natural world, have inspired artists and writers to express, in paint or in words, the shifting beauty of their landscape. It is these other aspects of light and the seasons that are the subjects of this section.

Although the solar calendar may seem commonplace to us, since we use it on a daily basis, its discovery was not intuitively obvious to ancient man—rather, it was the more obvious monthly cycle of the moon that formed the basis for our earliest measure of time. The calendar helped ancient civilizations predict the changing seasons and decide when to plant their crops. A major problem with the lunar year, which consisted of twelve months, was that it fell short of the 365-day solar year by several days. As a result, the lunar year shifted gradually out of phase with the seasons. In an attempt to correct these shifts, certain societies inserted extra months at intervals into their lunar calendar to keep it in line with the solar one.

The Egyptians have been given credit for developing the solar calendar. They used their ability to predict where the sun would fall on a given day to illuminate their obelisks and add drama to their religious festivals. Many societies have since used the similar principle of knowing where a slab of light or shadow would fall on a particular day—for example, the winter or summer solstice—to enhance their sense of awe at a mysterious, yet predictable, universe. The solar calendar, as measured, for example, by the sundial, worked well, and still does, in predicting the changing seasons.

The problem of anticipating seasonal changes in the world around us has not been exclusively a human one. For many animals, especially those that live at some distance from the equator, it is crucial to be able to anticipate when it will be cold or hot, when food will be scarce or plentiful, and when to mate, migrate, or hibernate. The sheep needs to anticipate when to give birth so that there is food enough to enable the newborn lamb to survive. The weasel must anticipate when to transform its dirty brown coat into one that is sleek and white for camouflage against the snow. The deer needs to time the growth of his antlers so that they will be at their full splendid size by the end of the summer to fight his competitors for the right to mate with the doe of his choice. In order to time such events correctly, all these animals have evolved complex physiological programs that depend for their accurate timing on information from the physical world. The environmental time cue of greatest importance across a multitude of species is the length of the day, which is a function of the solar year.

We know now that seasonal changes are not confined to animals, but occur in humans, too. Many normal individuals surveyed in the northern United States report that their energy and activity levels are highest in the summer and lowest in the winter; that in winter they eat more, gain weight, sleep more, and prefer sweet and starchy foods. These behavioral changes, similar in nature to those seen in SAD patients, though milder in severity, could be viewed as adaptive to the energy demands of

winter, since they appear to have an energy-conserving function. These
seasonal changes are probably triggered by certain environmental factors
such as day length or temperature, which vary seasonally. Thus our solar
calendar and the calendar of our biological responses both follow the
annual course of the sun across the sky. The discovery of the solar
calendar by the Egyptians, the product of human intellect, and the
seasonal patterns of human biology, shaped over thousands of years by
the forces of evolution, have thus both used the sun and the seasons as
the most dependable and meaningful markers for charting time over long
periods.

Quite apart from the practical need to measure it, man has also had to
deal with the emotional impact of time passing. Over the course of time
we receive the gifts of life, health, youth, children, and the rewards of
our labors; yet, in time, we lose them all. We are subject to aging,
disease, the destructive forces of our fellow human beings, and finally,
death. How do we come to terms with all these losses, as well as with
the burden of the errors we have made?

These are age-old problems, and ancient man found a novel solution
to them—simply abolish time. Wipe it out, and start all over again. Thus
in ancient times, at the end of each year, people engaged in cleansing
rituals, purifying themselves of the dirt and sin they had accumulated
over the previous year. They could then enter the new year fresh and
clean. All manner of complex rituals were developed. For example, sins
would be transferred to a goat, and the animal would be driven out of the
area—the proverbial scapegoat. Not only were one's sins abolished, but
the slate of time was, itself, wiped clean. Ancient man lacked a sense
that one year led to the next—a concept of time that has been termed
linear or historical. Instead, he believed in cyclical time, "the myth of
the eternal return," which happens to be the title of a fascinating book
on the subject, by Mircea Eliade.

Around the time of the winter solstice, it was traditional to extinguish
and rekindle fire. Even in modern times, the festivals that take place
around the time of the winter solstice are celebrated with lights: the
colored ones on Christmas trees and the candles on a Hanukkah menorah.
In some cultures the winter solstice coincides with the new year, and the
extinguishing and rekindling of fire could also be regarded as symboliz-
ing the obliteration of time past and the start of new time. Alternatively,

such activities might be viewed as a celebration of (or prayer for) the return of the sun's light following the winter solstice. The use of light in these rituals may also serve to lift our spirits during the darkest days of the year.

Cyclical time was common in many ancient societies. The Greeks conceived of history as cyclical and developed the idea of a "Great Year" many thousands of solar years in length. The Great Year, which they believed corresponded to the rotation of the heavens, had a Great Summer, when planetary forces would combine to destroy the earth by fire, and a Great Winter, when the world would be overwhelmed by water. The Indians had a similar concept of a cosmic cycle, called a Mahayuga, which was thought to last four million years.

It seems likely that the obvious seasonal changes in the world around us, and our internal changes in mood and behavior, together perhaps with the wish to abolish the past, all contributed to the development of a cyclical sense of time. In the past few centuries, however, a linear or historical one has prevailed. This sense of time is familiar to every schoolchild who has had to construct a dateline showing how certain events occurred over the years. An integral part of this concept is that these events took place in a certain sequence and that, in certain critical ways, the clock or calendar cannot be turned back. Thus World War II took place, in part, because of unresolved issues from World War I. Dropping the atom bombs on Japan put an end to World War II, an event that could not have happened four years earlier, since the atom bomb had not yet been invented. The dropping of the bomb ushered in an age in which nuclear warfare is an ever-present possibility. That has changed the nature of war and the whole way in which we view our world. Thus, nowadays even schoolchildren become thoroughly familiar with the concept of linear or historical time that moves in one direction only.

The Jews have been credited with the development of the sense of linear time. Calamities that beset the children of Israel were interpreted by the prophets as the result of the wrath of God, proof that the people needed to reform their ways. The prophets thus forced the people to turn away from a purely cyclical and ever-renewing sense of time and face the consequences of their actions. This concept was continued in Christianity, which sees time as a straight line that traces the course of humanity from its Creation through Redemption to the present. The

Chinese, in their descriptions of successive dynasties, have been credited with independently coming up with a linear sense of time, and such a sense was surely present in the mind of the thirteenth-century Japanese sage, Dogen, who observed, "Time flies more swiftly than an arrow and life is more transient than the dew. We cannot call back a single day that has passed."

According to Eliade, the conflict between the two different perceptions of time—cyclical and linear—continued into the seventeenth century, after which the latter view gained ascendance. This was in keeping with the development of science, the theory of evolution, and the idea of human progress, all of which were believed to proceed in a linear way. Despite this linear trend, both Jews and Christians have continued to celebrate cyclical time in the form of seasonal rituals and festivals. There has been a renewal of interest in cyclical time in the twentieth century. Historians, such as Spengler and Toynbee, have considered the problems of periodicity in history. The work of two important modern writers, T. S. Eliot and James Joyce, are, in Eliade's view, "saturated with nostalgia for the myth of eternal repetition and . . . the abolition of time."

One of the reasons it took modern psychiatrists so long to rediscover SAD might have been the ascendance of linear over cyclical time. According to a linear way of thinking, a psychiatrist might consider, for example, a patient with three episodes of winter depression as follows: Three years ago, in October, she broke up with her boyfriend and became depressed for several months. By April she recovered, moved, and found a new job. She was not able to function for a prolonged period in this position, however, became depressed, and lost the job in December. The next March she entered into a new relationship, which seemed to lift her spirits. She was well until about a month ago (October), when her relationship difficulties resurfaced, and she has since become markedly lethargic, withdrawn, and depressed.

In the past few decades, however, psychiatrists have once again become interested in cyclicity in the form of biological rhythms. It was this developing interest that served as a major precursor to the rediscovery of SAD.

13

Polar Tales

I have frequently been asked, "Haven't they studied SAD in Scandinavia? Don't they get a lot of it over there?" In recent years, since our work from the NIMH first appeared, several Scandinavian research groups have begun work on the subject. Before then, however, there was little or nothing about it in Scandinavian medical literature. Given the degree of light deprivation so far north, one wonders about this gap. Does it mean that the condition—or indeed, any seasonal change in mood or behavior—is very rare in those people, or is there some other reason they have not studied it? One Swedish psychiatrist provided a witty answer to my question about the prevalence of SAD in Scandinavia. "Either everyone there has it," he replied, "or no one does."

It certainly appears as though some Scandinavians have the problem. Dr. Tront Bratlid in Norway has come across many patients with the symptoms of SAD, and Dr. Andreas Magnusson in Iceland notes that, "Everyone seems to have some relative who takes to bed for the whole winter." Cases that sound like SAD can also be found, according to him, in Icelandic myths. Seasonal changes in behavior are reportedly rife in the population as a whole. According to some observers, these seasonal rhythms seem to be so widespread that most people just take them for granted. This may be why they did not gain the attention of the medical community until reports started appearing from other parts of the world.

In fact, some of the best descriptions of the behavioral effects of circumpolar winters come from outsiders. One early outsider, Dr. Frederick Cook, who went on a nineteenth-century expedition to Antarctica as ship's doctor to the *Belgica,* described how the ship was trapped in the ice during the Antarctic winter and how the crew suffered from isolation and the harsh weather conditions. Of all of these, the darkness appeared to affect the men most, and according to Cook, they "gradually . . . became affected, body and soul, with languor." He described other psychiatric problems among the crew and concluded that, "The root cause of these disasters was the lack of the sun." He treated his men with direct exposure to an open fire and found that this seemed to help them, perhaps more because of the heat than the light. For sixty-eight days the sun was not seen until, once again, it appeared above the horizon "like a small, withered orange."

Dr. Cook also provided us with a description of seasonal rhythms of sexual drive among the Eskimos:

> The passions of these people are periodical, and their courtship is usually carried on soon after the return of the sun; in fact, at this time, they almost tremble from the intensity of their passions and for several weeks most of their time is taken up in gratifying them.

Such shifts in sex drive, with a surge of interest in the spring, continuing into the summer, almost certainly affect people living at lower latitudes, though to a lesser degree. Many societies have created spring rituals that incorporate elements of sexuality or fertility, which coincide with the burgeoning of nature outside and rising sexual passions within.

An excellent description of the psychological effects of the dark days on the people of Tromsö in northern Norway was provided by Joseph Wechsberg, who wrote an article in *The New Yorker* called "Mørketiden," which means murky times. Tromsö, which lies 215 miles north of the Arctic Circle, has forty-nine sunless days during the winter. Wechsberg observed that "the people talked a lot about *mørketiden*, and at the same time protested that they were not affected by it." He reported that people felt tired, had difficulty getting up in the morning and accomplishing their work, and suffered from disturbed sleep, low energy level, and actual depression. In other words, many of these people complained of the symptoms of SAD. One man he interviewed even observed that the depression seemed to be a problem particularly among women.

Wechsberg described an opposite pattern of behavior in the summer. People rarely seemed to feel tired and often did not feel like going to bed. They were active at all hours of the night. There was widespread celebration as people headed for the country to "fish, hunt, have fun." As a result, it was difficult to get any work done. I have experienced similar effects of the long Arctic summer days myself while visiting Alaska in May, when the days were over twenty hours long. My family and I were extremely energetic and didn't get the feeling of winding down that ordinarily comes at the end of the day. We had to remind ourselves to go to sleep at two o'clock in the morning, or else we would have stayed up all night.

Wechsberg observed that in winter, the people of Tromsö kept their indoor lights on constantly during the day. One woman reported missing the sun so much that she gravitated toward the window. The return of the sun after forty-nine dark days was celebrated as *Soldag,* or *Sunday*. Children were sent home early from school that day and all work stopped by noon. The first rays were greeted with tears, prayers, and special wishes. Some people, unwilling to wait for this day, flew to southern Norway to see the sun.

Apparently, the physicians of Tromsö agreed that a study of the effects of *mørketiden* was long overdue. This was in 1972. Since then, some work has been done in Norway on midwinter insomnia, but it was only after SAD was described and treated with light in the United States that studies began in Tromsö. Why did it take so long? It is possible that the investigators' own seasonal rhythms interfered with their ability to study the problem. In the winter, it is conceivable that their low energy level did not provide them with the creativity or enthusiasm to undertake such a study, whereas in the summer, they might have been too busy enjoying the long, sunny days. It is possible that the stoicism of the northern people caused them to understate the difficulties associated with *mørketiden* and to deny the extent of the problem. Finally, it might have required an outsider, such as Joseph Wechsberg, who did not take *mørketiden* for granted, to describe the full extent of the problem. This may account for why the Scandinavians were not the first to describe SAD. I believe that my own upbringing, in a climate where the seasons were mild, enabled me to recognize the dramatic nature of the seasonal changes in North America. As in Edgar Allan Poe's story of the purloined letter, sometimes that which is right under one's nose is most difficult to observe.

14

SAD Through the Ages

The relationship between depression and the seasons was first observed over two thousand years ago by Hippocrates, who noted, "It is chiefly the changes of the seasons which produces diseases." Aretaeus, in the second century A.D., recommended that, "Lethargics are to be laid in the light and exposed to the rays of the sun, for the disease is gloom." Yet it is only in the late twentieth century that seasonal depression has entered the diagnostic manual of psychiatric diseases, and light therapy has been seriously considered as a treatment for winter depression. How can we account for this long hiatus? Why did it take medical science so long to rediscover the wisdom of the ancients? This rediscovery is not the result of some technological breakthrough, examples of which are to be found in so many other areas of medicine, for the elements needed to make this discovery—our powers of observation, the charting of mood changes over time, and bright light—have been available for ages. Rather, this rediscovery was a result of advances in our understanding of psychiatric diseases and our changing concepts of time.

The following are three historic cases of SAD, described some three centuries apart. Clinically, they have certain distinct resemblances to one another and to modern-day descriptions of SAD. What I find fascinating about these cases is how they illustrate the different ways in which the physicians of the time conceptualized SAD and what that can teach us about the changing concepts of time and mental illness over the centuries. During the era when the first case was described—the seventeenth century—medical science was still under the powerful influence of the humoral theories of disease that had held sway since the times of ancient Greece. The second case was described in the nineteenth century, at a time when the impact of the physical environment on mental illness was considered of great importance to those suffering from mood disorders. The final case was described in the middle of our own century, when psychoanalytic theories had the greatest influence on our approach toward mental illness.

ANNE GRENVILLE

She was the daughter of the Bishop of Durham and the wife of a reverend, but it was not for these reasons that Anne Grenville, who lived in England in the late 1600s, is remembered in history. Rather, it is because of her extraordinarily well-documented psychiatric problems and the prominence of the physicians whom she consulted. We owe this thorough documentation to an ongoing battle between her father and her husband. Her father claimed that she had always been healthy and, according to her sister, she had been driven to madness by her husband. Her husband's annoyance at Mrs. Grenville's psychiatric problems was compounded by financial difficulties, which were further aggravated by his father-in-law's reluctance to pay the expected dowry.

Mrs. Grenville appears to have suffered from a cyclical mood disorder. According to one physician she consulted, "There are twin symptoms, which are her constant companions, Mania and Melancholy, and they succeed each other in a double and alternate act; or take each other's place like the smoke and flame of a fire." Her problem would probably not have received so much medical attention—at least nine prominent physicians saw her—had it not been for the troublesome nature of her manic episodes. According to one physician:

> The first oncoming of this recurrent disease shows itself by mild insomnia, unusual talkativeness, propensity to laughter, practically continuously. . . . But as the illness increases, her periods of wakefulness become more extended, or if she does fall asleep, her condition is worsened as a result of the sleep; silence succeeds talkativeness, morosity, laughter . . . and finally, she sometimes rages against her attendants and attacks anyone she meets in a petulant manner.
>
> Dr. Peter Hunauld, Rector of the University of Angers, 1673

It is not uncommon for mania to begin as a euphoric condition and progress to a state of irritability and anger. As the following description of the alternate phase of Mrs. Grenville's condition indicates, she also suffered from recurrent depressions:

> From time to time the symptoms of melancholia proper also put in an appearance; she carries on her ordinary tasks and duties in a gentler manner, sometimes taciturn, timid, and sorrowful, without a trace of savageness. ˙ . .
>
> Stephen Taylor, M.D.; Robert Wittie, M.D., York, 1670

The seasonality of her symptoms—particularly her tendency to become manic in the summer—was well documented. For this reason, one of her doctors suggested special treatments "at the approach of the dog days." The dog days are the six hottest weeks of the year, named after the dog star, Sirius, the brightest star in the firmament. Once a year the dog star rises in direct alignment with the sun, and the ancients believed that around this time, its effects combined with those of the sun to produce the intense heat of July and August.

Mrs. Grenville's case was not exactly typical of most SAD patients I have seen, whose manic symptoms are generally less prominent. In addition, although her manias clearly occurred in the summer, and we are told that these alternated with her depressive episodes, we are not told specifically that the depressions occurred in the winter, though it seems likely that they did. Her depressions were probably less well documented than her manias because depression is often regarded as less of a problem by a patient's relatives. The patient frequently takes the opposite point of view, seeking help when depressed, but not when manic.

Many theories were advanced to explain Mrs. Grenville's condition, and on the basis of these, several treatments were suggested, all, unfortunately, to little avail. The theories of her illness showed the continuing influence of the humoral theories of the ancient Greeks, according to which Man was composed of four humors: blood, yellow bile (choler), black bile (melanchos), and phlegm. These humors were thought to be associated with the four seasons: spring, summer, autumn, and winter, respectively. Different types of climates—cold or hot, moist or dry— were thought to act upon the different humors, altering their relative influence on a person. So were different constellations and planets. The result of these influences on an individual's innate disposition was thought to result in one of four temperaments: sanguine, choleric, melancholic, or phlegmatic.

Melancholia, as its name implies, was considered to be due to an excess of black bile. The planet Saturn was thought to exert an influence on this condition. In one artistic portrayal of the four humors, the melancholic describes his nature as follows:

> God has given me unduly
> In my nature melancholy.
> Like the earth both cold and dry,
> Black of skin with gait awry,
> Hostile, mean, ambitious, sly,
> Sullen, crafty, false, and shy.
> No love for fame or woman have I;
> In Saturn and autumn the fault doth lie.

The idea of black bile being responsible for melancholia was extended by Aristotle to account for mania, as well. According to him, black bile, which he regarded as being naturally cold, "produces apoplexy or torpor or despondency or fear." However, if the black bile became overheated, "it produces cheerfulness, accompanied by song and frenzy." In keeping with this thinking, several of Mrs. Grenville's doctors attributed her condition to "atrabilious ferment"; in other words, black bile. According to one of the doctors:

The whole aim of our treatment must be at least to blunt that ferment, if we cannot entirely destroy it. This was the purpose behind the treatments proposed by the learned Doctor Bellay of Cleves: namely, cooling medicines, aperients, gentle evacuants, and occasionally hypnotics. The hope is, by these remedies to be able to suppress the force and energy of that atrabilious humour; for which purpose, especially as a preventive measure, you must see that every year at the beginning of spring you use the well-established remedies to provoke a flow of the haemorrhoids by the application of leeches.

The twin legacies of the ancient Greeks to the treatment of Anne Grenville were the humoral theory of disease, which tied melancholia to the seasons, and a cyclical view of time. The Greeks saw history as cyclical, with the rotation of the stars in the heavens resembling the rotation of the seasons, but on a much larger scale. With these theoretical views of the world, it was quite natural for them to emphasize the influences of the seasons on the lives of men.

THE CASE OF M

Approximately 150 years after Anne Grenville was treated for her problems, a patient whom we know only as "M" consulted the famous French psychiatrist, Esquirol, who described his case as follows:

M, a native of Belgium, forty-two years of age, of a strong constitution and transacting a very large business, consults me at the close of the winter of 1825. Observe the account which is given me by him. "I have always enjoyed good health, am happy in my family, having an affectionate wife and charming children. My affairs are also in excellent condition. Three years since, I experienced a trifling vexation. It was at the beginning of autumn, and I became sad, gloomy, and susceptible. By degrees I neglected my business, and deserted my house to avoid my uneasiness. I felt feeble, and drank beer and liquors. Soon I became irritable. Everything opposed my wishes, disturbed me, and rendered me insupportable, and even dangerous to my family. My affairs suffered from this state. I suffered also from insomnia and inappetence. Neither the advice nor tender counsels of my wife, nor that of my family, had any more influence over me. At length, I fell into a profound apathy, incapable of everything except drinking and grieving. At the approach of spring I felt my affections revive. I recovered all my intellectual activity, and all my ardor for business. I was very well all the ensuing summer, but from the commencement of the damp and cold weather of autumn, there was a return of sadness, uneasiness, and a desire to drink, to dissipate my sadness. There was also a return of irascibility and transports of passion. During the last autumn and the present winter, I have experienced for the third time the same phenomena, which have been more grievous than formerly. My fortune has suffered, and my wife has not been free from danger. I have now come to submit myself to you, sir, and to obey your directions in every thing."

After many questions, I offered the following advice. A hospital will not benefit, but on the contrary, injure you. . . . In the month of September, you should go to Languedoc [in the South of France] and must be in Italy before the close of October, from whence you must not return until the month of May. This counsel was closely followed. At the close of December he was at Rome. He felt the impression of the cold, and the beginnings of a desire to drink were manifest, but shortly disappeared. He escaped a fourth attack by withdrawing himself from the coldness and moisture of autumn. He returns to Paris in the month of May, in the enjoyment of excellent health.

This beautiful early description of SAD and the inspired treatment, so successful in the case of M, is impressive to a modern psychiatrist. It appears that Esquirol's treatment of patient M with climate modification was not an isolated event, for he observed that it was the practice of English physicians to send their melancholic patients into the southern provinces of France and Italy, "thus protecting them against the moist and oppressive air of England."

Esquirol acquired his enlightened approach from his mentor, Phillipe Pinel, the French psychiatrist renowned for removing the chains from patients in a Paris mental hospital. Pinel had strong reservations about "the usual routine of baths, bloodletting, and coercion," the standard treatment for mood disorders at the time, but suggested instead a "moral treatment" that relied more on empathy, understanding, and encouragement. Pinel also drew attention to the importance of the physical environment in modulating mood. For melancholics, he pointed out "the urgent necessity of forcibly agitating the system, of interrupting the chain of their gloomy ideas, and of engaging their interest by powerful and continuous impressions on their external senses."

With such a renowned mentor behind him, Esquirol went on to make his own original contributions to psychiatry. He noted that depression could result from many different causes and ought to be treated in different ways, "not . . . limited to the administration of certain medicines." In his view, "Moral medicine, which seeks in the heart for the cause of the evil, which sympathizes and weeps, which consoles, and divides with the unfortunate their sufferings, and which revives hope in their breast, is often preferable to all other." However, he also stressed the importance of the physical environment, recommending "a clear sky, a pleasant temperature, an agreeable situation with varied scenery."

The late nineteenth and early twentieth centuries saw the development of bright artificial light as a therapeutic modality. In fact, Niels Finsen of Sweden was awarded one of the first Nobel prizes for medicine for his work on the effects of artificial light on the tuberculous bacillus. Bright light was used for many conditions, including depression. A leading British psychiatrist observed:

> Since the energising influence of sunlight on all living matter is so well known, it is surprising that therapists have not made greater use of this natural curative agent.
>
> In the province of psychological medicine it is generally accepted that no institution, from a structural point of view, is complete without its solarium. . . . In addition . . . several mental institutions have already installed apparatus for the production of artificial sunlight.
>
> Even to the lay mind, it is obvious what a stimulating and beneficial influence artificial sunlight can exert on those whose fund of energy is seriously depleted by nervous or mental disorder, especially during the dull, sunless, and depressing months of our British winter.
>
> Dr. J. G. Porter Phillips, Bethlehem Hospital, London, 1923

THE UNMARRIED CLERK

The next published case of SAD was reported one century after Esquirol's description of patient M, and on the other side of the Atlantic. In the United States in 1946, a certain Colonel George Frumkes published in the *Psychoanalytic Quarterly* the case of a thirty-year-old clerk. Dr. Frumkes describes the patient's history as follows:

[He] was recovering from a depression of a type he had had each year for the past ten years. Although he knew he would be better in the spring and summer, he wanted to be treated so that the depressions would not recur. They began in August or September and continued about six months. During the spring and summer he was overactive and too confident, without excitement or unseemly behavior. After the recurrence of the first few cycles, he was never free from the fear of the autumnal depression. This constant threat interfered with his freedom of action in his business and in his relationship with women.

The depressions were heralded by the observation that he was sweating excessively; then he felt vague anxiety, followed by the fear that he would not be able to do his work. Later came feelings of unworthiness and inefficiency. He was convinced his work suffered because he was slow, because he had to check his work four times, and he dreaded anything new and avoided making decisions. He tried to evade as much work as possible without attracting attention, and he avoided contact with superiors and fellow workers. Despite the great effort it cost him, he never missed a day's work. He felt he had no right to indulge himself. He was certain that his deficiencies were apparent to everyone. If he could have afforded to do so he would have remained in hiding in the South for six months. If criticized, he would suffer keenly and be incapable of defending himself. Praise or affection caused him suffering because he felt he was an impostor not deserving such consideration.

He was especially uncomfortable in cold weather, but there was not a constant relationship between the depth of the depression and the drop in temperature. Certain signs foretold his recovery: he would take out his camera, make strokes as if he were playing tennis, and become interested in girls. In his overactive phase he was with as many as four girls a week; he was restless, prided himself on doing the work of three men, and devised new office systems.

Dr. Frumkes follows up this excellent description, which will sound familiar to all SAD sufferers, with an extensive history of the patient's background: his parentage, family relationships, childhood, and employment background are all reviewed. His sex life is a particular focus of attention. His sexual development, the sleeping arrangements in the family, masturbatory practices, dating patterns, and dreams and fantasies about sex take up well over half the article.

In attempting to explain the patient's depressions, Dr. Frumkes departs from the simple and straightforward prose used to describe the patient's symptoms and launches into a convoluted psychoanalytic interpretation. According to his formulation, the patient's depressions "began about the time he learned that masturbation was not a unique sin of his; when there was a decrease in the intense, conscious feeling of guilt. The depressions represented a redistribution of the punishment in the psychic economy. . . . Masturbation for him was an unconscious infantile sexual striving for his mother, and the associated hostile impulses connected with this drive." Dr. Frumkes also suggests that the depressions might have represented "memorial observances of the births of his brothers and sisters." Such explanations for the development of U.S. manic and depressive episodes were frequently offered by psychiatrists in the 1950s and 1960s. I have read through many medical records of manic-depressives treated at the New York Psychiatric Institute during these years, and was impressed by some of the ingenious formulations, which purported to explain both depressions and manias in terms of childhood experiences.

Dr. Frumkes treated his patient with psychoanalysis. Although he did not specify the frequency of sessions and length of treatment in his paper, I would assume he met with the patient four or five times a week over several years, as is customary in traditional psychoanalysis. Dr. Frumkes reports that "as the treatment progressed, the depressions diminished in regularity and intensity. The patient undertook work of a nature he had formerly dreaded. A year following treatment he wrote that he had had no disturbances of mood, that he was married and felt well."

It is difficult to know quite what to make of this reported outcome. It seems as though the patient did indeed have sexual conflicts, and it is quite conceivable that the analytic therapy was helpful for them. However, my experience with SAD makes me question the likelihood that the treatment made a significant impact on his annual depressions, though he might have worried less about them.

It is interesting to consider that in the same year in which Dr. Frumkes published his case, a German physician, Dr. Helmut Marx, reported using bright artificial light to treat four men who had become depressed in the dark days of an arctic winter. Marx's work was impressive in that he recognized the recurrent nature of winter depressions and even described the overeating that often accompanies the condition. Not only did he identify light deficiency as a trigger for this condition—and bright light as an effective treatment—but he also correctly suggested that light acted via the eyes to influence the hypothalamus. All these insights are in agreement with our views of SAD and light therapy some forty years later. Marx's report, however, was unknown to modern psychiatrists until very recently and had little influence on patterns of psychiatric treatment or research.

How, in the course of the century between the cases of Esquirol and Frumkes, did the importance of the physical environment get lost? In my view, the main reason for this was the powerful influence of Sigmund Freud. Although the discovery of psychoanalysis contributed enormously to our understanding of the human mind, it also obscured our consideration of alternative hypotheses—for example, the simple possibility that depressions could be related to regular changes in climatic variables.

Freud also made his mark on our view of time. He had two opinions on the subject. First, he asserted that the information that was repressed into the unconscious mind remained unaltered by the passage of time. His was a linear, historical view—of time as an arrow. Like the Dead Sea Scrolls, resting in their earthen jars in a cave until they were discovered, unaltered by time, so the repressed memories of childhood were buried in the unconscious, to be discovered later by the analyst. Freud's second opinion on time perception in the mind was that, "In the id there is nothing corresponding to the idea of time." He summarized these two views as follows:

> The processes of the system *Ucs* (the unconscious) are timeless; i.e., they are not ordered temporally, are not altered by the passage of time, in fact bear no relationship to time at all.

Although his colleague, Fleiss, believed in the importance of cyclical processes in the mind, there is little evidence that Freud regarded such a cyclical sense of time as being of any major importance.

So it was in the United States, as the second half of the twentieth century unfolded, that psychiatry lost its grip on time as an important consideration in evaluating psychiatric conditions, and this applied both to cyclical time and the longitudinal evaluation of individuals over time. Rather, the psychological associations of the moment were what mattered. Like a hologram in which a fragment contains an image of the whole picture, everything was contained in the present, in the cross-section of the mind that appeared there and then to the analyst.

As for the biological developments in psychiatry in the second half of the twentieth century, the big news was the development of psychotropic drugs, which could reverse psychosis, depression, and mania. These were the single most important factor in emptying out our state mental hospitals and "deinstitutionalizing" their patients. The consequences of such deinstitutionalization—for example, homelessness and street people—have caused new problems, but there is little question that the discovery of effective psychotropic drugs was a major breakthrough for psychiatry.

However, these drugs were regarded as suitable only for more disturbed patients, whereas those who were able to function in the outside world, like Dr. Frumkes's patient, were more likely to receive only psychotherapy. To some degree, a two-class system of psychiatric patients resulted. Since most patients with SAD do not require hospitalization, most would have been grouped in the healthier class and given insight-oriented psychotherapy.

Two trends in modern psychiatry were responsible for paving the way for the rediscovery of SAD and light therapy. First, standard ways of identifying discrete psychiatric conditions were developed; and second, cyclical time was rediscovered. The development of criteria for identifying psychiatric syndromes came from a group of psychiatric diagnosticians at Washington University in St. Louis. This group emphasized the importance of examining the longitudinal course of an illness, rather than relying primarily on the mental state of the patient as presented to the psychiatrist at any given moment. As to cyclicity and behavior, the great strides made in the past few decades in understanding biological rhythms in animals were applied to people. Pioneering human studies in Germany and the United States showed that humans had an endogenous circadian system resembling that of other animals—the medical importance of cyclical time had been rediscovered.

The NIMH group, led by Dr. Thomas A. Wehr, expanded on earlier observations by other circadian rhythm experts to develop the idea that disturbances of biological rhythms may underlie cyclical mood disorders. The cycle of day and night, light and dark, is crucially important in modulating daily rhythms in animals. It was logical, therefore, that light should recapture the interest of psychiatric clinicians and researchers, who had abandoned it some fifty years before. Into this environment came Herb Kern, scientist and patient, with fifteen years of documented seasonal cycles of depression and hypomania, to usher in the modern era of SAD and light therapy.

15

Creating with the Seasons

Great Wits are sure to Madness near ally'd,
And thin Partitions do their Bounds divide.
                                   —*John Dryden*

The association between genius and insanity is ingrained in our culture. We are told about the "thin line" that exists between the brilliant artist and the madman. Is there any truth to this assertion? Have great artists of the past indeed suffered from psychiatric disturbances and, if so, what forms have these disturbances taken? Where do seasonal responses fit into this picture, if at all? Does sensitivity to light—a cardinal feature of patients with SAD—seem to go along with sensitivity to our exterior and interior worlds?

THE LINK BETWEEN MOOD DISORDERS, CREATIVITY, AND THE SEASONS

The concept that genius and madness are somehow connected goes back at least to the time of Aristotle, who observed that, "No great genius was without a mixture of insanity." He added, "Those who have become eminent in philosophy, politics, poetry, and the arts have all had tendencies toward melancholia." The Roman playwright, Seneca, echoed

194

this view, noting that, "The mind cannot attain anything lofty so long as it is sane." For centuries this belief persisted, and melancholia was somehow endowed with cultural value. Genius was regarded as a "hereditary taint," transmitted in families, along with mental illness.

It is only in our century, however, that the subject has been a matter of serious study. Dr. Nancy Andreasen was the first researcher to study the relationship between creativity and mental illness, using modern psychiatric diagnoses. She interviewed thirty creative writers at the prestigious Iowa Writers' Workshop about their own backgrounds and those of their close relatives, and compared their responses with those of thirty control subjects. She found a substantially higher rate of mental illness among the writers and their family members. She had approached the study with the belief that there would be an association between schizophrenia and creativity. To her surprise, it was not schizophrenia but disorders of mood regulation—especially those involving a tendency to mania or hypomania, in addition to depression—that distinguished the writers from the control group. She concluded that the traits of creativity and mood disturbance appeared to run together in families and could be genetically mediated.

More recently, Dr. Kay Redfield Jamison studied a group of eminent British writers and artists for evidence of psychiatric illness, seasonal variations in mood and productivity, and the perceived role of intense moods in their creative processes. She selected these artists and writers on the basis of objective acclaim, in the form of prestigious prizes and other types of acknowledgment. She interviewed them extensively and found very high rates of mood disorders in the group. Over a third had been treated for mood problems, the great majority with medications or hospitalization. Poets were most likely to require medication for depression and were the only group to require treatment for mania. Playwrights had the highest total rate of treatment for mood disorders, but a high percentage of this group had been treated with psychotherapy alone. Exceptional among the writers in regard to their mood stability were biographers, who reported no history of mood swings or elated states. Although these writers were as outstanding as the others, in terms of their objective achievements, they were perhaps a less creative group.

Almost all subjects—with the exception of the biographers—reported having had intense, highly productive, and creative periods. Most of these lasted between one and four weeks. These episodes were marked by "increased enthusiasm, energy, self-confidence, speed of mental association, fluency of thoughts, elevated mood, and a strong sense of well-being." They sound very much like "hypomanic" episodes, without the behavioral disturbance that that term implies. It is extremely interesting that 90 percent of Dr. Jamison's group reported that very intense moods and feelings were either integral to, or necessary for, the development and execution of their work.

Investigating the association between seasons, mood, and productivity, Dr. Jamison found a strong seasonal pattern of mood changes among artists and writers, with highest mood scores in the summer and lowest in the winter. Peak periods of productivity, while also seasonal, occurred in the spring and the fall. It seemed as though as mood increased from spring to summer, so productivity declined to some extent, picking up again in the fall. Those who had been treated for mood disorders had a sharper decline of productivity in the summer than the other subjects.

How can one explain this drop-off in creativity in the summer, as mood continues to improve? A few possible explanations come to mind. When people are too euphoric, they are often not best able to produce. Their thoughts may race too quickly and their focus may be scattered. There is a tendency to start many tasks but not to follow through—distractability is a problem. Those subjects in Dr. Jamison's study who had been treated for mood disorders might have experienced more marked highs during the summer, with greater associated difficulties in focusing and carrying out tasks. Another possibility is that the artist might not wish to be creative during the summer. One writer with SAD whom I know said that she has so much fun in the summer that she doesn't want to spend her golden, sunny days bashing away at a word processor.

A new way of measuring creativity has been developed by Drs. Ruth Richards and Dennis Kinney, researchers at Harvard University. The advantage of this new Lifetime Creativity Scale is that it can be used to measure creativity in anyone, not just in those of exceptional talent. By means of this scale these researchers were able to show a higher rate of creativity among manic-depressives (bipolar patients) than expected. But even greater creativity scores were found among the relatives of bipolar patients—those with milder mood swings or no clear-cut mood swings at all. It is quite possible that this heightened level of creativity found in relatives of bipolar patients may explain why the illness has so successfully been transmitted from generation to generation. People who carry bipolar genes may be at an advantage to survive and reproduce, by virtue of their creative abilities. People with bipolar tendencies, and their relatives, seem more likely to take risks, such as emigrating, which may be highly adaptive in crisis situations.

All these studies suggest that Aristotle was correct in linking mood disturbance and creativity. It seems as though the most creative people are those with milder forms of mood disturbance, which is in keeping with my clinical experience. Severe depressions or wild manias are not conducive to productivity. The opposite is true for mild depressions alternating with hypomanias. During hypomanic periods, thoughts and associations flow rapidly, energy and confidence levels are high, the need for sleep is reduced, and ideas are more readily generated and pursued. During mild depressions, these ideas can be critically evaluated. Ideas that are too grandiose or unlikely to succeed can be discarded, and those that look more promising in the sober light of depression can be retained and developed. Mild depressions may be conducive to the drudgery that is required for any creative venture—the daily plodding necessary for the execution of any grand scheme.

The seasonal person will easily recognize this pattern of mood swings and its relationship to creativity, for the depressions of SAD are often relatively mild in severity, the hypomanias restrained and productive. As we now know, the mood changes in SAD patients are often driven by the amount of daylight present. Many creative artists have recognized the connection between changes in environmental light and their mood and productivity. The following section deals with famous creative people who suffered from mood disorders—especially those where there is evidence of strong seasonality or light sensitivity.

MOODY AND FAMOUS; SENSITIVE TO SEASONS AND LIGHT

The list of famous people with mood disturbances is impressive. Although there was no psychiatrist with a modern diagnostic handbook around to record the mental status of most of the people in this section, abundant evidence for mood disorders exists in most cases. It is not my purpose here to be comprehensive; only to select some illustrative examples of famous creative people with mood disorders. Among artists we have Michelangelo, Albrecht Dürer, and Vincent van Gogh; composers include George Frideric Handel, Gustav Mahler, and Robert Schumann; writers include John Milton, Edgar Allan Poe, Ernest Hemingway, and Virginia Woolf; politicians include Abraham Lincoln and Winston Churchill, who referred to his depressions as his "black dog." Sir Isaac Newton was perhaps the most eminent scientist to have suffered from manic depression.

How many of these people were strongly seasonal in their mood swings or sensitive to changes in environmental light? This is hard to say with any clinical certainty, especially since SAD as a distinct entity was described long after most of these artists were deceased. Statistically, it is highly likely that many of these people were seasonal. Figures for the rate of SAD among clinics of recurrent depressives range from one in six to one in three. For reasons noted above, highly creative people with mood disorders are more likely to have SAD than other forms of mood disorder, most of which are more disruptive to productivity. Beyond such general statistical information, however, we do have specific clues about seasonality and light sensitivity in several cases.

Among writers, Emily Dickinson is a likely candidate for a diagnosis of SAD (see chapter 14). T. S. Eliot might be another patient for this distinguished clinic. His poetry sparkles with references to light. We learn that Eliot was instructed by his doctors to go south each winter. Could that have been to treat his SAD? We can only speculate. Milton is reputed to have suffered from summer SAD and, according to his biographer, was able to work on *Paradise Lost* during only half the year, between autumn and spring.

Another writer with a mood disorder was Guy de Maupassant. Toward the end of his life he attempted suicide and went on to die in an asylum. The following extract is from a story called "Who Knows?", in which the narrator, who ends up in an asylum, recalls how he went to Italy, where the sunlight made him feel good. After that:

I returned to France via Marseilles, and in spite of the gaiety of Provence, the diminished intensity of sunlight depressed me. On my return to the Continent, I had the odd feeling of a patient who thinks he is cured but who is warned by a dull pain that the source of illness has not been eradicated.

Was de Maupassant seasonal? It seems like a fair bet.

Among musicians, Handel and Mahler were most clearly seasonal. Both, we are told, did most of their creative work during the summer months. One of the most prodigiously rapid feats of composition was Handel's *Messiah*, which he completed in twenty-three days, between late August and mid-September. Mahler, who called himself the "summer composer," was fortunately an avid letter writer. His seasonal mood changes are clearly reflected in his letters. Contrast the following two, one written in summer and one in winter.

> To Joseph Steiner, Puzsta-Batta, June 19, 1879
>
> Dear Steiner,
>   Now for the third day I return to you, and today I do so in order to take leave of you in merry mood. It is the story of my life that is recorded in these pages. What a strange destiny, sweeping me along on the waves of my yearning, now hurling me this way and that in the gale, now wafting me along merrily in smiling sunshine. What I fear is that in such a gale I shall someday be shattered against a reef—such as my keel has often grazed!
>   It is six o'clock in the morning! I have been out on the heath, sitting with Fárkas the shepherd, listening to the sound of his shawm. Ah, how mournful it sounded, and yet how full of rapturous delight—that folk-tune he played! Ah, Steiner! You are still asleep in your bed, and I have already seen the dew on the grasses. I am now so serenely gay and the tranquil happiness all around me is tiptoeing into my heart, too, as the sun of early spring lights up the wintry fields. Is spring awakening now in my own breast?! And while this mood prevails, let me take leave of you, my faithful friend!

Contrast that with a winter postcard, sent to Friedrich Löhr, January 20, 1883.

Dear Fritz,

Simply cannot find time to write to you properly. Sending the stuff soon. My address is: . . . . Am extremely depressed.

Very best wishes to you and your family,

Yours,

Gustav

But two years later, in spring, Mahler wrote to the same friend:

My dear Fritz,

My windows are open and the sunny, fragrant spring is gazing in upon me, everywhere endless peace and repose. In this fair hour that is granted me I will be together with you. . . .

With the coming of spring all has grown mild in me again. From my window I have a view across the city to the mountains and woods, and the kindly Fulda wends its amiable way between; whenever the sun casts its colored lights within, as now, well, you know how everything in one relaxes. That is the mood I am in today, sitting at my desk by the window, from time to time casting a peaceful glance out upon this scene of carefree calm.

There are many other letters that suggest that Mahler suffered from SAD.

Painters and sculptors are more difficult to diagnose in retrospect than writers, but Jamison's work would suggest that they are as susceptible to mood disturbances. Artists, perhaps more than any other group, have struggled to portray light. In fact, the works of some can be instantly recognized by the distinctive quality of the light they portray: Turner's swirls of light; Rembrandt's splashes of *chiaroscuro*, illuminating the pensive faces of his models; and, of course, the dazzling colors of Vincent van Gogh.

Of these three painters, the only one with a clear history of a mood disorder is van Gogh. It seems very likely that he suffered from manic depression, although his clinical picture was complicated by intoxication with absinthe, the French liquor that at that time had a toxic ingredient in it. Van Gogh's intimate understanding of depression is apparent in his famous sketches, *Sorrow* and *The Old Man in Sorrow*. In contrast to these sad figures is *The Reaper,* a young man striding boldly across a field with a huge, luminous sun shining in the background. Van Gogh's wonderful use of light and color might make one suspect that he was extremely sensitive to light, and indeed, his letters to his beloved brother Theo, appear to bear this out. They are filled with descriptions of his feelings of sadness and joy, and of his sensitivity to the weather, and to light and darkness in particular. Here are a few selections:

Autumn in Drenthe, 1883

When I look around me, everything seems too miserable, too insufficient, too dilapidated. We are having gloomy days of rain now, and when I come to the corner of the garret where I have settled down, it is curiously melancholy there; through one single glass pane the light falls on an empty colour box, on a bundle of brushes the hair of which is quite worn down. It is so strangely melancholy that it has, luckily, almost a comical aspect—enough not to make one cry over it.

As long as the weather was fine I did not mind my troubles, because I saw so many beautiful things; but with this rainy weather, which we must expect to continue for months, I see more clearly how I have got stuck here, and how handicapped I am. . . .

Winter in Nuenen, 1883

Hardly ever have I begun a year of gloomier aspect, or in a gloomier mood. It is dreary outside; the fields are a mass of lumps of black earth and some snow, with days mostly of mist and mire. . . . This is what I see in passing, and it is quite in harmony with the interiors, very gloomy these dark winter days.

Spring in The Hague, 1892

Spring is coming fast here. We have had a few real spring days; last Monday, for instance, which I enjoyed very much. I think the poor people and the painters have in common this feeling for the weather and the change of the seasons.

In February of 1888 Vincent van Gogh left Paris for Arles, in the south of France, at least in part to escape the north and seek out the brilliant and dazzling light of Provence. In van Gogh's own words, "I came to the south for a thousand reasons. I wanted to see a different light, I believed that by looking at nature under a bright sky one might gain a truer idea of the Japanese way of feeling and drawing. Finally, I wanted to see this stronger sun . . . because I felt that the colors of the spectrum are misted over in the north."

Here is a description to his brother Theo, written from Arles in the summer of 1888:

> The loneliness has not worried me, because I have found the brighter sun and its effect on nature so absorbing. . . .
>
> Yesterday at sunset I was in a stony heath where some very small and twisted oaks grow, in the background a ruin on the hill and corn in the valley. It was romantic, like a Monticelli; the sun was pouring bright yellow rays upon the bushes and the ground, a perfect shower of gold, and all the lines were lovely. . . .

Here is another description of the sun by van Gogh:

> Now there is a glorious fierce heat, a sun, a light which for want of a better word I can only call yellow, pale sulphur yellow, pale lemon gold. How beautiful yellow is.
>
> Life is almost an enchantment. Those who do not believe in the sun here are without faith!

To sum up, creativity appears to be more common among patients with mood disorders, especially those whose condition is relatively mild, as well as among the relatives of such patients. It is quite conceivable that genes for creativity and mood disorders are transmitted together. It is important for treating psychiatrists to understand this. Eradicating all mood swings may diminish creativity in some people, though it is likely to improve matters greatly for those whose mood swings are severe. Nowadays, when an understanding of the human genetic makeup is close at hand, and the possibility of preventing certain undesirable genes in the new generation is scientifically conceivable, we would do well to consider the beneficial aspects of certain types of emotional disturbance, while never forgetting the pain they can cause. Had the birth of all depressives in history been successfully prevented, the world we live in would be a far different place today, though not necessarily a better one.

Prominent seasonal changes in mood and behavior seem particularly conducive to creativity, and there is evidence that many creative artists, both past and present, have experienced them.

16

Words for All Seasons

For centuries the seasons have inspired poets and songwriters, who have left us a glorious legacy describing the changes that occur, both in the world around us and in ourselves as, year after year, the earth tilts and rotates around the sun. What is it that has so inspired writers over the ages? I believe it is, first, the intense feelings with which the changing seasons imbue us; second, the capacity of seasonal images to evoke memories in us; and third, the appeal of the cycle of the seasons as a metaphor for a person's life.

The seasonal changes in energy, feelings, and drives that we now recognize to be a common part of the human experience are accompanied by prominent changes in the world around us: varied colors, fragrances, temperatures, and sounds. By reminding us of these specific sensations, the poet can evoke in us the feelings that often accompany them. Beyond the recreation of these feelings, and the nostalgia that comes with them, the seasons remind us of cyclical time, loss, and recovery, birth, death, and renewal.

In poetry, spring has usually been portrayed as representing reawakening, rebirth, sexuality, and joy, and for some this is true. Yet others find spring to be a difficult and painful season. Summer is seen as a time of happiness and generativity. Autumn engenders mixed feelings—nature is intensely beautiful and summer's harvest abounds, but there are also hints of the approach of winter, and melancholy often accompanies them. Then winter comes, and with it the death of vegetation; cold, inhospitable temperatures; food shortages; the disappearance of birds and animals; and, of course, the waning of the sun's light.

The cycle of the seasons has often been compared by writers and artists to a person's life. This is a strange metaphor. One might think that a person's life would be better conceptualized as linear—a straight line from birth to death. But perhaps it is more difficult for us to think of our lives in such a linear way—as a segment snipped out of a long string, with a finite beginning and end. Instead, we once again embrace the concept of cyclical time—ashes to ashes, dust to dust—to create the more comforting image of life as a ring, round and complete.

In connecting the seasons with the cycles of a man's life, poets have linked spring with youth, summer with the prime of life, autumn with declining powers, and winter with old age.

SEASONS AND PASSION

In spring, as the saying goes, a young man's fancy lightly turns to thoughts of love, and this applies to women, too. So it has been since biblical times, when Solomon, poet and lover, sang out to his beloved:

> For lo, the winter is past,
>   the rain is over and gone.
> The flowers appear on the earth,
>   the time of singing has come
> and the voice of the turtledove
>   is heard in our land.

The passions of spring continued unabated for thousands of years. As Shakespeare observed:

> Between the acres of the rye
>> With a hey, and a ho, and a hey nonino,
> These pretty country folks would lie,
>> In the spring time, the only pretty ring time,
> When birds do sing, hey ding a ding, ding:
> Sweet lovers love the spring.

Yet the spring has not always been associated with unmixed joy. With spring comes the revival of desire, which has lain dormant through the winter. There may be an inertia to overcome before the energy of spring can be fully enjoyed. Emily Dickinson, one of our most seasonal poets, described this sensation:

> I cannot meet the Spring unmoved—
> I feel the old desire—
> A Hurry with a lingering, mixed,
> A Warrant to be fair.

T. S. Eliot, in his famous lines, expressed a more painful form of spring fever:

> April is the cruelest month, breeding
> Lilacs out of the dead land, mixing
> Memory and desire, stirring
> Dull roots with spring rain.

More recently, blues singer Betty Carter observed:

> Old man winter was a gracious host,
> But spring can really hang you up the most.

Summer has been regarded by some as a season of heady delight. Emily Dickinson writes:

> Inebriate of Air—am I—
> And Debauchee of Dew—
> Reeling—thro endless summer days—
> From inns of Molten Blue—

She compares herself to a bee, drunk on the light of the sun, an influence more intoxicating than any liquor brewed.

Although autumn has been regarded by some, like Keats, as a "season of mists and mellow fruitfulness," a time of beauty of fulfillment, others have seen it as a sad time—a time of waning light, and a harbinger of the coming winter. Matthew Arnold, for example, wrote:

> Coldly, sadly descends
> The autumn evening. The Field
> Strewn with its dank yellow drifts
> Of wither'd leaves, and the elms,
> Fade into dimness apace,
> Silent.

While poets have had their differences in their views of autumn, winter has been almost universally treated as a season of despondency and unremitting gloom. According to Shakespeare, "a sad tale's best for winter." James Thomson, in his poem, "Winter," of 1726, encapsulated the common view of this season:

> See! Winter comes, to rule the varied Year,
> Sullen, and sad.

SEASONS AND MEMORIES

The poet can depend on the reader to have powerful memories and emotions associated with the seasons. The distinctive colors, smells, and characteristics that each brings serve as cues to memories of poignant events that have occurred in that season. Conversely, the memory of a significant event is often colored and modified by the season in which it happened. We can perhaps recall the quality of the sky, the weather, and the specific smells of the season. Associations such as these were emphasized by Freud in his models of how the mind works. The importance of such associations continues to be recognized by both writers and mental health professionals. They are in no way incompatible with our more recent understanding of the biological changes in mood and behavior associated with the seasons.

Such memories, reawakened by a particular time of year, are described, for example, by Edgar Allan Poe in his poem, "Ulalume":

> The skies they were ashen and sober;
>   The leaves they were crisped and sere—
>   The leaves they were withering and sere;
> It was night in the lonesome October
>   Of my most immemorial year, . . .

As the poem continues, it emerges that the poet, driven by some compulsion that he does not understand, seeks out a path to the tomb of his beloved, whom he buried on that same October day the year before. He has repressed this memory until he comes across the tomb with the name of his beloved, Ulalume, upon it. At this sight, the sad memory of her loss penetrates him and he recalls now why the autumn, with its crisped and sere leaves, sent such a chill through his heart. Poe thus provides us with a powerful example of how we associate important events in our lives with the seasons in which they happen.

So does Shelley in his poem, "Adonais," where he laments the death of Keats, which occurred in late winter. He writes:

> Ah, woe is me! Winter is come and gone,
> But grief returns with the revolving year.

THE SEASONS OF A MAN'S LIFE

The seasons as metaphor for the stages of a man's life was succinctly expressed by Keats:

He has his lusty Spring, when fancy clear
  Takes in all beauty with an easy span:
He has his Summer, when luxuriously
  Spring's honey'd cud of youthful thought he loves . . .
His soul has in its Autumn, when his wings
  He furleth close; . . .
He has his Winter too of pale misfeature,
Or else he would forgo his mortal nature.

Shakespeare also compares the final stages of a man's life to winter and finds both barren and dreary:

That time of year thou may'st in me behold
  When yellow leaves, or none, or few, do hang
Upon those boughs which shake against the cold,
  Bare ruin'd choirs, where late the sweet birds sang.

Seasonal imagery has also been used to evoke feelings about an era, as Dickens did when he labeled the period of the French Revolution as "the spring of hope . . . the winter of despair." Likewise, Thomas Hardy, looking out over the landscape at the end of the nineteenth century, saw in its dreary, wintry features a metaphor for the dead century and a confirmation of his sense of hopelessness for the future:

I leaned upon a coppice gate
  When Frost was spectre-grey
And Winter's dregs made desolate
  The weakening eye of day. . . .

The land's sharp features seemed to be
  The Century's corpse outleant;
His crypt the cloudy canopy,
  The wind his death lament.

The ancient pulse of germ and birth
  Was shrunken hard and dry,
And every spirit upon earth
  Seemed fervourless as I.

THE LOVELINESS OF THE LIGHT

Just think of the illimitable abundance and the marvelous loveliness of light, or of the beauty of the sun and moon and stars.
    St. Augustine, City of God

Light has many meanings for us, and poets and authors have used images of it to illustrate them. Besides revealing our world to us, light can, in itself, influence the way we feel. In addition to the effects of light shining from the world outside, much has been written about the "inner light."

The capacity of light to induce in us a sense of wonder and joy may be new to scientists, but writers have recognized it for centuries. In the second verse of Genesis, we are told:

And God said, "Let there be light"; and there was light. And God saw that the light was good.

Later on in the Bible, in Ecclesiastes, we are advised:

Truly the light is sweet, and a pleasant thing
    it is for the eyes to behold the sun.

Just as light has been associated with joy, so has darkness been associated with sorrow. Perhaps no poet could understand darkness so well as the blind Milton, who wrote:

Seasons return, but not to me returns
Day, or the sweet approach of ev'n or morn,
Or sight of vernal bloom, or summer's rose,
Or flocks, or herds, or human face divine;
But cloud instead, and ever-during dark
Surrounds me, from the cheerful ways of men.

But even to the sighted, the dim light of winter could prove depressing. If the reader is not by now convinced that Emily Dickinson suffered from SAD, the following verse should settle the question:

There's a certain Slant of light,
Winter Afternoons—
That oppresses, like the Heft
Of Cathedral Tunes—

Heavenly Hurt, it gives us—
We can find no scar,
But internal difference,
Where the Meanings, are.

Dickinson's intuitiveness is astonishing. She not only connects her heavy mood with the quality of the light—specifically, its low angle—but she recognizes that one can be hurt without any external manifestations; that inside the mind there are places where the meanings of things are recorded, where joy and suffering are experienced. Although Dickinson points out that the weak and fading light can be oppressive, she also observes that:

We grow accustomed to the Dark—
When Light is put away—
As when the Neighbor holds the Lamp
To witness her Good-bye—

. . . .
Either the Darkness alters—
Or something in the sight
Adjusts itself to Midnight—
And Life steps almost straight.

Again, this brilliant poet is observing something within herself that corresponds to the physiological changes that occur in the eye—and perhaps the brain—when we are surrounded by darkness. The eye adapts to the dark—the pupil enlarges and the rods, the most light-sensitive receptors in the retina, take over from the cones, which are responsible for ordinary vision. It is quite conceivable that a corresponding adaptation to the dark occurs in the brain.

Flooding the dark-adapted eye (and perhaps brain) with light may have a powerful effect on mood. Such an effect, as is produced by bright snow on a dark winter's day, was described by T. S. Eliot in "Little Gidding":

Midwinter spring is its own season . . .
When the short day is brightest, with frost and fire,
The brief sun flames the ice, on pond and ditches, . . .
A glare that is blindness in the early afternoon.
And glow more intense than blaze of branch, or brazier,
Stirs the dumb spirit: . . .
In the dark time of the year . . .
The soul's sap quivers.

The capacity of light to affect mood was recognized by William James in his book, *The Varieties of Religious Experience*. He cites an example from the autobiography of J. Trevor, in which the author describes how, one Sunday morning, he felt unable to accompany his wife and sons to church, "as though to leave the sunshine on the hills, and go down there to the chapel, would be for the time an act of spiritual suicide. And I felt such need for new inspiration and expansion in my life." So reluctantly he bid his wife and sons farewell and headed for the hills with his stick and his dog.

> In the loveliness of the morning, and the beauty of the hills and valleys, I soon lost my sense of sadness and regret. . . . On the way back, suddenly, without warning, I felt that I was in Heaven—an inward state of peace and joy and assurance indescribably intense, accompanied with a sense of being bathed in a warm glow of light, as though the external condition had brought about the internal effect—a feeling of having passed beyond the body . . . by reason of the illumination in the midst of which I seemed to be placed. This deep emotion lasted, though with decreasing strength, until I reached home, and for some time after, only gradually passing away.

Architects have recognized the important influence of interior lighting of a building on the way its inhabitants feel. For example, in a recent restoration of a small London church designed by Christopher Wren, the architects went to great lengths to create the effect of daylight in the church's dome. One lighting consultant noted that he was seeking "that magical moment when you feel light becomes a material rather than something only to be in." Had similar pains been taken with the lighting in the church of Mr. J. Trevor, who is quoted above, he may not have chosen to spend his morning in the sunlight of the hills.

Mr. J. Trevor's response to the sunlit hills, is reminiscent of the reactions of the people of Tromsö on *Soldag* or, for that matter, of the reports by many patients with SAD following treatment with bright light therapy. Just as the darkness oppressed Emily Dickinson by acting on the place "where the meanings are," so perhaps the light exerts its uplifting effects by acting on the same part of the brain to reverse the oppressive effects of darkness. It seems reasonable to postulate, as Emily Dickinson did; the existence of a part of the brain capable of being stimulated by light entering the eyes, and thereby registering feelings of wonder and joy. That same part of the brain, if deprived of light, might lead to sadness and despair. I would speculate that this part of the brain, so sensitive to the presence or absence of light, is located in the hypothalamus at the base of the brain.

Besides the many descriptions of the way in which light from the world outside affects our mood, there are also many reports of internally perceived light, often associated with powerful emotions and, at times, with religious conversions or other major life changes. Eliade, who called this experience "the mystic light," described many reports of such experiences by holy men of all religions, as well as by apparently ordinary people. Famous examples of mystic light experiences appear in the New Testament, where Saul of Tarsus, on the road to Damascus, experienced blinding light, which resulted in his conversion to Christianity; and in the Bhagavad Gita, where Krishna appeared to Arjuna "with the effulgence of a thousand suns." The poet, Henry Vaughan (1622–1695), described such an experience as follows:

> I saw Eternity the other night
> Like a great *Ring* of pure and endless light,
>   All calm as it was bright.

How can we understand mystical visions of light if we do not ascribe these experiences to divine intervention? I believe that the clue may lie in their resemblance to the euphoriant effects of bright light therapy in SAD patients, or to the effects on those in the far north or south when the sun returns after many weeks of darkness.

During light therapy, light enters via the eyes, and acts on a part of the brain "where the meanings are," inducing feelings of energy, reawakening, tranquility, harmony, and joy. Under certain circumstances, the same part of the brain might perhaps be activated either spontaneously or by some stimulus other than light.

Whatever the mechanism of such mystical light experiences, and whatever their influence on the individual might be, there seems to be little question that they occur. Their profound emotional effects are compatible with the idea that light can powerfully modify mood and behavior—a lesson I have learned from my experiences with the treatment of SAD patients.

17

Seasonal Artists of Our Time

I have enjoyed working with SAD patients for several reasons—the condition is eminently treatable, and the idea that light affects mood and behavior has always fascinated me. But beyond these considerations have been the people themselves. I have seldom met a more sensitive, artistic, and creative group. I have learned a great deal from them, starting with the very first seasonal patient, Herb Kern, a creative scientist, who discerned the patterns of his moods and wondered about their relationship to changes in light. I have learned to look at light in a new way: to discriminate between different shades of fluorescent lamps, to observe the angle of the sun, the degree of cloud cover, and the quality of fog.

Among the strongly seasonal people I have known are artists of all types. Some of them have incorporated their sensitivity toward light and the changing seasons into their art, and this chapter deals with two such people. One collects wildflowers in the summer and shapes them into wreaths and garlands, to which the memories of long, sun-filled summer days adhere. The other tells stories, in which changes in light are intimately associated with changes in mood, as they are in his own life. Their stories follow, and illustrate how SAD as a condition and seasonality as a creative gift can be opposite sides of the same coin.

"JESSICA": A FLOWER ARTIST

Jessica is a woman in her mid-forties with blond hair flowing around her face in curls, blue eyes, and a broad smile. She has suffered from SAD for years and has benefited from light treatment. But Jessica, like all seasonal people, defines herself in a much larger context than "having SAD." She is a professional, a mother, a devoted friend, and a support to many in her community—an eminently likable woman. In this chapter I do not discuss Jessica as a patient, but as an artist.

She has always felt the urge to create, but resisted it for years because it was not regarded as an acceptable way of life in her family, where her father was a doctor and her mother a nurse. Life had to be devoted to service, and art, insofar as it was acceptable, had to be a hobby. She struggled to become a counselor, but the artist in her prevailed.

I spoke with Jessica on her porch at the height of summer. She served iced, fruit-flavored tea, garnished with mint. Bees were buzzing all around us, attracted to the flowers hanging from baskets and craning toward us in splashes of color from all sides. Jessica creates her artwork from these flowers. The artist was in her studio.

Jessica did not always work with flowers; she was a photographer first. But in her creative work she has always felt in harmony with light and the seasons. Her whole body, she feels, resonates with the seasons. As she describes it:

My body is part of the day and the night. In a dry spell, when the earth is dry, I feel dry. When it is wet, I feel clogged and wet and soaked. When it's dark, I feel dark; and when it's light, I feel light. I love nature because somehow I am biologically tied to it. When the days get shorter, I almost feel a silent buzzing in my ears. It's just a presence that gets heavier and heavier as my body gets heavier and heavier. In the spring I am aware of a lightness, a peeling off, the way we peel off our clothes. As the days get lighter, I get lighter. By March I am like a plant. I can't wait to get outside and get my hands into the earth. As I water a plant and see it growing in the sunshine, I think to myself, "I am that plant. That plant is me."

Even though she suffers with the changing seasons, Jessica would hate to lose them. Even the sad, drab winter holds for her its magical images—the sun shining off snow, a fire crackling at night, the architecture of the trees, stripped of their leaves—and she would miss them if she were to move to a seasonless climate. She was once diagnosed manic-depressive and offered lithium to level out her moods, but she was reluctant to relinquish the buoyancy of the summer and the creative impetus provided by her alternating mood states.

Jessica is fascinated by portraying the dark, and the light gleaming out of that darkness. As a photographer, she loved working with lighting and had a burning desire to master taking pictures in the dark. She thought of photographing the winter landscape at sunset, when there was snow on the ground and little lights would come on in all the houses. How could she make a picture where there was no light—except these? She became obsessed with the desire to capture the darkness on a photograph. Now that she is no longer doing photography, her urge to capture the light within the darkness has been transformed into a wish to create a Christmas decoration of a miniature papier-mâché house built under the roots of a huge tree. Inside there will be little caverns and rooms, covered with soft moss and furnished, peopled with little animals—mice and moles—and illuminated by tiny lights. The object is to portray the peaceful hibernation of the winter, the comfort of not having to do anything when you don't want to, but instead to be warm, snug, and resting inside some dark cavern in the earth.

This is quite opposite to images that Jessica wanted to convey in the summer: photographs with too much light in them. She enjoyed letting the sunspots show—"those little dappled, octagonal things you get when your lens is too close to the sun." She wished to create an effect in the viewer that would cause him to exclaim, "Look at all this sun! How it shone! Incredible!"

After the photographic phase of her life, Jessica worked in her husband's flower shop and developed a new way of creating with the seasons. She began to resonate with the progression of the year, as reflected in the changing flowers available at the market:

Every week something new has arrived and something else has died off. In May you have to get flowers from California: statice and caspian, but in June the yarrow starts—white yarrow and green dock. Those are the first things you watch for by the road, and suddenly, now that June is beginning, there they are. That's the beginning of the picking season. By July the dock has turned from green to brown, and then it's time to pick that. Then there's goldenrod. In late July and early August many things arrive. I go north, picking tansy from the Catskills and pearly everlastings from the Berkshires. There are about fifty varieties of goldenrod, which I pick along the way. There are grasses to pick all summer long. Then in September comes hydrangea. You have to wait until it's dry on the vine. In October there's rabbit tobacco from around Williamsburg, and pussytoes, an everlasting from the Cape Cod area. There are things to pick all summer long. I've even taken the family out on picking trips at Thanksgiving.

Flowers are Jessica's medium. She dries them and twists them into wreaths, and makes arrangements and decorations for Christmas. She also creates little animals of papier-mâché. She has used her mood changes and swings of productivity, which resonate with those in the world around her, to create from nature's own bounty. She marks the changing seasons with the flowers, and they provide her with her art and her livelihood.

ROBERT WILHELM: TALES OF DARKNESS AND LIGHT

Robert described himself as a storyteller when he called to apply for the NIMH seasonal program. Even on the phone I could imagine him spinning out his tales in his deep, sonorous voice, and his storytelling was on my mind when I went to interview him in his apartment. There is nothing about his appearance—or his apartment—that would suggest that he is an artist. He is in his mid-forties, with a ruddy complexion, a mustache, and a full head of black hair, graying slightly. One might easily mistake him for a college professor or a minister—and he has been both. After spending some hours together, it was easy to see the artist emerge, for he regaled me with stories—his own, and those he tells for a living.

The son of European immigrants, Robert learned the art of storytelling from his mother, who told stories as she cooked dinner. From his father he developed his love of books. His earliest memory is of staring at the single candle on his brother's first birthday cake when he was three. Memories of the seasons are also strong:

> As a child I remember being sensitive to the seasons. I was always uncomfortable in the summertime, with the heat and humidity, but I loved spring. I loved water, and the clear, snowy days that were rare in New Jersey.

His early winters on the East Coast were "delightful, very bright and clear and cold, very crisp." It was only much later, at age twenty-three, when he went with his wife, Mary Jo, to take up his first college teaching job in Minnesota, that the seasons began to be a problem for him. He became so depressed and physically ill the first Christmas there that he vowed he would move to California the next year, even though it was not a wise career decision to leave an academic position so soon after taking it.

He and his wife moved to northern California, choosing a place where there was a small amount of high fog. Robert enjoyed the mixture of sunlight and fog. He and Mary Jo had three children, all of whom suffered from a rare genetic illness. All died in infancy. Robert reacted to the loss of his children more with anger than depression. He remembers raging at the unfairness of it, being angry at the universe and at God. Mary Jo was also grief-stricken and went into extensive therapy for several years to deal with the losses.

Robert completed his doctoral studies in theology and interviewed for a job in Niagara Falls. It was Christmastime when he flew up for the job interview, and he returned knowing that he had the job, yet weeping because he did not want to go back north. He remembers walking to the edge of Lake Ontario on a gray day and seeing the faint outlines of the Toronto skyline in the distance. "It was terrible," he recalls, "but that's where my job offer was." He loved teaching, and the couple lived in

Niagara Falls for three winters—difficult times for himself and his wife. He went into Gestalt therapy and worked on his ambivalent feelings toward his father, whom he resembles. Although the therapy was helpful, he is doubtful whether he would have gone into it had it not been for the gloomy winter weather. Summers in Niagara Falls were a total delight. It was then that he came in contact with the outdoor storytellers, who were to shape his final career choice.

In January of his third winter, he returned to the San Francisco Bay area for a workshop. He walked through Golden Gate Park on a bright, sunny day, lay on the grass, and wept as he "felt the greenness," wondering, "What am I doing in upstate New York?" Robert and Mary Jo moved back to San Francisco and lived there for five years. By then he had dropped out of two tenure-track academic positions and was questioning his future. He later worked briefly as a Roman Catholic lay minister, but ruled that out as a realistic career option. Mary Jo, who had always had a love-hate relationship with San Francisco, was eager to leave the city where her children had died. Robert had not yet learned to take his winter difficulties seriously, for the couple went to Seattle, one of the darkest cities in the United States. They moved in the summer, to a lovely house in the middle of a Douglas fir forest. All around the house were tall evergreens, and in the summer the sun streamed in through a high opening between the treetops. Robert did not realize that when winter came and the angle of the sun was low, the trees would block out all the light.

They spent two very difficult winters there. Robert recalls sitting by the window, watching the rain come down, and weeping. He thought of Dante again and again, saying to himself, "Suddenly, in the middle of my life's journey, I find myself literally in a dark wood. I have failed in my work. My academic career is gone. I will never have a career in the ministry. But I have not failed as a person." That last observation was a core discovery for him. He felt that having survived the loss of his children, this mid-life crisis was insignificant by comparison. He appreciated his parents, perhaps for the first time since adolescence—that they had loved him and felt good about him as a person. "In the midst of all the grayness," Mary Jo got a job offer to return to the Washington, D.C. area.

It was there that Robert finally decided to make storytelling his career.

He would take people on tours to places that served as dramatic settings for his stories—for example, the British Isles and Canada. But his seasonal difficulties interfered with his ability to create. He would engage in "a surge of scheduling and planning that begins in the spring and goes wonderfully into early autumn. And then there is the real agony of going through the winter months." He would not have the energy to carry out his plans and would feel "incredible fatigue" as he dragged himself from one engagement to another. In addition, he would become physically sick with flu and colds, which would drag him down further.

Robert joined the NIMH seasonal program at the urging of his wife. He had never really thought consciously that light might be important to his mood, "even though everything about my preoccupation with it should have led me to agree with her conclusion. It was so obvious, but I could not see it."

Robert did well on light therapy. Within a few hours of starting treatment, he felt dramatically better, and remained well through the winter. He was skeptical about the effect, and wondered whether it might not be a placebo. However, he became convinced that it was genuine after he went traveling without the lights a few times during the winter, and relapsed each time within days of stopping the treatment. He feels pleased that in the future he won't be at the mercy of intense periods of depression. On the other hand, he is worried that his creativity will be damped down if he is too even all year round. But this is not a serious concern for him, and he plans to use lights again next winter.

Robert has for some time been fascinated by stories of the North, of winter journeys, Siberian shamanism, and the northern Indians, from Canada and the Northwest. Many of these stories embody the idea of light as a precious essence, connected with love and life, as darkness is connected with loss and despair. Robert has also studied Nordic and Celtic mythology, which is preoccupied with light. He told me the following stories in his deep, resonant voice, alternating between the drama of the story, in which he would become lost from time to time, its meaning to himself, and comments about how he achieves his effects. I relate the following stories as Robert related them to me.

The Selfish Seagull

This tale is told by the Nootka Indians of British Columbia.

When the world was created, gifts were given in the potlatch tradition of the Northwest Indians, in cedar boxes. In this imaginative story the animals all receive gifts of creation, the boxes are all opened, and they are shared. In this land of heavy cloud cover, one box that was not opened was that containing sunlight. It's an important aspect of this particular story that getting the sunlight out somehow requires pain. What happens is that Seagull, who has the light, is not willing to share it. Raven, who is the trickster of this culture, knows that Seagull has the sunlight, and tries to get it out of him by all possible means. He tries to flatter Seagull, to beg him, but no matter what he does, Seagull keeps saying, "It's mine, it's mine."

So Raven has a thought: Seagull is causing so much trouble that it would serve him right if something awful happened to him—if he got a thorn stuck in his foot. No sooner has Raven thought this than it happens, and Seagull cries out in pain. Raven then says, "Let me help you," and goes to pull the thorn out of Seagull's foot. The crucial part of the story is that he doesn't pull the thorn out; instead, he pushes it in farther, and then has the opportunity to say, "I'm sorry, but I can't see what I'm doing"—the hinge of the story—"I need more light if I'm to pull it out. Open the box." And then, in the form of storytelling, the box is opened only a little bit, and the scene has to be repeated. This happens a second and a third time, so the drama builds. But the key is that at each opening a lesser light comes out, followed by a greater light. At the first opening only the stars emerge; at the second, the moon; and only after the third opening does the sun come out. The world is filled with light. The story ends as other traditions would have it begin: in the beginning there was the light.

"And does Seagull get the thorn removed?" I ask, like a child after a bedtime story.

"There are different versions," he tells me. "It depends how you choose to tell it. This story always troubled people in religious circles. They always felt it was cruel. But I knew somehow that it was valid, though I didn't know why. But now I realize that it was the connection between the lack of light and pain that caused me to resist changing it.''

In an Estonian version of the story there are four sets of light ranging in brightness from least to most adequate. The additional ones are the northern lights. As a flickering light, it is even less powerful than the stars. In this particular story a woman searches for her husband. The four sets of lights are a personification of her lovers, who range from least to most satisfactory, from the northern lights to the sun.

As I listen to Robert's stories—and he is a spellbinding storyteller—I think of our research studies and how we have found that in order for light to have a powerful effect on mood, it has to be bright, approaching the intensity of sunlight streaming through a window. Lesser light, equivalent perhaps to starlight or moonlight, just doesn't work. So we reach the same conclusion by widely different approaches—an ancient folk tale or a modern scientific study.

Where the Spirits Go

The Ojibwa Indians say that the first day was seventy years long. The sun shone. There was joy until the first night. People were afraid, and some died.

Trickster was sad, and wanted to be with those friends who died. Then he saw a new light—a round, pale one—rise from the waters. Owl said the name of this light was "Moon."

Trickster paddled a canoe across the waters and saw that Moon was housed in the lodge of those who died. But they were not sad. They ate, danced, and laughed. Owl and Trickster disguised themselves and joined the feast. At dawn, Frog pulled Moon down from the lodge pole and hid it under a blanket, and all the spirits went to sleep.

But Trickster and Owl were awake. Trickster put each of the sleeping spirits into a moose-hide pouch and paddled the canoe across the lake. But Trickster could not wait to reach the Land of the Living, and opened the pouch to peek in. All the spirits flew high to the heavens, and floated back to the Lodge of the Dead.

Owl then perched on Trickster's canoe and spoke: "You will never trick them again into letting you into their Great Lodge. You will never see them again." Trickster was saddened, but then a little smile came into his heart. He said, "Owl speaks the truth, but I will now speak a deeper truth. Every night I—and all people—will fly across the Great Lake on the wings of Owl and Owl's brothers and sisters. We will not be welcomed into the Lodge of the Dead, but we will sleep outside. And we will hear the voices of the past. We will remember those we have lost. We will hear them laughing and dancing and telling stories. And the nights will be filled with memories and adventures for all people in the Land of the Living."

Trickster became quiet and still. Owl blinked, and said, "And what shall this be called?" A little smile came into Trickster's heart: "This shall be called . . . dreaming." And that is how dreaming came to be.

I think about the association between darkness and loss, about the wish to recover loved ones who have departed. There is a universal need to find a way to come to terms with such losses. I think of Robert's three children, lost in infancy. In the Ojibwa story, death is associated with the first sunset, or loss of the sun. It makes one wonder whether there is a relationship between the chemical changes that take place in the brain as a result of loss and sorrow, and those that result from darkness. Dylan Thomas, in a poem to his dying father, writes:

> Do not go gentle into that good night
> Rage, rage against the dying of the light.

There is a Scottish storyteller, so Robert tells me, who in his tales of winter journeys uses the saying, "Where there is light there is life," at repeated points in the narrative to build up the drama, step by step.

Brother Wolf

There's a story that I tell, and it's one of my favorites, in which the feedback from the audience or workshop members is always the same.

The heart of the story is a legend about St. Francis of Assisi speaking to a wolf who lives in the darkness and comes and devours people in a certain town. The townspeople live in dread of this wolf and consult St. Francis about their problem. St. Francis decides to go meet the wolf. Everyone is terrified, but he goes into the woods anyway.

When I describe that scene, I'm very clearly describing the darkness. And I'm describing how Francis goes into the woods without any light or weapons. He goes into the darkness—I always close my eyes when I get to this part of the story—and I say he goes to the part of the woods that *feels* the darkest. When he reaches the place that feels the darkest, he stops. He knows that if he reaches out in front of him he could touch the wolf. The two of them are silent until Francis speaks. He says just two words—"Brother Wolf."

The two of them understand each other. Francis comes back into town and tells the people that the way for them to deal with the wolf is to feed him. St. Francis then goes back to his own village. The people are confused about what he has said and they debate about it, but then night falls. The wolf comes into the village and prowls around the streets and alleys in the darkness. All the doors are shut, the windows are closed, and everything is barred and dark. Suddenly, as the wolf comes around a corner, a door opens and—I use this phrase because I see it so clearly—*light pours out*. Someone steps out and puts a platter of food in the roadway, and the wolf with burning eyes looks up at the person, then turns to the food and devours it.

The story goes on from there. But after it is done—and it is about twenty-five minutes long—three out of four people will always say that the image they recall most clearly is when the door opens and the light pours out. That image comes about twenty minutes into the story, and I really think that after being, essentially, in different levels of darkness throughout, I can really see the light. My eyes are open and I'm looking at my audience, but it is as if somewhere I've been in a dark night and I open a door, or I walk in and turn my light on. It just floods. It's overwhelming—there's an emotional response that is instantaneous with the appearance of light.

Robert regulates the amount of light that comes into his eyes as he tells the story—it seems to influence his mood and how he conveys it to his audience. When he describes the darkness in his tales, he closes his eyes and feels it. When he talks about light, he opens his eyes and sees it. The most dramatic moment in this story, and in other stories of winter journeys, is coming upon bright light, suddenly and unexpectedly, in the midst of the dark landscape. I wonder whether the receptors in the eye, having been starved of light—and the chemical changes light induces— might pour out these chemicals in response to the light that pours suddenly out of the darkness, flooding our senses.

Robert shared with me just a small sample of his life. When I think back over the forty years that he covered in just a few hours, I am struck by his first memory—that of a three-year-old boy on a winter's day, staring at the flame on his brother's birthday cake. Only three, and already mesmerized by the light on a dark day!

As I listen to Robert's tales, I think of all the people united within the pages of this book: Peggy driving through the dark New England countryside, tired and sad and craving cookies; Alan missing school on dark winter days; Neal, who used to be too tired to keep his appointments, now emphatically selling light fixtures; Angela working on her book in front of. her light box; Jessica picking wildflowers at high noon in the summer; and now Robert telling stories of winter journeys, of light pouring out of the darkness. These people, with their unusual sensitivity to darkness and light, tell us something about our world and our reactions to it that otherwise might have passed us by completely.

Epilogue

It is small wonder that we are affected by the physical world in which we live: the dome of the sky, alternately brilliantly blue or dark as sleep; the quality of the air—full of moisture or crisp and dry; heat and cold; the loveliness of the light or the oppressive shadows of a winter afternoon. We are affected by our physical environment because we have evolved under its influence over thousands of years. It orchestrates the internal rhythms of body and brain, the seasons of the mind.

In their infinite variety of nature, people, like other creatures, are all different. Some show little change with the revolving year, while others react to seasonal changes with exquisite sensitivity. There is no shortage of examples in the plant and animal world of creatures reacting to changes in light, heat, or moisture. People who experience marked seasonal changes have no reason to feel alone. Even among our fellow humans there are millions with such strong reactions. We have estimated that perhaps as many as 20 percent of the U.S. population—thirty-five million people—experience some diminished function or impaired quality of life in response to winter.

It is important for a seasonal person to recognize that there are millions of others who suffer from the same changes and to have faith in the legitimacy of the messages that come from inside the body and mind. This was a major problem for people suffering from SAD before it was recognized by the medical establishment. A series of standard examinations and tests is conducted in an attempt to diagnose the symptoms of SAD. When the results of these tests are negative, the sufferer is left with the impression that the problem is not real or valid. Now we know that even without any positive chemical tests, it is possible to diagnose the condition of SAD and treat it. These discoveries are relatively new, so not all medical practitioners are aware of them. If you suffer from SAD and encounter such a practitioner, bring this information to his attention, and see whether you can resolve the problem together. If you encounter further skepticism, or a lack of open-mindedness about the powerful effects of the seasons and our capacity to reverse them, I suggest that you move on to another practitioner, rather than mistrust the messages that come reliably and powerfully from your mind and body.

In this book I have shown how you can evaluate the seasons of your mind, how strongly they express themselves, and what form and pattern they take. If they are a problem for you, there is much that can be done about them. The physical environment can be changed—most obviously by adding extra light, but in many other ways as well. Likewise, the psychological environment can be modified to good effect. Stresses can be reduced. Friends and family can help. Understanding the problem is valuable in its own right, and your view of the world and your relationship to it can be considered and modified, if you choose to do so. It is vital to our mental health that we do not feel helpless, that we believe we can do something to influence our destinies and the way we feel. How fortunate it is, therefore, that seasonal people can do so much to improve their lives.

There is, however, a limit to the degree to which we can change ourselves, and there may be much—our seasonality included—that we do not wish to alter. Many may regard their seasonality as an important part of themselves, integral to their rhythms of joy and sorrow, to their creativity, and to the pulse that makes them feel alive. From such heightened sensitivity has come some of our most beautiful poetry and art. Had all such creative rhythms and fluxes been flattened out by some omnipotent therapist, our lives would be the poorer for it.

I believe that we should use our seasonality to tune in to nature and to the creative forces within ourselves; that we should create with the seasons and share the products of our creation with others. This book is my seasonal creation, and if it brings you even a single shaft of light on a winter's day, my mission has been accomplished.

Standard light box. Contains eight fluorescent tubes which virtually duplicate sunlight.

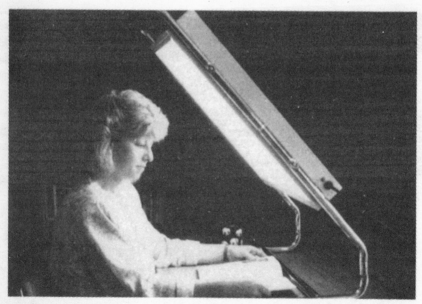

Recent findings show that the smaller, angled light box is as or more efficient than the standard box.

Resources

1. **Where to get further help**
   1. Where to purchase light fixtures
   2. Practitioners and Research Programs for Supervision of Light Therapy
   3. Support Group for SAD
   4. Further Sources of Information

2. **Dietary Advice, Menus, and Recipes**

3. **Further Reading**

Resources

Where to Purchase Light Fixtures

The technology of light fixtures is bound to change over time. Currently, most effective fixtures are metal light boxes, some with surrounding wooden frames, with fluorescent light bulbs in them. Some are full-spectrum, including a small amount of ultraviolet light; others omit this wavelength, probably without significant loss of efficacy.

The light fixtures vary in size and are correspondingly more or less portable. Some have special frames or brackets that allow them to be positioned in such a way as to give off light that is more powerful than the traditionally used 2,500 lux. Increasing the brightness seems to enable people to respond with shorter sessions. We have less experience with the brighter light, and though it appears to be quite safe, its long-term safety is less well established. We should have better answers to these and other questions over the years to come. Discuss the latest

233

developments with the professional supervising your treatment and obtain information from different lighting suppliers.

The number of lighting companies supplying suitable fixtures increases with each year. Many of them will ship to all parts of the United States. The three companies with which I have the most experience are:

The Sunbox Company
1132 Taft St.
Rockville, MD 20850
301-762-1786

Apollo Light Systems, Inc.
320 West 1060 South
Orem, UT 84058
801-226-2370

Medic-Light, Inc.
Yacht Club Drive
Lake Hopatcong, NJ 07849
201-663-1214

Practitioners and Research Programs for Supervision of Light Therapy

The following programs and individual practitioners have an active, ongoing interest in administering light therapy. The list should certainly not be regarded as comprehensive, nor are any of these people necessarily the best therapists for you. They are simply people who, I believe, can probably help people suffering from SAD. As light therapy becomes better established, the list of practitioners competent to supervise it is bound to grow. Although I have taken care to ensure the knowledge, competency, and interest of the practitioners and programs listed, I cannot take responsibility for the unsuccessful outcome of a consultation with any particular individual. I would also like to emphasize that if you already have a therapist with whom you are pleased, and if that therapist is willing to consider learning about phototherapy, it probably makes more sense for you to continue to work with him or her than to switch to someone else, simply on the basis of knowledge in this specific field.

If your geographical area is not represented in this list, you might find it helpful to contact the Psychiatry Department of your local medical school and ask for a suitable referral.

United States

Alaska

Bruce N. Smith, Ph.D.
2550 Denali, #1306
Anchorage, AK 99503
907-272-4741

Arkansas

Frederick Guggenheim, M.D.
Chairman, Department of Psychiatry
University of Arkansas for Medical Sciences
4301 West Markham, Slot 589
Little Rock, AR 72205
501-661-5483

California

Los Angeles

David A. Sack, M.D.
3340 Los Coyotes Diagonal
Long Beach, CA 90806
213-425-7747

Michael J. Gitlin, M.D.
Robert H. Gerner, M.D.
Center for Mood Disorders
1990 So. Bundy
Los Angeles, CA 90025
213-207-8448

San Diego

Daniel F. Kripke, M.D.
Scripps Clinic
10666 N. Torrey Pines Rd.
La Jolla, CA 92037
619-554-8087

Barbara L. Parry, M.D.
Department of Psychiatry, T-004
UCSD, 225 Dickinson St.
San Diego, CA 92093
619-543-5592

San Francisco/Palo Alto

Hugh Ridlehuber, M.D.
215 North San Mateo Drive
San Mateo, CA 94401
415-579-5785

Colorado

Anthony Gottlieb, M.D.
180 Cook St.
Denver, CO 80206
303-333-9007

Connecticut

Edward W. Allen, M.D.
504 Goose Lane
Guilford, CT 06437
203-453-5554

Walter Keckich, M.D.
Institute of Living
400 Washington St.
Hartford, CT 06106
203-241-6889

Francine C. Howland, M.D.
45 Trumbull St.
New Haven, CT 06510
203-624-3516

Charles S. Mirabile, M.D.
Box 683, Upper Main St.
Sharon, CT 06069
203-364-0740

SAD Program
Lawrence & Memorial Hospital
365 Montauk Ave.
New London, CT 06320
203-444-5125

Washington, D.C. Metropolitan Area

Norman E. Rosenthal, M.D.
Thomas A. Wehr, M.D.
Seasonal Studies Program
National Institute of Mental Health
Building 10, Room 4S-239
9000 Rockville Pike
Bethesda, MD 20892
301-496-2141 or 496-0500

Florida

Robert G. Skwerer, M.D.
1650 South Osprey Ave.
Sarasota, FL 34239
813-366-6070

Georgia

S. Craig Risch, M.D.
Emory University School of Medicine
Department of Psychiatry
1701 Uppergate Drive
Atlanta, GA 30322
404-727-3030

Hawaii

Douglas L. Smith, M.D.
1188 Bishop St., Suite 3405
Honolulu, HI 96813
808-544-0919

Idaho

Winslow R. Hunt, M.D.
155 2nd Ave.
Pocatello, ID 83201
208-232-3423

Illinois

Charmane I. Eastman, Ph.D.
Biological Rhythms Research Laboratory
Rush Presbyterian St. Luke's Medical Center
1653 West Congress Parkway
Chicago, IL 60612
312-942-8328

Indiana

John I. Nurnberger, Jr., M.D., Ph.D.
Professor of Psychiatry
The Institute of Psychiatric Research
791 Union Drive
Indiana University Medical Center
Indianapolis, IN 46223
317-274-8382

Boghos Yerevanian, M.D.
Kingwood Hospital
3714 South Franklin St.
Michigan City, IN 46360
219-873-1610

Richard H. Spector, M.D.
9250 Columbia Ave.
Munster, IN 46321
219-836-0810

Iowa

Bill Yates, M.D.
Keith L. Rogers, M.D.
Department of Psychiatry
University of Iowa
500 Newton Rd.
Iowa City, IA 52242
319-353-6218

Kentucky

Edward Goldenberg, M.D.
Behavioral Medicine Group
1401 Harrodsburg Rd., Suite A-420
Lexington, KY 40504
606-278-8999

B. Kishore Gupta, M.D.
Suite 125, Owens Medical Ctr.
4122 Shelbyville Rd.
Louisville, KY 40206
502-895-6368

Maryland

Seasonal Studies Program
National Institute of Mental Health
(See Washington, D.C. metropolitan area)

J. Raymond de Paulo, Jr., M.D.
Department of Psychiatry
Johns Hopkins University
Meyer 4-181
Baltimore, MD 21205
301-955-3246

Mary Ackerley, M.D.
100 Owings Ct.
Reistertown, MD 21136
301-833-1510

Michael Edelstein, M.D.
Shepherd Pratt Hospital
Towson, MD 21204
301-938-3000

Massachusetts

Martin H. Teicher, M.D., Ph.D.
McLean Hospital
115 Mill St.
Belmont, MA 02178
617-855-2970

Boston

John P. Docherty, M.D.
(See New Hampshire)

Janis L. Anderson, Ph.D.
Center for Circadian and
    Sleep Disorders Medicine
Harvard Medical School
Brigham & Women's Hospital
221 Longwood Avenue
Boston, MA 02115
617-732-7993

Gary S. Sachs, M.D.
Massachusetts General Hospital
Clinical Psychopharmacology Unit
Boston, MA 02114
617-726-3488

Michigan

John Greden, M.D.
Professor and Chairman
Department of Psychiatry
University of Michigan Medical School
Ann Arbor, MI 48109-0704
313-763-9629

Atul Pande, M.D.
9D9702 UH, Box 0118
University of Michigan Hospital
Ann Arbor, MI 48109-0118
313-936-4400

Minnesota

Minnesota Regional Sleep Disorders Center
Hennepin County Medical Center
701 Park Ave.
Minneapolis, MN 55415
612-347-6288

Mississippi

Mary B. Wheatley, M.D.
234 Highland Village
Jackson, MS 39211
601-982-8531

Missouri

Dale J. Anderson, M.D.
Psychiatric Center of Creve Coeur
12520 Olive Blvd.
St. Louis, MO 63141
314-576-6692

Montana

Michael J. Silverglat, M.D.
554 W. Broadway
Missoula, MT 59802
406-721-6050

Nebraska

Robert G. Osborne, M.D.
2221 S. 17th St., Suite 110
Lincoln, NE 68502
402-476-7557

Kay M. Shilling, M.D.
7602 Pacific St., Suite 302
Omaha, NE 68114
402-393-4355

New Hampshire

John W. Raasoch, M.D.
331 Main St.
Keene, NH 03431
603-357-4400

Michael Purcell, M.D.
P.O. Box 559
Littleton, NH 03561
603-444-5358

John P. Docherty, M.D.
Brookside Hospital
11 Northwest Blvd.
Nashua, NH 03063
603-886-5000

New Jersey

Robert K. Davies, M.D.
47 Maple St.
Summit, NJ 07901
201-522-1320

Steve Resnick, M.D.
Carrier Clinic Medical Assn.
Belle Mead, NJ 08502

Benjamin Natelson, M.D.
Department of Neurosciences
New Jersey Medical School
185 South Orange Ave.
Newark, NJ 07103
201-456-5864

Jeffrey T. Apter, M.D.
Princeton Psychiatric Centers
330 North Harrison St., #6
Princeton, NJ 08540
609-921-3555

Robert E. McGrath, Ph.D.
Department of Psychology
Fairleigh Dickinson University
Teaneck, NJ 07666
201-692-2445

New Mexico

Robert Buser, M.D.
1325 Wyoming Blvd., NE
Albuquerque, NM 87112
505-291-5300

New York

New York City

Michael Terman, Ph.D.
Light Therapy Unit
New York Psychiatric Institute
722 West 168th St., Box 50
New York, NY 10032
212-960-5714 (Research volunteers)
     960-2469 (Private practice referrals)

Leslie L. Powers, M.D.
15 West 75th St.
New York, NY 10023
212-724-5222

Lauren Gorman, M.D.
15 West 81st St.
New York, NY 10024
212-548-0568

Henry McCurtis, M.D.
Associate Director, Department of Psychiatry
Harlem Hospital
506 Lenox Ave.
New York, NY 10037
212-491-8481

Norman Sussman, M.D.
20 East 68th St, #204
New York, NY 10021
212-737-7946

Michael Wainstock, M.D.
928 Middle Neck Rd.
Great Neck, NY 11024
516-466-6996

New City

James W. Flax, M.D.
2420 North Main St.
New City, NY 10956
914-638-3358

Syracuse

Richard Kavey, M.D.
725 Irving Ave., Suite 406
Syracuse, NY 13210
315-470-7367

Geoffrey Margo, M.D.
Department of Psychiatry
750 East Adams St.
Syracuse, NY 13210
315-473-5633

Westchester

Joseph Deltito, M.D.
21 Bloomingdale Rd.
Cornell University Medical Center
White Plains, NY 10605
914-997-5967

North Carolina

Dan Blazer, MD., Ph.D.
Affective Disorders Program, Box 3215
Duke University Medical Center
Durham, NC 27710
919-684-4128

Tobin Jones, M.D.
Albemarle Mental Health Center
P.O. Box 791
Edenton, NC 27932
919-482-7493

Michael A. Hill, M.D.
Dept. of Psychiatry
UNC School of Medicine
Chapel Hill, NC 27599
919-966-4473

Ohio

Joseph R. Calabrese, M.D.
University Hospital of Cleveland
Case Western Reserve
School of Medicine
Director, Mood Disorders Program
11400 Euclid, #200
Cleveland, OH 44106
216-721-4600
1-800-729-4601

Ruth Ragucci, M.D.
11201 Shaker Blvd., #204
Cleveland, OH 44104
216-721-6770

Steven Dilsaver, M.D.
5973 Shadow Lake Circle
Columbus, OH 43235
614-457-5025

Gregory G. Young, M.D.
1735 Big Hill Rd.
Dayton, OH 45439
513-293-2507

Oregon

George C. D. Kjaer, M.D.
132 E. Broadway, Suite 301
Eugene, OR 97401
503-686-2027

Sleep and Mood Disorders Laboratory
Department of Psychiatry
University of Oregon Health Sciences Center
3181 S.W. Sam Jackson Park Road
Portland, OR 97201
503-494-7746

Pennsylvania

Philadelphia

George Brainard, Ph.D. 215-928-6939
Karl Doghramji, M.D. 215-955-8285
Sleep Disorders Center
Dept. of Psychiatry and Human Behavior
Jefferson Medical College
1015 Walnut St.
Philadelphia, PA 19107

Mark S. Bauer, M.D.
Bipolar Disorders Program
University of Pennsylvania
133 S. 36th St.
Philadelphia, PA 19104
215-662-2307

William Sonis, M.D.
Medical Director, Outpatient Clinic
Child Guidance Center of Philadelphia
Philadelphia, PA 19104
215-243-2620

Pittsburgh

David B. Jarrett, M.D., Ph.D. 412-624-2018
Michael Thase, M.D. 412-624-0752
Western Psychiatric Institute and Clinic
3811 O'Hare St.
Pittsburgh, PA 15241

David E. Thomas, M.D.
401 Shady Ave #B-208
Pittsburgh, PA 15206-4409
412-363-7368

Steven D. Targum, M.D.
Crozer-Chester Medical Center
Upland PA 19013
215-874-8491

Rhode Island

Martin Furman, M.D.
Butler Hospital
345 Blackstone Blvd.
Providence, R.I. 02906
401-455-6369

South Carolina

Timothy D. Brewerton, M.D.
Medical University of South Carolina
Department of Psychiatry and Behavioral Sciences
171 Ashley Ave.
Charleston, SC 29425–0742
803-792-7183

Tennessee

Kenneth O. Jobson, M.D.
Tennessee Psychiatry and Psychopharmacology Clinic
9401 Park West Blvd.
Knoxville, TN 37923
615-690-8190

David R. Daugherty, M.D.
Chamberlin Clinic
8001 Centerview Parkway, #102
Memphis, TN 38018
901-757-0568

Texas

John Cain, M.D.
John Rush, M.D.
Department of Psychiatry
University of Texas at Dallas
5161 Harry Hines Blvd.
Dallas, TX 75235-8890
214-688-3888

Cynthia Desmond, Ph.D.
730 Inwood
Bryan, TX 77802
409-846-8321

Philip M. Becker, M.D., A.C.P.
Sleep/Wake Disorders Center
8200 Walnut Hill Lane
Dallas, TX 75231
214-696-8563

Utah

Joanne L. Brown, Ph.D.
Breck Lebegue, M.D., Assistant Clinical Professor
Department of Psychiatry, School of Medicine
50 North Medical Drive
Salt Lake City, UT 84132
801-581-5111

Vermont

Ray C. Abney, M.D.
75 Linden St.
Brattleboro, VT 05301
802-257-7785, ext. 218

Edward Mueller, M.D.
Rutland Mental Health Center
78 South Main St., Box 222
Rutland, VT 05701
802-775-2381

Virginia

Washington D.C. Metropolitan Area (see above)
Seasonal Studies Program
National Institute of Mental Health

Fredericksburg

Bruce E. Baker, M.D.
150 Olde Greenwich Drive, Suite J
Fredericksburg, VA 22401
703-898-5533

Washington

Michael Norden, M.D.
18631 Olderwood Mall Blvd., #102
Lynnwood, WA 98039
206-775-0509

David H. Avery, M.D.
Harborview Medical Center, ZA-99
325 9th Ave.
Seattle, WA 98104
206-223-3425

Carla Hellekson, M.D.
Providence Sleep Disorders Center
550 16th Ave, #304
Seattle, WA 98122
206-320-2575

Wisconsin

Steven V. Hansen, M.D.
1220 Dewey Ave.
Milwaukee, WI 53213
414-258-2600

Joseph A. Heaney, M.D.
Rt 3, Box 101
Cumberland, WI 54829
715-234-4535

Nancy E. Barklage, M.D.
Center for Affective Disorders
Dept. of Psychiatry
University of Wisconsin Hospital and Clinics
600 Highland Drive
Madison, WI 53792
608-263-6087

Canada

Alberta

Chris P. Gorman, M.D., FRCPC
704 3031 Hospital Drive, N.W.
Calgary, Alberta T2N 2T8
403-270-8222

Carl A. Blashko, M.D., FRCPC
402-11523-100 Avenue
Edmonton, Alberta T5K 0J8
403-488-5821

British Columbia

Raymond Lam, M.D., FRCPC
Department of Psychiatry
University of British Columbia
2255 Wesbrook Mall, Room 2C-9
Vancouver, B.C. V6T 2A1
604-228-7325

Manitoba

Mark Lander, M.D., FRCPC
Health Science Center, Outpatient Psychiatry Dept.
697 McDermot Ave.
Winnipeg, Manitoba R3A 1R9
204-787-3367

Nova Scotia

Paul M. Sheard, FRCPC, MRCPsych.
98 Regent St.
North Sydney, Nova Scotia B2A 2G5
902-562-5006

Ontario

Russell T. Joffe, M.D.
The Clarke Institute of Psychiatry
250 College St.
Toronto, Ontario M5T 1R8
416-979-6933

Edward R. Horn, M.D., FRCPC
Royal Ottawa Hospital
1145 Carling Ave.
Ottawa, Ontario K1Z 7K4
613-724-6500

Meyer Steiner, M.D., Ph.D., FRCPC
McMaster Psychiatric Unit
St. Joseph's Hospital
50 Charlton Ave.
East Hamilton, Ontario L8N 4A6
416-522-4941

Quebec

N.P. Vasavan Nair, M.D.
Douglas Hospital Research Center
6875 Lasalle Blvd.
Verdun, Quebec H4H 1R3
514-766-1967

Hani Iskandar, M.D.
(same address as above)
514-761-6131

Support Group for SAD

The National Organization for SAD (NOSAD) was developed to support the interests of patients with SAD. Its membership is open to patients, friends, relatives, interested professionals, and any others who wish to further its goals. These include: (1) disseminating information about SAD by means of a regular newsletter; (2) offering support groups to patients and their families in a manner that has been successful for many other medical and psychiatric illnesses; and (3) working for things that are important to people with SAD—for example, insurance reimbursement for light fixtures.

The parent body has been established in the Washington, D.C. metropolitan area, but members are eager to develop satellite groups across the country. If you are interested in finding out more about NOSAD, or in starting your own local chapter of the group, write to:

NOSAD
P.O. Box 40133
Washington, DC 20016

Further Sources of Information

For further information about SAD and light therapy, write to:

Seasonal Studies
National Institute of Mental Health
Building 10/4S-239
9000 Rockville Pike
Bethesda, MD 20892

Sun Net
P.O. Box 10606
Rockville, MD 20850

Society for Light Treatment and Biological Rhythms
P.O. Box 478
Wilsonville, OR 97070
503-694-2404

For information on climatic conditions—day length, amount of sunshine, and temperature—in different parts of the United States, contact:

The National Climatic Data Center
Federal Building
Asheville, NC 28801
704-CLIMATE

DIETARY ADVICE, MENUS, AND RECIPES

Dietary Advice

The following diets—1200, 1500, and 1800 calories—are designed for gradual weight loss in people whose ideal weights are 120, 150, and 180 pounds, respectively. Those whose ideal weights fall between these amounts may make calorie adjustments accordingly, allowing for 10 calories per pound of ideal weight per day. In practice, however, most people do fine on one of the three diets. The menus provided are just examples of the type of foods that will add up to the desired number of calories, while providing appropriate proportions of the different major nutrients. If you wish to substitute your favorite foods for those mentioned below and would like to maintain the basic calorie and nutritional structure of the diets, contact your local branch of the American Diabetes Association for a copy of its Diabetic Exchange List. This lists foods that are calorically and nutritionally interchangeable.

The diets below contain approximately 57% carbohydrate, 22% protein, and 21% fat. They may seem to contain too little protein. The reason for this is that there is a general tendency for us in the United States to eat more protein than necessary. Fat almost invariably accompanies the protein—especially that derived from animal sources. For this reason, even if we stick to the less fatty animal proteins, such as chicken and fish, we will still be getting too much fat if we consume large volumes of protein.

The total calorie counts include three snacks, and a suggested list of snacks is provided below. In addition, any items recommended as part of a meal can be held back and eaten between meals, if preferred. A list of "free beverages" that can be consumed at any time is also provided.

Menus

1200 Calories

Day	Breakfast	Lunch	Dinner
1	1 cup cooked oatmeal ¼ cup skim milk	2 ounces roast beef with mustard on a large (2-ounce) roll large raw vegetable salad with 2 tablespoons reduced-calorie dressing	1 cup lentil spaghetti sauce (recipe follows) 1 cup cooked spaghetti 1 cup steamed zucchini
2	2 slices toast 1 ounce cheese	½ cup water-packed tuna with 1 tablespoon reduced-calorie mayonnaise 2 slices rye bread 2 cups raw vegetable sticks	1 cup beanpole stew (recipe follows) ½ cup brown rice 1 cup steamed spinach and mushrooms
3	¾ cup cooked lentils with 1 ounce grated cheese	1 ounce sliced turkey breast with mustard 2 slices rye bread 1 green pepper, raw, cut in strips	2 ounces broiled fish with lemon and basil 1 large baked potato with ½ cup fat-free, plain yogurt 1 cup steamed broccoli

Day	Breakfast	Lunch	Dinner
4	1 cup bite-sized shredded wheat ½ cup skim milk	1 ounce lean ham 1 ounce cheese with mustard 1 pita bread 6-inch pocket, filled with raw vegetables such as alfalfa sprouts, tomato, green pepper, cucumber	2 cups curried barley and lentil soup (recipe follows) 1 slice pumpernickel bread large raw vegetable salad with 2 tablespoons reduced-calorie dressing
5	1 cup cooked Wheatena cereal	3 ounces boiled shrimp mixed with 1 cup diced raw vegetables (cucumber, green pepper, tomato) mixed with 1 tablespoon reduced-calorie mayonnaise, and stuffed into 1 pita bread 6-inch pocket	medium chicken breast (1 piece) baked 1 cup lima beans large sliced tomato with vinegar
6	1 bagel (2 ounces) ⅓ cup low-fat cottage cheese	1 cup canned lentil soup 4 Ry-Krisp crackers 1 cup canned asparagus on lettuce with vinegar	2 ounces broiled hamburger on hamburger bun with mustard 1 cup cole slaw made with 1 tablespoon reduced-calorie mayonnaise ½ cup fat-free, plain yogurt, flavored with vanilla and artificial sweetener

Day	Breakfast	Lunch	Dinner
7	2 slices toast 1 egg, fried in non-stick spray	⅓ cup white beans with herbs and tomatoes ⅔ cup brown rice 1 cup steamed broccoli	3 ounces broiled lamb chop with garlic salt and rosemary 1 cup noodles with ½ teaspoon margarine, ⅓ cup chopped tomato, and basil 1 cup steamed green beans

1500 Calories

Day	Breakfast	Lunch	Dinner
1	1 cup cooked oatmeal	3 ounces roast beef with mustard on a large (2-ounce) roll large raw vegetable salad with 2 tablespoons reduced-calorie dressing	1 cup lentil spaghetti sauce 1½ cups cooked spaghetti 1 cup steamed zucchini
2	2 slices toast 2 ounces cheese	½ cup water-packed tuna with 1 tablespoon reduced-calorie mayonnaise 2 slices rye bread 1 cup cream of tomato soup made with water 2 cups raw vegetable sticks	1 cup beanpole stew ⅔ cup brown rice 1 cup steamed spinach and mushrooms

Day	Breakfast	Lunch	Dinner
3	1 cup cooked lentils 1 ounce grated cheese	2 ounces sliced turkey breast with mustard and sliced tomato 2 slices rye bread 1 green pepper, raw, cut in strips	3 ounces broiled fish with lemon and basil 1 large baked potato with ½ cup fat-free, plain yogurt 1 cup steamed broccoli 1 slice bread
4	1½ cups bite-sized shredded wheat 1 cup skim milk	2 ounces lean ham 1 ounce cheese with mustard and 1 tablespoon reduced-calorie mayonnaise 1 pita bread 6-inch pocket, filled with raw vegetables such as cucumber, alfalfa sprouts, tomato, green pepper, etc.	2 cups curried barley and lentil soup 4 Wasa crackers large raw vegetable salad with 2 tablespoons reduced-calorie dressing
5	1 cup cooked Wheatena cereal 1 cup skim milk	6 ounces boiled shrimp mixed with ½ cup diced raw vegetables (cucumbers, green pepper, tomato, etc.) mixed with ½ cup cooked macaroni and 2 tablespoons reduced-calorie mayonnaise and stuffed into 6-inch pita bread pocket	medium chicken breast (1 piece) baked ½ cup lima beans 1 large baked potato with ½ teaspoon margarine 1 medium sliced tomato with vinegar and basil

Day	Breakfast	Lunch	Dinner
6	1 bagel (2 ounces) ⅓ cup low-fat cottage cheese	1½ cups canned lentil soup 6 Ry-Krisp crackers 1 cup canned asparagus on lettuce with vinegar	3 ounces broiled hamburger on hamburger bun with mustard 1 ear corn with ½ teaspoon margarine 1 cup cole slaw made with 1 tablespoon reduced-calorie mayonnaise 1 cup fat-free, plain yogurt, flavored with vanilla and artificial sweetener
7	2 slices toast 1 egg, fried in non-stick spray ½ cup skim milk	⅔ cup white beans with herbs and tomatoes ⅔ cup brown rice 1 cup steamed broccoli	3 ounces broiled lamb chop with garlic salt and rosemary 1½ cups noodles with 1 teaspoon margarine, ¼ cup chopped tomato, and basil 1 cup steamed green beans mixed with dill and ½ cup fat-free, plain yogurt

1800 Calories

Day	Breakfast	Lunch	Dinner
1	1 cup cooked oatmeal 1 cup skim milk 2 slices toast 2 teaspoons margarine	3 ounces roast beef with mustard on large (2-ounce) roll large raw vegetable salad with 2 tablespoons reduced-calorie dressing	1½ cups lentil spaghetti sauce 2 cups spaghetti 1 cup steamed zucchini
2	2 slices toast 2 ounces cheese ½ cup bite-sized shredded wheat ½ cup skim milk	½ cup water-packed tuna with reduced-calorie mayonnaise 2 slices rye bread 1 cup cream of tomato soup made with water 2 cups raw vegetable sticks	1½ cups beanpole stew 1 cup brown rice 1 cup steamed spinach and mushrooms with 1 teaspoon margarine
3	1 cup cooked lentils with 2 ounces grated cheese	2 ounces sliced turkey breast with mustard 2 slices rye bread 1 green pepper, raw, cut in strips	4 ounces broiled fish with lemon and basil 1 large baked potato with ½ cup fat-free, plain yogurt 1 cup steamed broccoli 2 slices bread

Day	Breakfast	Lunch	Dinner
4	2 cups bite-sized shredded wheat 1 cup skim milk	2 ounces lean ham 2 ounces cheese with mustard and 1 tablespoon reduced-calorie mayonnaise 1 6-inch pita bread pocket, filled with raw vegetables such as alfalfa sprouts, tomato, green pepper, cucumber, etc.	2 cups curried barley and lentil soup 6 Wasa crackers large raw vegetable salad with 2 tablespoons reduced-calorie dressing
5	1½ cups cooked Wheatena cereal 1 cup skim milk	6 ounces boiled shrimp mixed with ½ cup diced raw vegetables (cucumber, green pepper, tomato, etc.) mixed with ½ cup cooked macaroni and 2 tablespoons reduced-calorie mayonnaise, stuffed into a 6-inch pita bread pocket	large chicken breast (1 piece) baked 1 cup lima beans 1 large baked potato with 1 teaspoon margarine 1 medium sliced tomato with basil, vinegar, and 1 teaspoon olive oil

Day	Breakfast	Lunch	Dinner
6	2 bagels (2 ounces each) ⅔ cup low-fat cottage cheese	1½ cups canned lentil soup 6 Ry-Krisp crackers 1 cup canned asparagus on lettuce with 1 tablespoon reduced-calorie mayonnaise	3 ounces broiled hamburger on hamburger bun with mustard 1 6-inch ear corn with ½ teaspoon margarine 1 cup cole slaw made with 1 tablespoon reduced-calorie mayonnaise 1 cup fat-free, plain yogurt flavored with vanilla and artificial sweetener
7	2 slices toast 1 teaspoon margarine 1 egg, fried in non-stick spray ½ cup skim milk	1 cup white beans with herbs and tomatoes 1 cup brown rice 1 cup steamed broccoli	3 ounces broiled lamb chop with garlic salt and rosemary 1½ cups cooked noodles with 1 teaspoon margarine, ¼ cup chopped tomato, and basil 1 cup steamed green beans mixed with dill and ½ cup fat-free yogurt 1 teaspoon margarine over green beans

Beverages Allowed

Coffee, tea, club soda, seltzer water, water, diet soft drinks.

Snacks

In addition to your three meals, you may have three snacks per day. The following list provides only a few examples; many other foods may have similar caloric and nutritional properties. Recipes are provided below for the items with an asterisk.

½ cup Very Spicy Chick Peas*
2 rice cakes
⅓ cup kidney beans with chopped onion
4 Ry-Krisp crackers
1 oat bran muffin*
3 cups air-popped popcorn (no oil)
¾ ounce matzoth
1 slice bread without butter

Recipes

Oat Bran Muffins

2¼ cups Mother's Oat Bran cereal, uncooked
¼ cup raisins (may omit if desired)
2 teaspoons baking powder
½ teaspoon salt (optional)
¾ cup skim milk
⅓ cup honey
2 eggs, beaten
1 tablespoon vegetable oil

Heat oven to 425°. Coat 12 medium muffin cups with nonstick spray or line with paper baking cups. In large bowl, combine oat bran cereal, raisins, baking powder, and salt. Add remaining ingredients; mix just until dry ingredients are moistened. Fill prepared muffin cups almost full. Bake 15 to 17 minutes or until golden brown. Makes 1 dozen muffins.

Very Spicy Chick Peas

2 teaspoons olive oil
3 small garlic cloves, minced
1 teaspoon minced fresh ginger
1 large onion, chopped
4 medium canned tomatoes packed in tomato juice
3 teaspoons coriander
½ teaspoon cumin
½ teaspoon cinnamon
¼ teaspoon salt
¼ teaspoon freshly ground black pepper
¼ teaspoon ground cloves
⅛ teaspoon cayenne pepper
2 15-ounce cans chick peas, drained and rinsed
¼ cup minced fresh parsley

In a large, heavy skillet, warm the olive oil over moderately low heat. Add the garlic, ginger, and onion; cook, stirring occasionally, until softened—3 to 5 minutes. Drain the tomatoes, reserving the juice, and add them, breaking them into pieces with the spatula. Add ½ cup of the reserved tomato juice, along with the coriander, cumin, cinnamon, salt, black pepper, cloves, and cayenne pepper. Cook, stirring occasionally, for 5 minutes, then add the chick peas. Cook 10 minutes. If the mixture gets too thick, add more tomato juice. Add the parsley and toss.
(Reprinted from *Nutrition Action Newsletter* which is available from the Center for Science in the Public Interest, 1501 16th St., N.W., Washington, D.C. 20036.)

Lentil Spaghetti Sauce

1 medium onion, chopped
1 clove garlic, minced
2 tablespoons oil
1½ cups dried lentils, washed
1 dried hot pepper, crumbled
1 teaspoon salt (optional)
½ teaspoon pepper

4 cups water and 2 beef bouillon cubes
  (or 4 cups fat-skimmed beef broth)
¼ teaspoon dried basil, crumbled
1 16-ounce can tomatoes
1 6-ounce can tomato paste
1 tablespoon vinegar

Saute onion and garlic in oil for 5 minutes. Add lentils, red pepper, salt, pepper, and water with bouillon cubes or beef broth. Cover and simmer 30 minutes. Add remaining ingredients and simmer uncovered for about 1 hour, stirring occasionally. Serve over regular or whole wheat spaghetti, or rice.

Beanpole Stew

2 16 oz. cans tomatoes
1 15½ oz. can red kidney beans
1 15½ oz. can northern beans
1 15½ oz. can garbanzo beans
3 medium onions, chopped
2-3 cloves garlic, minced
2 medium bell peppers, chopped
2 large stalks celery, sliced
1 medium zucchini, chopped
½ cup water
1-2 teaspoons chili powder
2 teaspoons basil, crushed
¼ teaspoon black pepper
1 bay leaf

Turn canned tomatoes, with their juice, into a large soup kettle. Chop into bite-sized pieces. Add undrained beans and all other ingredients. Bring to boil. Reduce heat, cover and simmer for 2 hours. Vegetables will be tender in 1 hour, but you will have a tastier stew after 2 hours of simmering. Makes 10 cups.

Curried Barley & Lentil Soup

1½ cups chopped onion
2 crushed garlic cloves

2 teaspoons olive oil
1½ teaspoons curry powder
8 cups water
¼ cup uncooked barley
½ cup uncooked lentils
1 teaspoon salt
2 cups stewed tomatoes
1 cup chopped celery
1 tablespoon white vinegar

Place water, barley and lentils in a 4-quart pot. Bring to a boil, cover and reduce heat. Meanwhile, spray a nonstick skillet with vegetable cooking spray and heat until medium hot. Cook onions and garlic until lightly browned. Add oil and curry powder and continue cooking for 5 minutes. Add onions to barley/lentil mixture and simmer for 45 minutes. After 45 minutes add tomatoes and celery and cook an additional 15 minutes. Remove from heat and let cool for 10 minutes. Blend in SMALL batches in the food processor or blender. (CAUTION: hot liquid tends to spurt, so be careful.) Return to pot, stir in vinegar and reheat to serving temperature. Makes 8 cups.

FURTHER READING

This is not intended to be a comprehensive bibliography, but rather, a list of some texts that the general reader might find useful and interesting. For an extensive list of articles on SAD and light therapy, the reader is referred to the first two scholarly works, each of which lists hundreds of references.

Part 1: Seasonal Syndromes

Rosenthal, N. E., and M. Blehar, eds. *Seasonal Affective Disorders and Phototherapy*. New York: Guilford Press, 1989.
Thompson, C., and T. Silverstone, eds. *Seasonal Affective Disorders*. London: CNS Neuroscience Press, 1989.

Part 2: Treatments

Diet and Exercise:

Brody, Jane. *Jane Brody's Good Food Book*. New York: W. W. Norton & Co., 1985.

Carper, Jean. *The All-in-One Calorie Counter*. New York: Bantam Books, 1974.

McCann, L., and D. S. Holmes. "Influence of Aerobic Exercise on Depression," *Journal of Personality and Social Psychology*. 46(5): 1142–47, 1984.

Schwartz, Bob. *Diets Don't Work*. Houston: Breakthru Publishing, 1982.

Wurtman, Judith J., Ph.D. *The Carbohydrate Craver's Diet*. Boston: Houghton Mifflin, 1983.

Psychotherapy and Advice to Friends and Family:

Burns, David D. *Feeling Good: The New Mood Therapy*. New York: Signet, 1981.

Papolos, Demitri F. and Janice. *Overcoming Depression*. New York: Harper and Row, 1987.

Storr, Anthony. *The Art of Psychotherapy*. New York: Methuen, 1979.

Part 3: Celebrating the Seasons

Boorstin, D. J. *The Discoverers*. New York: Vintage Books, 1983.

Cameron, I. *Antarctica: The Last Continent*. London: Cassell & Co., Ltd., 1974.

Cook, F. A. "Medical Observations among the Esquimaux," *New York Journal of Gynaecology and Obstetrics*, 4:282–96, 1894.

Dewhurst, K. "A Seventeenth-Century Symposium on Manic-Depressive Psychosis," *British Journal of Medical Psychology*, 35:111–25, 1962.

Eliade, Mircea. "Experiences of the Mystic Light," *Mephistopheles and Androgyne*. New York: Sheed and Ward, 1965.

———. *The Myth of the Eternal Return, or Cosmos and History*. Translated by W. R. Trask. Bollingen Series XLVI. Princeton, N.J.: Princeton University Press, 1954.

Esquirol, J. E. D. *Mental Maladies: Treatise on Insanity*. New York: Hafner Publishing Co., 1965.

Frumkes, G. "A Depression Which Recurred Annually," *Psychoanalytic Quarterly*, 65:351–64, 1946.

James, William. *The Varieties of Religious Experience*. New York: University Press, 1963.

Jamison, K. R. "Mood Disorders and Seasonal Patterns in Top British Writers and Artists," *Psychiatry*, 52(2): 125–134, 1989.

Johnson, T. H., ed. *The Complete Poems of Emily Dickinson*. Boston: Little, Brown and Company, 1960.

Jones, Jack Raymond. *The Man Who Loved the Sun: The Life of Vincent van Gogh*. London: Evans Brothers, Ltd., 1966.

Marsh, Michael. *Philosophy of the Inner Light*. (Pendle Hill Pamphlet 209.) Pendle Hill, Pa.: Pendle Hill Publications, 1976.

Martner, Knud, ed. *Selected Letters of Gustav Mahler*. London: Faber and Faber, 1979.

Stone, I., ed. *Dear Theo: The Autobiography of Vincent van Gogh*. New York: Signet, 1969.

Wechsberg, J. "Mørketiden," *The New Yorker*, March 18, 1972.

Index

Poe, Edgar Allan, 181, 198, 208
Polar regions, facts and myths
 about SAD, 178–81
Practitioners and research programs for light therapy,
 234–51
Premenstrual syndrome, 61–62,
 168–69
 relationship to SAD, 61–62
Productivity
 decreased, 9, 11, 19, 42, 57,
  58, 67, 74, 125, 177,
  196–97
 increased, 19, 107, 196–97
Prolactin, 166
Proust, Marcel, 150
Prozac, 85, 149–50, 166
Psychiatric Institutes of America,
 36, 77
Psychoanalytic Quarterly, 189
Psychotherapy, 127, 128, 130–33
 choosing a therapist, 138–40
 and SAD, 130–40
 types of, 134–38

Rape, 89
Reaper, The, 201
Recipe(s)
 Beanpole Stew, 264
 Curried Barley & Lentil Soup,
  264–65
 Lentil Spaghetti Sauce, 263–64
 Oat Bran Muffins, 262
 Very Spicy Chick Peas, 263
Recurrent depression, 85–86
Reference reading, 264–66
Rembrandt, 200

Remembrance of Things Past, 150
Research on SAD. *See also*
 National Institute of Mental
 Health, 113, 162–169
Richards, Ruth, 196
Risk factors, 45–51
 environmental, 45–46
Ritalin, 69
Rosen, Leora N., 77
Rovner, Sandy, 12, 82

SAD. *See* Seasonal Affective
 Disorder
Sadness. *See* Mood
SPAQ. *See* Seasonal Pattern
 Assessment Questionnaire
S-SAD. *See* Subsyndromal
 SAD
Sack, David, 14
St. Augustine, 210
Santa Ana winds, 91–92
Saul of Tarus, 213
Scandinavian origin and SAD, 47,
 178–181
Scarsdale Diet, 121
Schumann, Robert, 198
Seasonal Affective Disorder
 age groups, 17, 45
 antidepressant medication and,
  9, 61, 85, 127, 131,
  141–54
 behavior therapy, 136–37
 children and, 67–69
 cognitive therapy, 134–36
 conditions resembling, 65–66
 creative persons past and
  present, 194–226